Reflections of a **TEENAGE BARNSTORMER**

by Peyton Autry

Turner Publishing Company

Turner®
PUBLISHING COMPANY

Turner Publishing Company Staff:
Tammy Ervin, Editor
Shelley R. Davidson, Designer

Library of Congress Control No. 2002116930
ISBN: 978-1-68162-332-0

Limited Edition.

Reflections of a Teenage Barnstormer is dedicated
to Marty, my father Arch Autry and mother Nellie Baker Autry.
They conceived and enacted the aerial odyssey described
in the following pages.

ACKNOWLEDGMENTS

I have a host of people to thank for making this book possible. Among these are: my wife Leta Ellsworth Autry for her caring encouragement on this book as well as all of my other endeavors. I am grateful to Helen Krinke, my manuscript secretary and advisor of thirty years, for her professional proficiency, promptness and faithful caring. To the citizens and officials of dozens of communities in the Hoosier Ohio River and Wabash River Valleys, for their important assistance in confirming my 70-year-old memories of times, places and things. To all of my friends, especially James and Barbara Balentine, who have always taken a special interest in me personally and my technical and literary careers.

AN *INTRODUCTORY NOTE BY THE AUTHOR:*

Reflections of a Teenage Barnstormer is the story of a 1933 two-month barnstorming tour of the Ohio River Valley of southern Indiana when the author was 16 years old. It is told in a first person, present tense in the manner he would have told it at the time it occurred.

CONTENTS

Peyton Autry in Marty's Waco 10 in 1933 just before take-off on barnstorming tour.

CHAPTER I

O ur primary glider sits facing north at the south end of the freshly cut alfalfa field. A primary glider has no wheels for a landing gear, only a long wooden skid under its open trussed flat framework "fuselage." I am sitting here on the open board seat mounted atop the skid's nose fastening my safety belt while Jim at the left wing tip holds the wing level. Ray and Carl back the old Nash open touring car up to the glider, throwing out one end of the light 600-foot towline with its one-inch steel ring attached. The ring is snapped into the release hook mechanism on the nose of the glider's wooden skid. I tucked the lanyard cord for the release hook in my belt so I could reach it easily when it came time to yank it, which would drop the towline. Ray and Carl drove the Nash slowly up ahead, paying out the towline as they moved along. When the line was drawn up taut they waited for our signal. I nodded to Jim who waved a white cloth he was holding and we slowly moved along gradually gathering speed. I could hear the old Nash slowly changing gears. Jim's walk is now a trot. He must hang on to the wing tip until there is enough slipstream pressure on the ailerons so I can keep the wing level without his help.

There! Now, I shake the stick from side to side a little bit and the wing rocks back and forth. Jim gets the message, trailing way behind, waving as I went along. Now I can feel the elevators and rudder take hold with my feet on the rudder bar and both hands on the stick. I ease the stick back a little and she's off! Each time I fly this thing, it's a greater thrill than the last! Now, I ease the stick back more and we're climbing. Carl is a good tow car driver— there isn't a single tremor transferred up the towline from rough driving. He accelerates very slowly and smoothly. He has done this now for three years.

Gee, I'm climbing so fast I'm leaning way back on the seat. I'm now at about 150-foot altitude and the climb is beginning to slow because of the angular weight of the towline. I must be very careful now because this is the crucial moment of a ground towed ascent. If I jerk the towline release at this steep climb angle the considerable weight of the towline on the nose will be released suddenly and the nose of the glider will just as suddenly dart upward and she will stall, and at this altitude of 150 feet I would never recover and will crash. So, just a split second before releasing the towline, I push the stick forward in a momentary dive. There! The towline falls away, the nose rises sharply from the released weight and we are in a shallow glide. The tow car's motor below is idled. Now I can no longer hear anything but the gentle tranquilizing whir of the 40 M.P.H. wind in the wing brace wires. My air speed indicator is only the sound level of the wind in the brace wires and the wind on my face.

This glider was designed and offered in kit form by the Mead Glider Company of Chicago. Their claim was that the glider had a glide angle of 18 to 1, which would mean that at 18 to 1 we would at this point of 150 foot altitude, glide about a half mile. We found that it wasn't that good. It was something less than 18 to 1. At 150 feet we would glide about a third of a mile. It would be much greater than that if we had a longer field and a longer and lighter towline, perhaps a wire, piano wire, instead of the 600-foot cord, which we have been using. If that were a wire, of say 1500 to 2000 feet, and a long field, we could climb to 700 or 800 feet and then glide to nearly two miles from the point where we dropped the towline.

I am now passing over the wide ditch at the north end of the field. I am at an altitude of about 50 feet as I near the ground. This field is also alfalfa stubble. As I near the ground I rotate the stick backward and we slow, doing about 40 M.P.H. Gently the skid touches the alfalfa stubble and we decelerate and I feel myself lurch forward against the safety belt. The bottom of the skid has worn slick from use and it slides very easily over the stubble. We slide for about 100 feet, then come to a stop. The glider tilts over as the right wing tip drops over and rests on the ground. I unstrap the safety belt and crawl out, looking around to see if anyone approaches. Ray and Carl are going back across the first field and gathering up the towline, turning around and are heading back across the old wooden bridge over the drainage ditch. A short length of the towline is attached to the nose of the glider and the old Nash slowly drags it back over the bridge into the other field.

The north end of the first alfalfa field is an "L" shape cut into the corn field which extends all along the east side of both alfalfa fields. Beyond the corn, to the east is the Fairground. The tip end of the "L" forms a nice little secretive place to stake down the glider in the corn, hiding it from curious visitors and onlookers who drive along the highway at the south end of the field. Stakes are driven in the ground beneath the wing tips and tail to which we attached lengths of rope. The glider has a wingspan of 32 feet and a length of 18 feet and weighs only 118 pounds without the pilot. One of these southern Indiana windy thunderstorms would blow it away and tear it up if it were not staked down.

I feel lucky and good about the fact that as a 16-year-old BHS sophomore, I can do things like this. Two of us have taught ourselves to fly this thing the past two summers. It's the same thing as flying an airplane; it has the same controls as an airplane with the exception of there being no engine throttle as an airplane. Neither of us has ever flown an airplane. Gliders these days, in 1933, are pretty much what has been picked up from the youthful glider clubs in Germany following World War I. Today, gliders are of 3 basic types: The primary, the secondary, and the ultimate is the soaring glider or sail plane. The gliders of today got their start in the Rhon Mountains of Germany. The Mead Company dubbed our old primary the "Rhon Ranger."

Trademark of the primary is its open flat vertical framework fuselage. The secondary is usually strut braced instead of wire braced wings, with a fully fabric enclosed, but open cockpit, fabric covered the full length of the fuselage. The soaring glider has a much greater wingspan. Its wing is fully cantilevered, and is entirely aerodynamically super clean. Only a few are owned and flown and almost always by wealthier pilots. Some have been flown at Monteagle in the Smoky Mountains of North Carolina or the hill country of up state New York. They can stay in the air for hours, climbing on the rising thermal air currents in the mountains. Primary gliders, on the other hand, are being built and flown in profusion all over the country, not only by impromptu clubs like ours but by clubs formed in many colleges and universities.

Our little club started with a primary I built from German blueprints brought back from Germany by Marvin Northrop of Minneapolis. It was more rugged than our Mead "Rhon Ranger" but was heavier and more durable, but glide angle not as good as the "Ranger." I later sold it to a fellow in Ohio. Our later Mead was built from a "kit" by the Salem Glider Club. Recently I had a small home built monoplane powered by a 4-cylinder Henderson Motorcycle engine built by Al Hocker of Evansville. I tried to fly it but a poorly repaired broken wheel axle shimmied so badly I could not get it off the ground, a good thing perhaps. Meanwhile, I had struck up correspondence with Marvin Northrop, a World War I pilot with the British Royal Flying Corps, and an internationally known airplane dealer who operated out of Minneapolis. He purchased the Hocker from me sight unseen, with a mailed check. About six weeks later he showed up in a brand new flatbed truck to pick up his airplane, obviously surprised but enthusiastically friendly, to find that his correspondent was a 16-year-old aviation nut. Of course he is older than me, tall with blond Scandinavian hair, about 35 to 40 years old I would guess, well dressed in summer with a silky striped shirt, necktie and stylish sailor-straw hat.

It was a hot summer evening and my mother made up a large pitcher of lemonade. Northrop is a real hit with my parents. He told my father how he collected brewery posters for his recreation room in Minneapolis. My father made a hit with him by promising to send posters from three breweries in Evansville, which he later did. Northrop remembered selling me plans for the first primary glider and when he learned I built it, flew it, then sold it, his blue eyes told me he was about to make me a proposition. If I would return the check he'd sent for the Hocker, he would trade me a Mead "Rhon Ranger" Primary Glider for the Hocker. He had purchased the Rhon Ranger from the Salem Glider Club. I eagerly agreed. Next day we loaded the Hocker on his truck and drove the 125 miles to Salem. Next day we loaded my newly acquired Rhon Ranger on his truck and returned to Boonville where we had a second enjoyable visit again with Marvin Northrop. He told us that ten years earlier in 1923 he had purchased several war surplus training planes, offering them for sale at what would become Lambert Field in St. Louis. The trainers were used Curtiss Jennies and Standard J-l's. He sold them to enthusiastic non-pilots who aspired to fly their own airplanes. Mostly newly airminded Midwest farmers. Flight training sufficient to solo was included with each airplane for $300. Northrop hired a young barn storming pilot, also from Minnesota, to train the buyers and turn them loose on their own. The young pilot my friend Marvin Northrop hired to teach his customers was Charles Augustus Lindbergh (some 25 years later, Lindbergh would tell of his employment as an instructor working for Marvin Northrop in his book *The Spirit of St. Louis*. The book would become a motion picture of the same name featuring James Stewart as Lindbergh). Anyway, that is how I acquired this Mead "Rhon Ranger" glider.

Having a primary glider and flying it are two different things. You have to have three important things. No. 1, you have to have enthusiastic people to help you. The best way to do that is to let them take turns learning to fly it. Teamwork is essential. No. 2, you need a good long dry flat field of grass or hay stubble. No. 3, at least one of your team must be a smooth tow car driver. A lurching driver can easily stall the glider and cause a fatal crash.

My obsession with aviation and what makes airplanes tick goes back nearly as far as I can remember. At age 6-1/2 on the night of October 4, 1923, an unforgettable event of aeronautical history occurred in our little town. A native son, Commander (Cdr.) R.D. Weyerbacher had been chief constructor of the U.S. Navy's new 700-foot long rigid dirigible at the Navy's airship base in Lakehurst, New Jersey. It was the first dirigible built in the U.S.A. Only a month after its maiden flight, Commander Weyerbacher and his crew flew over Boonville in southern Indiana in the newly christened "Shenandoah" or ZR-1, its numerical designation. He dropped a parachute laden with flowers on his parents' Main Street lawn, and another parachute of greetings to the townsfolk and civic leaders on the Courthouse Square lawn.

From that day on I made it a full time project to learn and to read everything I could find or send away for in the mails on the subject of aviation of any kind. I regularly bought the lot of aviation magazines on the periodical stand at Kuntzman's Confectionery. Each acquisition revealed the existence of other publications, which I acquired through the mails. So, for the past ten years I have been reading such journals and magazines as *Popular Aviation, Aviation, Aero Digest,* the annual *Flying & Glider* manuals of Fawcett Publications which for 50 cents gave detailed construction plans for homebuilt airplanes and gliders. Such airplanes as the Pietenpol Air Camper, the Heath Parasol by Ed Heath in Chicago, the Longster by Les Long out in far away Oregon, the Corben Junior Ace by O.G. Corben of Madison, Wisconsin, and last but not least, Marvin Northrop's primary glider, the same plans as the blueprints I had purchased from him. I exhausted the local library collection of aeronautica and related technical texts. An old favorite was Grover Loenig's 1910 *Monoplanes & Biplanes.*

In those past 10 years I have taken rides with every barnstormer who showed up around Boonville. The first was in a raunchy, oily, tattered old Standard J-1 with Hall-Scott water-cooled engine with its leaky, ungainly radiator slung under the upper wing over the rear of the engine. I returned from that ride with my face smeared with oil and hot water. My father roared with laughter when I extricated myself from the forward cockpit. Another time was in a Curtiss JN-4 "Jenny" powered by the venerable old OX-5. In 1929, another ride was in a brand new beautiful Waco "10", owned by an Illinois airmail pilot, relative of a family in our town. The pilot's name was Ed Hamman. Not long afterward he was killed in a storm flying the mail between Chicago and St. Louis. On every airplane I came in contact with, I queried the pilots on every detail of those airplanes: name, model number, manufacturer, engine make, horsepower, and many questions even the pilots could not answer.

On another occasion in September 1929, I encountered a real windfall! The local Chamber of Commerce, along with other such chambers throughout the state had organized a statewide air tour. On a scheduled date, each member town was to be visited by an organized fleet of 35 private or commercially operated airplanes. A long field was selected and marked for visibility from the air. Our field stretched out north from Highway 62 east of Boonville and four miles from our house on Oak Street. It lay directly next and east of the Warrick County Poor Farm.

It turned out that the poor, aged and indigent had a veritable "field day" watching the exhilarating "commotion" next door as they excitedly rocked back and forth in their rocking chairs on their broad veranda. I rode out there early on my bike. Two hours later they began to show up, landing one at a time and parked in rows at the direction of white clothed flagmen. My father likened my response to all of this as like "a blind dog in a meat house." I stayed until long after the last plane departed near sunset.

I examined each and every one of those 35 airplanes and pestered each pilot with my usual well-memorized list of questions. The fleet was a real cross section of what was being built by a host of manufacturers and licensed between 1927 and 1929 by the Department of Commerce under the newly enacted Air Commerce Act of 1926. To name just a few, there was the big 3-engine Ford Trimotor. Then the Waco "10," Waco "9," American Eagle, Alexander Eaglerock, Lincoln-Page, Monocoach, Monocoupe, General "Aristocrat," Swallow, Travel Air 2000, Curtiss "Robin" (OX-5), Cessna "AW," "Bird" Model A, Ryan "Brougham," Lincoln-Standard and two dozen others I could name.

A week later a lone big biplane arrived at this same field. A lone pilot barnstorming rides. Seeing it in the air I lost no time on my bike. The airplane was a big 5-place Lincoln-Standard being built by the Lincoln Company in Lincoln, Nebraska. It was a modern 1929 version of the old Standard J-1 trainers of 1917 and 1918, but powered by the big Hispano-Suiza ("Hisso") engine of 150 to 200 horsepower. The rear open cockpit, as usual, carried the pilot. But the forward open cockpit was unusual for it seated four. Two side by side at the rear faced forward while the two forward faced rearward. Me and one adult stranger were the only customers.

We sat on the ground under a big oak tree next to the road with the plane nearby. I remember vividly the shiny riding boots of the pilot as he preached a sermon of dissent against President Herb Hoover and the Republicans, ignoring too many of my important unending questions about the airplane. His political tirade disappointed me. How could he be so absorbed in politics when he obviously owned this beautiful big grand old Lincoln-Standard and could fly it? But I thought my testy Grandma Autry (a devout Democrat) would love this pilot, but Grandpa (a devout Republican) would detest this upstart who would surely kill himself in this big "contraption!"

Another early mentor was Roscoe Pope, the son of our next door neighbors on Oak Street. He had moved to a new job in St. Louis. At that same time and place "Marv" Northrop and Lindbergh were selling Standards and Lindy was training the eager buyers just well enough so the new owners could fly them home—wherever in the Midwest that might be. But before St. Louis, Roscoe had first flown an hour or two of dual instruction with a barnstormer who had an old Standard J-1 and who had hung around their former place, a farm near Richland, Indiana not far from Boonville. This was several years before the parents moved to Boonville and he to St. Louis. In one of his trips home from St. Louis in about 1925, Roscoe gave me his collection of *Aero Digest* magazines. They opened up an entirely new era for me. I began saving nickels for a subscription.

The types of airplanes that predominated in the September 1929 air tour were tandem open cockpit biplanes powered by the old standby Curtiss OX-5, an 8-cylinder, V-type engine of 90 horsepower with long overhead valve rocker arms exposed to the windstream on some airplanes. Most of these biplanes typically were 3-place, seating two passengers side by side in the front cockpit, such as the Waco "9," Waco "10," Travel Air 2000, American Eagle, Alexander Eaglerock and many others. This air tour and other experiences recounted above took place several years before I took up building and flying gliders.

That air tour was 4 long years ago, and some of the other flights with barnstormers even before that when I was just a kid. Now I'm 16, and soon a junior at B.H.S. Now, already, it is summer of 1933. Hard to believe I'm getting so old so fast. The annual big Boonville Fair is about to take place. The Fairground fence is only a quarter of a mile east of the corn and alfalfa fields where I have been flying my glider. I have the glider staked down and hidden from the highway by the corn in a little patch of alfalfa stubble cut out of the north end of the cornfield. A little present of the kindly landowner, Mr. Hart. During the weeklong Fair each summer, our field is sometimes used by barnstormers to attract the nearby Fair goers over to take a 10-minute ride for $5.00 or whatever the traffic might bear. A yearly path had been worn through the cornfield from the Fairground to the alfalfa field by the curious, the brave, as well as the brave with a spare $5.00. The likely possibility of these Fairgoers traipsing along the path to the alfalfa field has me very worried. I am afraid they will discover my glider in its secluded notch and from there who knows? A glider is a frail contraption, if exposed to the heavy-handed. They might take it apart, tear it up, or otherwise damage it just in their enthusiasm to examine it. I'm thinking this on the day before the opening of the Fair as I ride my bike north through the field on the west edge of the corn heading for where my glider is staked down in the hot sun.

The Fair runs for seven days from 7:00 a.m. to 10:00 p.m. So what to do? I suppose I must camp out here day and night. Sitting in the shade of the wing all day in 95' heat and be eaten up by mosquitoes all night for seven nights? To make matters worse, Jim, Ray and Carl had only yesterday gone on a 3-week vacation trip with their families. I trust no one else and who else would suffer chiggers and mosquitoes all night to protect something in which they had no interest. My sympathetic father believed in my working my own problems. "Not the first time you ever camped out," he said.

I lay down my bike and walk around the glider the ailerons, rudder, elevators, and control runs. Then the wing lift-wire bracing under the wings and the wing dead-weight wires above the wing. There are a few tears in the fabric on the wing tips where I had let the glider tip to the side on landing. I patch those with fabric and nitrate dope from a kit I carried on my bike. I sat down in the shade under the wing, contemplating the boring week ahead. Even though the Fair does not open until tomorrow, there are transient Fair people who are setting up food stands, entertainment acts, fortunetellers and you name it.

They are already over there a quarter mile on the other side of the corn-field. I'm still concerned. Somebody could explore around over here and discover this thing. But it is well hidden. The A-frame atop the wing is 6 feet above the ground and the corn is even taller. After a few hours I decide I'm going to take the risk and go home for dinner and return early tomorrow. Dad said he would drive down in his Essex to provision me daily with food and drink as I carried out my vigil of protection for my precious "Rhon Ranger."

As I headed down to the highway on my bike I heard something! I know that it is a sound that means a great deal to me! What is it? Gosh, it sounds like an airplane! Barnstormers do not always show up for the annual Boonville Fair. Half the time they don't show up at all! What is it? I look all around and run out into the open hay field away from the tall corn, peering eastward. There it is, at an altitude of 500 feet, I see a biplane. The sound is unmistakable. It's a good old OX-5, a distinctive, peculiar combination of exhaust noise and two-bladed propeller clatter at about 1200 r.p.m.

As he heads this way I can see the single bay struts and the almost even span of the two wings. Silver wings and tail. A red fuselage. I am really excited. He turns to the north flying about 2 miles. My heart is sinking. Is he passing up the Fair? Then he begins a slow, gentle, 180-degree turn, then heads straight for our alfalfa field, losing altitude to about 75 feet, flies right by my bike and me! Good Lord! It is a Waco "10"! The pilot's arm is extended above his head as he sits in the rear cockpit giving me a little wave, his head going from side to side as he peers around the windshield for oncoming obstructions. He pulls up and climbs to the south about 3 miles, making a wide 180-degree turn to the west and heads back north. He is coming in for sure, losing altitude, engine r.p.m. noticeably reduced. He fishtails from side to side by kicking the rudder pedals from side to side to reduce his speed as he comes in over the 2-lane highway, clearing the phone wires by 50 feet, then touching down ahead in a perfect 3-point landing, rumbling and modestly bouncing along in the hay stubble right by me and my bike.

Coming to a halt down by the drainage ditch, he guns the engine, depresses the elevators, raises the tail, kicks the rudder and, keeping the skid off the ground, turns it around to the south, drops the tail and taxis toward me. Obviously, he's spotted my glider from the air, because it is bright orange and the span is 32 feet with a wing chord width of five feet. He taxies up to my little niche in the corn field, urging the OX-5 up in little nudges of the Waco's throttle, cuts the switch, the prop kicks back and forth a couple of times and stops. I am beside myself! I rush over alongside the cockpit. A slender fellow of about 35 stood up in the cockpit, helmetless, goggleless, straight dark hair combed straight back on the rare occasion it was combed, small dark moustache; lean face; dark, alert, enthusiastic eyes. He threw one leg over the side to find the step on the side of the fuselage, dropped to the ground. He wore a faded dress shirt that showed stains of oil that had defied laundry. His rumpled trousers showed only signs of once being pressed in a crease. Once rather elegant dress shoes had been relegated to a summer of barnstorming. I think to myself hoping he had warmer clothes bagged away in the front cockpit. He shakes my hand, saying, "I'm Marty." In return I stuttered my name to him.

"What you got over there?" he asked. "Looks like a primary glider. And I think it's a Mead, isn't it? A 'Rhon Ranger' I think they call it up in Chicago."

I ran around the Waco like my dad had said "like a blind dog in a meat house." I asked if I could climb on the fuselage step, peer into the rear cockpit of the Waco. He replied, "Sure, kid!" I blushed, said I was 16, going on 17. He chuckled, pushing his unruly hair back, then his eyes narrowed in a good-humored frown, beckoning over to the glider.

"You fly that thing?"

"Two years," I said.

His eyes told me he had added a few years to my 16 even though they did believe I was 16!

Looking back at the Waco again, I asked, "When was it built?" He thought a moment, obviously crediting me with a good question. "About 1928," he replied.

"In Troy, Ohio," I added.

"He replied, "Yes sir!" giving me a friendly punch on the shoulder.

He led me around the Waco, offering, "Note that I've installed a new ground adjustable all metal Hamilton-Standard propeller on the OX-5. It can be set for short field performance, which it is now, for on these barnstorming tours, field length can be short and the turf can sometimes present a lot of tire drag. Or the prop can be set for a better cruise performance and fuel mileage. But you can't have it both ways. More advanced planes than this old Waco are having props in which pitch can be changed in flight. Then you can have it both ways! The wood factory prop I removed was factory installed, painted red with copper sheathed tips to eliminate rain erosion on the tips of the blades."

I asked him if he planned on giving the Fair goers rides during the coming week. He said, "Sure, kid, but I have to charge $5.00 a head to pay expenses." Then he asked, "How do they get over here? They see the Waco land over here, but if they have to lose their car parking gate ticket to get over here, they'll never come. Is there any way they can walk over here?"

I knew right then that he had never barnstormed at Boonville before. In my hero-worship, I could not hide the truth about the old path through the corn of past barnstormers. The Fair goers would leave the grounds either by pure stealth or, on one occasion, the Fair officials saw the barnstormers as a lucrative free attraction (to them), and they posted a porter at the path to check the people's paid day tickets so they could go back and forth. When I told Marty all the details he gave me a quizzical look. He said, "Kid, you seem to have some reservations about telling me of that path through the corn?" and I told Marty of my concerns of vandalism rendered upon my precious "Rhon Ranger." He smiled broadly, but again returned to the quizzical look. Then I told him my plans to camp here all week.

After a full minute, he smiled again and softly said, "I think we can work something out." He looked south toward the highway, then back to my glider in its corn field niche. He said, "You have it as far back in there as it will go, but I think if we can lay a dozen corn stalks, the glider's tail will go further back and we can then push in the Waco and stake it down in front of your Rhon Ranger. Sound okay, Kid?"

"You bet!" was my eager reply. We went to work breaking off enough stands of corn to accommodate the span of the Ranger's elevators, then moved the glider back and re-staked it. We then lifted the tail of the Waco, pushing it into the corn niche and staking it down.

The day was now winding down and the sun was getting low. We sat under the glider's wing while Marty thoughtfully rolled and lit a cigarette out of a sack of Bull Durham. "You're staying here twenty-four hours a day for a week?" he asked incredulously.

I replied, "Yes, I figure I got no other choice."

He pressed his lips together, shaking his head, saying, "Kid, if you'll look after both ships tonight, I'll make it worth your while, okay?" I nodded and he asked the whereabouts of the nearest hotel. I told him, "The St. Charles, northwest corner of the Court Square. Walk down to the highway and turn left. It's only about a mile."

I have made my decision to camp all week at the field but I have yet to tell my parents I would start tonight. And I need food, drink, flashlight and a mosquito netting. I hate to leave the Waco and the glider but I'll wait until near dark, speed home on my bike and hurry back. Nearly an hour has passed. Sun is now below the horizon. I gotta go. I pick up the bike, push it out onto the field. Then I see a car coming down into the southeast corner of the field. Dad's Essex! Good old Dad! Reading my mind again! I ride down to meet him and he and I turn back up to where the planes are tied down. He has brought along a box of sandwiches, jugs of water and lemonade, a flashlight and mosquito netting.

"I saw the Waco over town, and was sure it would land for the Fair and it being so late and all..." he says.

"The Pilot's name is Marty. He walked to town. I sent him to the St. Charles!" I bragged.

"I know. I just met him at Rudolph's Sinclair Station on First and Main. He was arranging for Rudolph to drive his gas truck down here tomorrow and gas up the Waco. I introduced myself as your dad. You know, I said I was the dad of the boy down here with the glider."

Doggoned it, I like my dad a lot, but he is always calling me a boy. Heck's alive. I'm nearly 17 for gosh sakes! I asked him, "You're kidding me! How in the heck did you know he was the Waco pilot? He is a stranger in town and I don't think Mr. Rudolph would bother to introduce him."

Dad gave me that smug look he often gets. "Simple. I know every soul in this little town. Sure he is a stranger. So he had to be the Waco pilot. Then I heard him ask Rudolph to gas up his plane. I told him I'd pick him up tomorrow morning to come down here. And that you and I wanted the first ride in the Waco before the Fair yokels started breaking down the corn to get over here."

We had some sandwiches and lemonade, but Dad has now left me to fend off the mosquitoes. Sitting half prone in the Waco with the rear cockpit covered with the net has staved off the "skeeters." Now I yearn to stretch out and sleep. Prone in the grass, I slumber dead as a stone, but the net is not large enough draped over the Ranger's wing tip. Now slips in the big "skeeter" fighter-bombers droning in my ears, then the stings as they loosen all their machine guns on my neck and ears and even their blood-sucking stingers pierce my shirt and trousers. Finally it is sun-up and the vampires retreat to wherever it is the doggoned bloodsuckers go at dawn of day. In the box I search out mother's cold biscuits and a cup of lemonade. I find a thoughtfully supplied tube of Unguentine for my "skeeter" bites. I spent all of last night going back and forth between trying to sleep half sitting up and half lying down in the rear cockpit or by stretching out under the Ranger's wing. Under the wing, otherwise blessed sleep was thwarted. Thwarted by these bloodthirsty savages of the night. In the cockpit I had the suckers foiled except for one or two who slipped under the netting when I climbed in. I gleefully smashed their vicious little bodies between my palms with a sadistically satisfying whack! Sleep came easily for an hour until the yearning to become prone and lack of the blessed ability to turn over became unbearable. Then I would climb out, try to arrange the net once more over the Ranger's wingtip, but all to no avail. Only ten minutes of prostrate bliss, then the droning bombers found their way under the canopy. Then a hasty retreat back to the cockpit. Repeated over and over again all night long.

Then comes the blessed dawn. Low sun in the east, warming dew on the upper wing of the Waco created little wisps of rising mist. The smell of taut doped fabric and a host of other mystic scents that make up the wonderful mesmerizing pastoral odor of a wood, steel tube and fabric airplane in a rural field. How lucky I was to be visited by this beautiful ship and its pilot.

Sitting right here in my care, no less, on this beautiful summer day! Soon now I would fly in this Waco. The horrors of the night rapidly faded. How happy I was! Heck, if I can be so lucky as all this—flying my own glider at 16, a new friend in a Waco "10," a great Dad—if I could do all these things, I could certainly overcome a nocturnal mosquito problem. For starters, I could use Unguentine before being bitten instead of afterward. Maybe it would taint my youthful flesh, hopefully turning their voracious little appetites away from me and incite them to the vast human supply of blood that would tonight be available over at the evening Fair.

Thoughts of my swollen bites are happily dispersed at the sight of Dad's Essex parking at the south field just off the highway. A small red truck has parked behind the Essex. I recognized the truck as belonging to Mr. Hart, owner of the alfalfa field. Two men get out of the Essex. Marty had ridden down with Dad as my father had promised last evening. The three men conversed for a moment, then Mr. Hart drove away before I could reach them on my bike. I knew that Mr. Hart did not allow motor vehicles to traverse the field except for a few occasional barnstorming airplanes. People taking rides with the pilots had to park along the highway and were loaded into planes at the south end near the road with takeoffs made to the north. Dad and Marty are rapidly getting acquainted. My approach, mosquito bites and all, seemed not to attract their attention at all. Marty was telling him that Rudolph would soon be arriving next to the Essex in his gasoline tank truck and he'd best get up to the Waco and taxi it down to the truck. As we made our way north along the edge of the field, Marty began telling me he wished my help in getting the OX-5 cranked up. He had spied some heavy chunks of wood to which he would tie some lengths of rope I had with the glider. The chunks would be safety wheel chocks which could be remotely pulled away from the rotating propeller without the de-chocker getting his head split wide open. Something of an inarguable necessity. After loosing its staked tie-down ropes, we lifted the tail of the Waco and pulled it out into the open field, placing the chocks ahead of the wheels with ropes played out well behind and to one side of the propeller. Marty thoughtfully stood surveying us with his hands on his hips.

Then he turned to Dad, "Sir, when we get the engine started, only on my signal, pull the chocks only on the left wheel, then run around behind the plane and pull the right chock. Never get any closer to the propeller than the end of the rope. Stay far away from the propeller at all times. As you know, the Waco has no starter like your Essex. I will swing the prop by hand and your son will help me with the engine controls in the cockpit."

Now he is leading me around to the rear cockpit, gesturing for me to climb in as he stands alongside on the cockpit step. He now speaks in a new curt, no nonsense manner, asking me if I have ever done this before? I shake my head.

"Okay. Now listen carefully. This is the Ignition Switch, see? Off and on, here and here. It's the only thing I want you to touch on the instrument panel. I am going to set the magneto in Retard. Don't touch it. I am also going to position the throttle where I want it. Don't touch the throttle. When the motor starts it will be running at a low r.p.m. speed. Stay in the cockpit until I come around and take your place. Now, the Switch is off, keep it there until I call out to you from up front. I will have to swing the prop two or three different times to prime the engine. When I do that the Switch must be off. Otherwise you could break my arms if the engine fires while I am trying to prime it. Okay. When I get up front, before I touch the prop, I will call out 'Switch Off!' You make certain the switch is off. Then you answer loud; 'Switch is off.' I will then swing the prop a couple of times, making sure I keep my arms and legs clear. When I am ready I will call out, 'Switch on!' Throw the switch to on, then call out loudly, 'Switch is on!' When I swing the prop the engine should start. If it doesn't we may have to repeat the process. When it starts I will run around to you. You climb out and I climb in. Then I'll taxi down to the south end to meet the gas truck."

Well! I feel like a real airplane pilot now. In the driver's seat and about to fire up! Okay, Peyton, knock off the foolish nonsense, I tell myself. Marty calls out up front and we go through the priming procedure. Then at the "switch on" phase, he pulls her through and I feel a blast of wind around the windshield as the OX-5 coughs and sputters a small cloud of exhaust smoke. The entire framework of the plane is alive and vibrant. Sounds of all kinds from all kinds of places. "R-r-r—R-r-r" of the rotating crankshaft. The air-flailing patter of the prop blades. The vibrant drum of taut fabric. I put my face around the windshield into the air stream. I feel a confident exhilaration that leaves me extremely reluctant to leave this seat.

My dream is abruptly halted by a rap on the head. It's Marty. Jerking his upturned thumb over his shoulder. "Out!" I hurriedly extricate myself. He climbs in and with uplifted arms signals Dad to pull the chocks.

He then taxis slowly south, rumbling along with little spurts of low r.p.m. power he throttles from the OX-5. Mr. Rudolph is waiting with the tank truck as Marty pulls up, blasts the tail skid up off the ground with the elevators and turns around with the Waco headed north, props the tail and switches off the engine.

The gas tank and filler cap is behind the engine and ahead of the front cockpit. With the truck in front of the airplane, Marty climbs up with the hose. After he completes the job and Rudolph drives the truck away, Mr. Hart shows up again. Mr. Hart is a prosperous Warrick County farmer, as prosperous farmers go. But he is also an air minded farmer. He is no pilot or expert on planes like me. But he loves planes and aviation people. He has let me and my glider friends use the field and drive the old Nash through the fields as a tow-car as long as we do no damage. We know his rules and we follow them. For example, we never fly or drive the tow-car on the field after a heavy rain. I have briefed Marty on Mr. Hart. Marty shows his appreciation by telling Mr. Hart he will fly him as a free passenger any time during the coming week that he wishes.

Mr. Hart quickly allows as how this is as good a time as any, making the sage observation that very soon the Fair yokels will be taking up all of our intrepid pilot's time. He had overheard Marty's remark that he would fly Dad and I first as a gesture of appreciation for my watchdogging his Waco all night. Mr. Hart would not think of going first even though Dad insisted. Instead, he would watch my glider while we were aloft, then take his turn when we returned.

The three of us repeated the earlier procedure of starting up the OX-5. Marty beckoned us to climb aboard. He had briefed me earlier on how to occupy the front cockpit which seated two people side by side with a wide safety belt which stretched across both our laps. Entry was on a reinforced step or walkway area of the inner lower left wing. A small hinged door and latch was cut in the side of the cockpit to allow easy entry without bumping noggins on the upper wing. The "10" had forward dual controls which were disconnected when flying non-pilots or passengers. The wood joystick had been removed from its socket in the floor and the cables to the rudder pedals disconnected from those in the rear cockpit. Other engine controls and panel instruments were either disconnected or absent altogether. After we were aboard and belted in, I raised my arm that we were ready as Marty had instructed me to do. The OX-5 came to life from a sputtering idle to its full 1400 r.p.m. and 90 horsepower. The tail came up to a level attitude and we began to slowly gather speed, the gentle rumbling sound of rolling wheels over the hay stubble is now drowned out by the engine and propeller. I can feel the wing lift us gently into the warm still air and the noise of the airplane once it is aloft only 50 feet seemed to subside and became markedly serene by comparison. Why is that? The pilot has not cut back power. The OX-5 needs almost all it can put out to climb up to an altitude where it can be cut back. So I'm thinking that when taking off the noise a passenger or a pilot hears is louder because it is reflected against the ground. When aloft even at an altitude of 50 feet the noise markedly begins to subside until at 500 or 1000 feet or more, it is instead a serene noise that gives a feeling of security and exhilarating pleasure. I am making a mental point to ask Marty why this seeming decay in noise occurs. I will do better than that, I will advance my theory first and see if he agrees. Whether he agrees or not I will learn something either way. The thought gives that old smug feeling that feels so good. The feeling of being right even if you are wrong.

At 75 feet we pass by the old Rhon Ranger sitting there in its niche in the cornfield, the bright international orange color of its wings gleaming in the sun in sharp contrast to the five large black numbers 12846 of its registration with the Bureau of Air Commerce. Mr. Hart waves his straw hat as we whiz by. Off to the right, the first day of the great 1933 Warrick County Fair is at full tilt. Already lots of people are roaming the Midway. The Merry-go-round and Ferris Wheel are in full rotation, loaded with real kids and old kids. The race track tenders are dragging and watering the dirt one-mile track for the afternoon harness races for those graceful trotters and pacers and the color-fully dressed drivers on their handsome two-wheeled sulkies. For a moment I am distracted by the metal nameplate on the instrument panel; "Advance Aircraft Company, Troy, Ohio." The name of the company that builds Waco airplanes located northeast of Cincinnati. The original name was "Weaver Aircraft Company", which abbreviated formed the name that became per-manently attached to the firm's products even after it became Advance Air-craft Company. Waco is pronounced "Wah-co," not "Way-co."

Dad shouldered me out of my nameplate trance, pointing down and to the right. The old Elk-Horn Mill where he worked years ago and the 2-story frame house just next it to the east where I was born 16 years ago. Now! From here we can see the full length of First Street clear to the south end of town! On its northern end, below us at a 30-degree angle, is the eastern main entrance to the Fair. I laughed to myself that there must be a hundred auto-mobiles, mostly Fords lined up to enter. The Roth Brothers, Ford dealers on First and Main would be most happy to see this aerial view of their long time profits. We are heading east circling our hometown. I see the Boonville wa-ter tank tower up ahead where as kids we were always frightening the neigh-bors by climbing the 100-foot flimsy steel ladder. Now we bank more to the south, looking along Oak Street to the west at a 30-degree angle. I can see our house at 420 Oak Street. Tiny neighbors standing in the street. One is probably my anxious mother. Knowing dad, I'm sure he told her we were going flying today. Since our Waco is now the only airplane in the county she is without a doubt sure that it is we who are her "brave ones up there." I'm sure she is telling all the neighbors who will listen. Next, we head west over Old Lake. I can see the bathhouse, the pier, the diving platform and a dozen or so bathers and swimmers. I can even see a few leaping up and down and waving. Marty gives the girlish bathing beauties a thrill. He rolls the Waco from side to side and blips the OX-5 by gently jockeying the throttle about 200 r.p.m. up and down in speed. Enough so they can hear it real good. Dumb girls. They are probably now shrieking their heads off! Begging their split-second hero to dive down and carry them off to some heroic place where if he did they would scream for help after less than a half minute. I wish he hadn't done that. It's not what a real aviator like him should do.

We are now over the fields just out of the southwest edge of town. The Southern railroad tracks that run east and west through Boonville stretches out in the distance to the west to the city of Evansville where they join the Chicago and Eastern Illinois. The latter connects Chicago through the southern states all the way to Florida and its famous fast train the "Dixie Flyer." Marty banks to the right and north over the Southern tracks and I can see our field ahead as it stretches north beyond our Highway 62. The OX-5's steady staccato laboring lessens as Marty gradually cuts back on the throttle and noses down slightly, coasting down in a shallow glide. Then he cuts back on the throttle still more, the OX-5 giving off little minor coughing backfires. We are dropping a bit too fast and he increases the engine r.p.m.'s and pulls up a bit but still not to climb. We are still gliding. Then he cuts back again and fishtails the Waco in a right-left/left-right yaw to slow us down. We come in over the phone wires with seventy-five feet to spare. He cuts back on r.p.m. almost to idle, straightens her out and we touch down, trundling down through the hay stubble to where Mr. Hart is standing by the Ranger.

As we swing around and taxi back to the Ranger, I am concerned because at the end of our landing roll, I had seen a dozen people making their way through the cornfield trail. As we come to a stop I rise up and yell to Marty,

"Don't shut off the engine!"

Marty looks at me knowingly, then over to Mr. Hart, nodding his head. Dad and I climb out and I run over to Mr. Hart, shouting above the idling Waco.

"Mr. Hart, there are passengers coming. Marty will take you up now while he still can. I'll help you get in!"

I climb up on the wing walk, open the door, help him into the cockpit, making sure the safety belt is secured across his lap, take his straw hat and place it on the floor. As I jump down Marty guns the OX-5 and they start taxiing down to the south end of the field for their takeoff. A dozen people walk out of the corn and then curiously over to the Ranger. A few reach down with feigned nonchalance, pulling a weed to chew on, getting up nerve enough to ask a question or two. An older gent in well-washed denim overalls withdrew his weed, asking,

"Is the airyplane leavin' now? Don't the pilot feller know the Fair is jist startin'? Some of us'ns was hopin' we'uns could take a ride."

"No," I replied. "He is taking up a passenger. Back in about 15 minutes. I work for him. You just pay me and I will put you on the plane. First come first served. It's $5.00."

"Is it cheaper fer two?" he countered.

"Nope, it's $5.00 each, but he wants to take two at a time. The plane carries just two passengers. You can't all go up at once, nor can you go one at a time. Unless there is only one who is paid."

My explanation seems to have provoked a conference for they all form a little circle over near the corn, and out of earshot, to discuss the situation, all the while digging into their overalls to count their money. I know it is a serious decision for them. I know all too well that some of them must work for nearly a week every day to earn $5.00. They also know that going home to the farm next day to report a 15-minute ride over the county seat would earn extra respect and admiration from the other farm hands. "Worth it to have flewed," as one later said.

Then I saw five more coming out of the corn. With the Waco gone this second group turned their attention to my glider. One was a more youthful yokel than any of the others. I hate to admit that he is my own age, but a dumb country bumpkin probably from up around Lickskillet in the washed-out gully "farms" being reclaimed by old Roosevelt's New Deal WPA crews at taxpayer expense, or so says my grandpa, my dad's dad. Before I can stop the yokel he runs over and begins thumping on the taut fabric as if it was a drum solely constructed for him to beat.

"Boy! Shore is like a great big drum. If I had 'er in my yard I'd be beatin' tunes on 'er all day long. I seed 'er land jist a few minutes ago. How come she can fly with no engine? I'd a swore I heerd 'er runnin' an' a turnin' a perpeller! How come she's staked down?"

I dash over too late but yell at him,

"Keep back away from it! Stay behind the stakes and tie-ropes! Do not touch it or beat on it that way!"

He leaps back giggling, bug eyes all agog. I tell him it is a glider and what he saw was an airplane, which would be returning soon. I did not ask him if he wanted to ride for $5.00. Marty might not appreciate this idiot as a passenger. Obviously he was unpredictable. If alone and with a passenger as nutty as he was I could visualize the two of them unstrapping the safety belt and start climbing around in the wings of the biplane 800 feet above the town. His other four companions giggled and cavorted around at the ex-change between me and this Lickskillet bumpkin. They probably did not have 50 cents between them let alone $5.00. 1 looked forward to Mr. Hart's return. He'd chase them off his field, no questions asked or answered. I am worried that these five yokels will likely hang around the Fair all week, sleeping nights off the grounds after the 10:00 p.m. closing time. Now they have found the field and my glider and the Waco, I am more resolved than ever to camp here all week until the end of the Fair. The yokels keep some distance from the glider but they smirkingly grin their disdain of my protec-tionism.

Then the overall clad dozen come ambling over, give me six names and instruct me timidly on the order and pairing they wish in flying over their county seat, producing six $5.00 bills! Marty is going to be real pleased when I give him this money. I had better plan this carefully so I can unload and reload the passengers to save time without him having to shut down the OX-5 or get out of the pilot's cockpit.

There! Marty is gliding in over the highway to touch down. When he has taxied up to the glider niche I get up on the wing to help Mr. Hart out, then I yell above the OX-5's idling noise to Marty, showing him the $30.00. He gives me a thumbs-up salute and beckons me to bring on the next load, which I do. I see they are strapped in and off they go, slowly taxiing down to the south end for yet another takeoff. I go over to Mr. Hart and give him my verbal assessment of the loathsome five horsing around with my glider, now without actually touching it. Mr. Hart steps quickly over to them, mincing no words.

"You are on private property. If you have come over to take an airplane ride, then pay this young man. Otherwise, leave. We guard these airplanes all night. I use a sixteen-gauge shotgun on any trespassers after dark. So if you have any idea of camping here tonight or any other night, you can count on getting your loathsome butts so full of birdshot you won't be able to stand up for a month."

They lost no time heading back down the corn trail to the Fair. I just hoped they believed that Mr. Hart stayed here all night with his shotgun, but the look on their sober faces told me they did not yearn to find out. Fifteen minutes later Marty is taxiing up again to unload and reload passengers. The two de-planing are greatly excited, one telling their waiting friends,

"We'uns seen the whole county from up thar! I was skeered we was gonna nose-dive to the ground an' kill us both but that pilot feller kept 'er up thar the whole time. Yep, he was strugglin' to keep 'er from nose-divin' an' kept her good an' level. We got him to thank for savin' our lives!"

Good gosh! I hope no one else hears this yokel's overdone yarn. Not good for Marty's passenger-hopping business. But luckily his passenger buddy countered his overblown assessment.

"Aw, Clem, it was safe an' sound. He wasn't fightin' to keep it from nose-divin'! Shucks, I'd fly all day an' feel as safe as on the ground, if I had $5.00 for ever' fifteen minutes all day!"

CHAPTER **II**

A s I put a new load of passengers on board I see two dozen more fair goers coming out of the cornfield trail, all of them nonchalantly chewing on weeds they had plucked on the way. All wore well-washed denim overalls and straw hats. Good honest hard working farm folk to whom the Fair and an airplane ride were their only taste of entertainment all year. I feel a warm spot in my heart for them just like I have for these six we are flying now.

Of the new bunch, eight produce five dollars each and then patiently sit on the prickly alfalfa stubble in the hot sun waiting their turn, all nibbling on a weed or blade of grass. They sit there talking of past plane rides in this same field or of their labors in a harvest soon to come. God bless them, I'm thinking. They deserve a good plane ride, these good simple folk. I tell them if they are careful they are welcome to sit in the shade under the Ranger's wing. One responds in an "Aw shucks" manner.

"Naw, we'uns is used to the sun. 'Sides we'd be afraid we'd accidental puncture your glider machine. But it shore is a purty thing. We heerd you'uns flyin' it with a car pullin' it. That shore is somethin', I tell ya."

This first day of the Fair has been a busy one for me and Marty. He has flown thirty passengers today and I hand over the one hundred fifty dollars to him as he said,

"Kid, we did real good today, but I'm ready to quit."

People have now stopped coming through the cornfield.

They are all packed in the grandstand, viewing the entertainers on the platform next to the bandstand across the racetrack. We can hear it all. The sensational announcements, the band's steady stream of John Phillip Sousa renditions. Music for the acrobats and jugglers. In the background is the never ending, soul stirring pieces of the carousel merry-go-round's calliope.

We stake down the Waco for the night and I see dad walking his way up from the highway carrying something, after parking the Essex down in its usual place. One of the things is long and wrapped in one of my mother's thin quilts. The other is a large roll of mosquito netting. Boy! I sure welcome that. It is much larger than the one with which I suffered last night. Marty and dad proceed to drape one of the Ranger's wingtips with the netting, tucking and tying it here and there so the voracious vampires cannot enter and suck my youthful body dry of blood as they did last night. Now I can stretch out flat on mother's quilt and really sleep, protected from those vicious "skeeters"! Absolute bliss is what it will be! Yes, absolute bliss!

Then dad unwraps the long thing. It is about four feet long. My jaw drops in puzzlement. It is an old single barrel, sixteen-gauge shotgun, and dad hands me a half dozen shotgun shells.

"What in the world is this for?" I asked.

"Well, Mr. Hart said to give it to you along with the shells loaded with birdshot. He said if those punks come back and try to harm you or do damage to your glider to fill their butts with birdshot. But be careful not to shoot them in the head."

I shake my head wearily and tell dad,

"Aw, I won't need that. But if he wants me to keep it, lay it over there. I think he scared them pretty good today without this. But I tell you one thing, if they started tearing up my glider right here in front of me, I'd stop them somehow, shotgun or not."

He and Marty turn to walk to the Essex, telling me they'd see me tomorrow morning. I could tell Marty was ready to flop into his bed at the St. Charles. I am tired. I eat sandwiches from the box and drink lemonade from the thermos. Very carefully I enter the netting shelter and seal off every crack and cranny, for soon the "skeeters" will be out in full force. The netting is so roomy and far from my ears that I do not even hear their impatient buzzing. But I know they lust to drain me dry of every ounce of blood. I fall asleep in less than a minute and begin dreaming that by some glorious miracle I have been able to entrap every mosquito in the world into a diabolical chamber of my own ingenious design—a chamber conceived in such genius it would be the frantic envy of he who invented the pendulum for Edgar Allen Poe's inescapable Pit of Horrors. My chamber is a cube of only a few feet in width such that when it contains all the mosquitoes in the world those mosquitoes are so confined that they barely have room to roll over let alone to fly. The ingenuity of my chamber is its ability to reduce its size at my command as each of its six sides move inward to its center but yet maintains its geometric symmetry as a cube. In each of my commands I call for the precise dimensions of shrinkage I wish it to assume. Until at last I call for a cube size to which it can no longer respond because all the mosquitoes in the world are now a mass of compressed bodies and mosquito juice. All of the mosquito juice in the world is under such compressive pressure that it brings about the heat of combustion. All sides of the cube are blown apart and its contents are consumed in flames. And all the humans and animals in the world can rest and sleep in blissful tranquillity.

How can I be so blissfully asleep when I can see the orange underside of the Ranger's wing in plain daylight? And what is that infernal noise? I cannot believe it is dawn already. Any idiot would know I had just gone to sleep. The dew on the hay stubble beyond the netting is a perfect clue that it is early morning. The infernal noise is early morning carpentry over in the Fair's Midway. A wave of utter disappointment descends upon my rested conscience. My miraculous shrinking chamber was only a dream. Pure reflex brings me to double-check the security of the netting as I carefully extricate myself from its confines. The dawning sun has driven away the mosquitoes. I dig into the box for mother's biscuits and jam. I look around. There are no signs of intruders. Even the shotgun lay where I left it outside my cabin of netting. An intruder could have riddled me in my bed—or worse, riddled the wings of the Ranger and the Waco. Tonight I would either lay it under my make-shift pillow or hide it over in the cornfield. I amble over to the Waco, look into both cockpits, wiggle the controls and give it a general walk-around inspection. All okay. Then I hear the Essex parking and dad and Marty make their way up the field.

The three of us get the OX-5 cranked up. Marty taxis us down near the Essex as Mr. Rudolph arrives with his gas truck. The fueling complete, we are ready for another day hopping passengers. And none too soon. Two cars show up parking next to the Essex, four wanting rides. At the same time we can see six figures ambling out of the cornfield near the glider. We get the OX-5 cranked up and I load two from the cars into the Waco and Marty takes off with them and I hike up the field with the other two. All six from the cornfield want rides. The morning sun is still low and the air blissfully cool. What a gorgeous day and I thank my lucky stars at being able to do all this. Another day of barnstorming in Warrick County, Indiana.

At fifteen minutes after sundown we have flown thirty-two passengers. Another one hundred sixty bucks which I turn over to Marty. He gives me a look of real camaraderie, which makes me feel better than ever. He says, "Soon we will have some settling up to do." He looks up at the sky, then looks off to the west at the rays of the fading sunset.

"Now that we have no passengers, I wanted the two of us to take off late in the afternoon and scout out some of the local countryside. We can put the stick in up front and hook up the rudder pedals so you can feel the Waco and compare it to flying the Rhon Ranger. Your dad told me it's okay. Your dad and I also talked some more about you and how I could compensate you for all your help signing up all these passengers and looking after my plane all night. But we will go into that later. I want to talk to your dad some more about it. But anyway, the first chance we get, we will take a flight together. But we should do it late in the day when it's cooler. The passenger business slacks off late in the day anyway. How does that sound?"

I lost no time in giving him a response. "Wow! Sure! I'm ready any time you are! But I know you have to fly all the passengers you can first."

I didn't say it, but I should have, that just being here and doing this is all the payment I want. And to fly the Waco? Gosh, it is a real pleasant surprise that never occurred to me. And I had not even thought of getting a cut of that passenger money. I saw the amount of money Marty peeled off to pay Mr. Rudolph for his best grade of gasoline. The OX-5 was a temperamental engine with a distinct distaste for dirty, watery, low octane fuel. I had heard and read of careless 'Jennie' barnstormers who had suffered the OX-5's distaste for cheap, watery tractor gas by having to make forced landings in very inhospitable places. Such as the roofs of farmhouses, barns or trees. Marty had contrived his own fuel strainer and a funnel inserted into the filler neck of the 35-gallon tank. The Waco also had a 4-gallon oil capacity which required frequent replenishment. Fuel and oil were not Marty's only expenses. His hotel and restaurant bill at the St. Charles was much more expensive than my alfalfa bed under the Ranger's wing.

I sympathetically mentioned all of this to Marty. He seemed to be thinking carefully before surprising me with his response.

"Well, the reason I stayed at the St. Charles was to get some rest. I've been on this tour all summer and most of the time I sleep under the Waco's wings like you've been doing under your glider. But every once in a while I go into a town and sleep in a bed, take a bath, wash out some clothes. So I've concluded I'm rested up enough now at the St. Charles that tomorrow night I may want to use the other "room" of your place here—the opposite wing of your glider. That be okay with you?"

"Yeah!" I replied. "Sure! Dad left more of that netting. There is enough left to rig up another net tent on the other end of the Ranger's wings!"

The barnstormer threw his head back in a loud laugh.

"Okay, we'll do it. Tomorrow night. I want one more night of blissful slumber at the St. Charles."

With that he headed back down to the highway where he will turn left, go up Orphan's Home Hill on Locust Street, then four blocks to the Court Square, then left a block on the Square to the St. Charles at Second and Main. I sat in the cockpit of the Waco a while, wiggling the controls, watching the ailerons, rudder and elevators respond to my movements of the joy stick and rudder pedals, all the while dreaming of the upcoming crack at the real thing. Then the "skeeters" began to arrive for their nocturnal blood binge and I headed for my net cabin and fell asleep, the intrepid aviator.

I awoke early, had my biscuits, jam and lemonade. No signs of life all night. At least none that I knew of. Darn! I have forgotten the old shotgun again. It lay over there in the stubble where dad had put it. The sixteen gauge shells lay beside it. Alongside lay Marty's Spartan duffel, strainer funnel and gas can which he stowed in the front cockpit when flying cross-country without passengers. I occupied myself by un-staking the Waco and tending to a few minor repairs on the Ranger.

I thrust one arm deep into my trouser pocket to fish out my 'Pocket Ben' dollar watch. It was nine o'clock already and no sign of dad, Marty or Mr. Rudolph. The Waco would need gassing up judging by all the flying the day before. Now I'm really getting nervous because "wouldn't you know it" here comes four guys trudging along the cornfield trail from the Fair grounds. Probably wanting an early morning ride in the Waco.

The first is looking at me somewhat in disbelief.

"You the pilot?" he asked in a tone of distrust.

"No. Pilot is in town. He'll be here soon. I work for him. Rides are five dollars each. He takes two at once. Pay me and I'll get the first two on the first ride."

Then the existence of the Ranger dawns on his infertile brain.

"Haw-haw-haw! Ferd, looka over here at this thing! It ain't got no engine, not even a perpeller."

Then he turns to me and gurgles, "What in tarnation is it fer, if ye cain't fly it nohow?"

"Of course it flies. It's a glider. We tow it in the air with an automobile."

His face beams in disbelief as if I am lying through my teeth.

"Looka here! A dang automobile won't fly even if it has a engine. Neither will that contraption with no engine."

It's high time I change the subject so I say,

"How many of you want to fly? Pay me your five dollars. First come first served. But you'll have to wait 'til the pilot shows up and we get the plane gassed up." At that I turned my back and began fussing with things that needed no fussing. It was now nine thirty by the Pocket Ben. Just as I started a new round of worrying, Rudolph's red truck drove down off the highway. A minute later the Essex pulled up behind it.

My new companions saw the truck too. They began whispering briefly, then the doubting one offered, "We'uns all want to go flyin'," handing me four five dollar bills.

Dad and Marty ambled up as though they were early, both chuckling at my obviously anxious expression. Not the least wanting to be critical of my hero Marty, I instead frowned at dad, driver and chauffeur, who in our years of familiarity I could criticize. I said,

"It's late. Where've you been? I've got four customers waiting."

Dad looked over at the new customers who he obviously recognized.

"You already got their money? I know them. They're old man Turpin's boys. They probably stole that money. We better fly 'em and get 'em on their way. They're not dangerous. They just like to steal anything laying around."

We started the Waco and Marty and I taxied down to the truck while dad stayed with the untrustworthy four. After we gassed up, I helped Marty start the OX-5 but this time I had to do dad's un-chocking job too. We taxied up to the glider and I loaded on the first two of the Turpins. Thirty minutes later Marty had flown all four, dad sending them back through the cornfield to the Fair, telling them we had work to do—inferring unerringly that they were in our way.

It still nags me that dad took so long. He gets up at five O'clock without fail every morning. I feel left out of this new exciting relationship between the three of us. I've known dad for sixteen years, but Marty only three days. Now my relationship with dad has taken on a new meaning with his interest in this barnstormer on a par with my own. Dad has always pleased me very much. But he and Marty seem to have an amusing secret between themselves that they seem mischievously reluctant to share with me. And I am having a hard time hiding my jealousy even though I am.

"What took you so long this morning?" I asked grudgingly.

"I met Marty early and we had a long breakfast at the St. Charles," dad said matter-of-factly with an air of phony nonchalance. His statement of non-information has me stewing even more. Then he added,

"Oh yeah. After breakfast we went out to the house and he met your mother. I showed him the plans for your old glider and the airplane plans and figures that you have done."

I don't know what to say. My stuff? Without me to show it? He seems to delight in deepening some kind of mystery. And why have Marty meet mother? She has always trusted me, but had only a mother's non-technical interest in flying machines and depended on dad as well as myself to engage in gliders and planes, hopefully sanely and safely. But she hardly even knew my four local glider buddies, let alone the barnstormer of just three days acquaintance. But like me, dad knew and trusted the right people quickly.

It was still early and no additional passengers had shown up out of the cornfield or down on the highway. Marty switched off the OX-5, removed its top cowling, then climbed up straddling the engine and began fussing with the valve settings with a feeler gauge he withdrew from a pocket. Dad and I gathered around, looking up as our pilot friend did his little inspection. Dad then asked, "Marty, you think we ought to tell him now?"

"Don't see why not. There are plenty of things to do before we leave— for both of us. If he goes along with me," he says looking down at me with a wide grin.

What is going on here? Who goes where? I feel a pang of disappointment when I realize that I had not reckoned with the fact that Marty, like all barnstormers, would remain here in Boonville only a few days. I had become so imbued with this exciting partnership I guess I figured it would last forever, without even thinking about it. Then Dad laid a hand on my shoulder. He was saying,

"Okay, Marty is leaving in a few days to continue his barnstorming tour for the rest of the summer. He would like to take you along and will come back through here about the middle of September when school starts. We kicked it around with your mother too. So it's all up to you if you want to go. But there are some things you will need to do. The main one is what to do with your glider? Your buddies won't be back here for a month to look after the Ranger. I suggest we remove the left and right wings and also the tail right here tomorrow and I'll have Roedel come down with his horse-drawn dray and we'll haul it over to your Uncle John's tobacco barn on Division Street and store it until next summer. Mr. Hart said it would be okay to drive the team up through the field to load it up. I can take care of all that if you will help me dismantle the glider. How does all of this sound to you?"

"Sound to me?" I'm too flabbergasted to speak, let alone in any detail. But then I force myself when I realize I don't want a second to pass before I yell "Yes!" for fear he or Marty may change their minds. Then it is all I can do to stop talking and asking questions. When will we leave? Where will we be going during the six weeks until mid-September? What will be my job? Will I be able to do it? How and where will I eat? Where will I sleep? Will I fly the Waco? How much? The only license I had was a glider certificate from the Bureau of Air Commerce, which I acquired through the mail by filling out and mailing in a form. Marty had finished his valve check, was closing up the top cowl and securing it. He was answering a few of my more basic questions.

"We leave in two or three days. First, we'll see how many more passengers we get from the Fair next door. Our tour will be a very much zigzag loop through the southern half of Indiana and maybe a little of southwestern Ohio and later maybe a bit of southeastern Illinois. I usually play it by eye, ear and gut. A lot depends on what we learn along the way from other pilots. As to eating and sleeping, that's easy. It will be what you and I both have been doing the past few days. Bring along a very small soft cloth bag of belongings. No suitcases. You will have to share the front cockpit with our necessary junk. Emphasis on the necessary. A little daily eating money is one of the necessities. I'll pay you at times when I can. But you have to understand that more often than not our passenger revenue doesn't even buy the gas and oil for the OX-5. Your main payment is the dubious distinction of suffering the rest of the summer by barnstorming this old Waco with me— what some reservedly refer to as fun and experience! Also, depending on how you do, you will get a little dual time en route from place to place keeping the ship straight and level while I get some fitful shut-eye in the rear hole!"

Now dad is leaving, he says, to make arrangements for Mr. Roedel to come down tomorrow for the glider.

Hark! We have four more customers coming out of the corn. Two fairly well dressed gentlemen and two primly dressed ladies. All four are distracted by the irksome fact that their polished footwear has accumulated no small amount of dust from the corn field trail. But true gentlemen the gentlemen are. One whips out his white handkerchief, proceeding on bended knee to restore the brilliant polish on the ladies' dainty slippers. Without hesitation the gents whip out a twenty-dollar bill. Marty and I then get the Waco fired up. The ladies wanted the plane rides to be completely "proper"! They wanted to fly together rather than with their beaus, leaving the gents to do the same. I saw a mirthful twinkle in Marty's eyes and I wondered if he was thinking what I was thinking. I wondered if all had been as properly "proper" on that quarter mile trip through the cornfield? A cornfield with adjacent row upon row of eight-foot high corn.

I loaded the ladies into the Waco first and fifteen minutes later their gentlemen friends took their turn, leaving me, the blushing young aviator alone with their ladies as they asked dozens of irrelevant questions about my glider, me, the Waco and their exciting flight, and last but not least about Marty, the handsome, mysterious barnstorming pilot to whom they had entrusted their very lives! I let each one try out the seat on my glider, strapped them in and let them wiggle the stick and rudder bar as they watched the control surfaces move in response to their titillated will.

Now! Marty is taxiing up and I help the two sartorial gentlemen deplane. The four gather, make their way into the cornfield trail, the ladies tittering anxiously about the coming dust on their slippers, and pleading with the handkerchief one to repeat his kneeling duties on entry back into the Fair grounds. Marty shakes his head but smiles when I hand him the twenty. He calls me over to the rear cockpit as the propwash whips our hair. "Climb in," he shouts. "Looks like there are no more passengers today. It's already 6:00 o'clock!"

He is gesturing downward toward the front cockpit, his lips telling me to "Hook'em up," above the OX-5's noise. He has shown me how to do this before. I pull the stick from under the seat and pin it into its socket, then connect and fasten the rudder pedal cables, turn and give Marty a thumbs-up signal. We taxi down to the south end and he raises the tail with a blast from the OX-5, turning around heading north. Full power from the OX-5, tailskid up and level and we are gathering speed. As we pass the Ranger we are off and up, heading out northwest of the Fair grounds.

We have discussed several times before about my doing a little flying of the Waco. It is agreed and understood that when he wants me to take the controls he will shake the stick from side to side. He will do the same when he wants me to turn control back to him. The front cockpit throttle also has a ground disconnect but he has instructed me to leave it disconnected until later on after I have had some experience just flying the Waco straight and level and in making gentle banks and turns.

Now! Marty is making a one eighty turn, heading back south over our field. I can see the Ranger below, its bright orange wings with the bold black registration numbers **12864,** a sharp contrast to the faded green and yellow of our hayfield and adjacent cornfield.

We are passing over the highway with its few autos going back and forth between Boonville, Chandler and Evansville. My airplane rides up to now have been just circling Boonville with barnstormers. Now I am seeing familiar countryside, which I have not seen before from the air. There below is the Pursley farm and the rich soil of its bottomland. And to the east is the high hill topped by Ira Nichols' old ramshackle place where dad and I roamed the fields with our pointer and setter bird dogs. I am seeing things now in two minutes, which took us thirty minutes to reach in dad's 1926 Essex. Gosh! There below is Red Brush Chapel and its surrounding fields where Charlie Derr and I hunted with our bird dogs.

Ahead in the distance I can see the Ohio River and can barely make out the tiny settlements of Yankeetown and Hatfield. Fond memories for a moment fill my mind of summer annual fishing camps on the Ohio just beyond Yankeetown when I was a little boy! Never dreamed I'd be looking down on it from the air. But here I am!

My aeronautical doldrums are rudely awakened by a sudden drop in noise from the OX-5 up front, followed by a lateral shake of the straddled stick as it hit my knees. I raised my arm in signal and took the stick and pedals as Marty restored power to its former r.p.m. The Waco seemed to slowly roll to the left, which I corrected with the stick. The feel of the stick and rudder were more sensitive than the Ranger. Of course we were doing 75 miles per hour not the 45 of the Ranger and as I'd read in my aerodynamic studies the air forces on the control surfaces increased with the square of the speed. In anticipation of some day flying a plane like the Waco, those air forces at 75 miles per hour would be nearly three times as much as the Ranger. To me the Waco seems to require constant attention to keep the nose level and on the horizon and the engine torque, or whatever, has a sneaking stealthy way of wanting to roll to the right or left. In the front cockpit it's difficult to exactly know where the nose is in relation to the horizon. Which part of the nose? Marty has kept the throttle at the same setting. When the nose slowly and sneakingly drops I can hear the OX-5 speed up a little in response because the airplane is in a slight glide. Conversely, when the nose creeps up the engine slows down a few r.p.m.'s, laboring because it is climbing. I am not really surprised because Marty had told me he has trimmed the stabilizer for carrying two passengers. Of course, he is now carrying only one passenger. It seems to confirm what I'd heard about the Waco Models 9 and 10, that they were quite docile but you had to fly them every second and were a far cry from being a so-called inherently stable airplane, even with the stabilizer trimmed to suit the load of passengers, fuel and baggage you were carrying. Much like taking your eyes off the road for a second or two when driving an automobile.

Suddenly Marty grasps control and has the Waco in a shallow turn and banked to the left. Then he lets go, obviously urging me to complete the turn. Coordination of stick and rudder pedals is not too unlike the Ranger so I don't badly sideslip or crab in the turn. I'm too absorbed in doing it right that I overlook where I am in my directions. We are heading back north toward Boonville in the distance but still turning. This is fun. Let it turn. Then we are headed south again and I straighten out, or so I believe. The dang thing has ended up in an obvious fifteen or twenty degree nose-down attitude and the OX-5 is revving up and we are picking up speed and the Waco wants to roll right. I ease the stick back and left and the nose comes up too far and the left wing rolls too far left.

So with some nudging back and forth and sidewise I've got her straight and level back to where it was before Marty started the turn. We are headed south. My elation during the turn has cooled. Now I realize I was not doing it as good as it seemed. We are over the Ohio River and downstream I can see the picturesque old town of Newburgh and my thoughts go back to its Civil War history. Then suddenly Marty is up to his old tricks again. He throws the Waco over into a right turn this time, releasing the controls to me. I try hard to concentrate this time on tracking my changing directions, staying neutral between a sideslip and a skid, keeping an eye on the rotating horizon and ears tuned to the change in engine speed. We make a three-sixty heading back south and by now are about a mile south of the river into Kentucky. Marty nudges the Waco over into a left turn this time and leaves it to me until we are headed north, then he shakes the stick and takes back control.

Suddenly he noses down and cuts the OX-5 back to almost "idle." The engine gives off a couple of little backfiring sputters as the long prop windmills. The noise level is now radically changed. Most of the sound now is slipstream noise through the struts and tie rod wires and the coasting sound of the OX-5's crankshaft bearings.

Now Marty is raised up and pounds on the cowl behind me, yelling, "Better head back! Getting late! A lot darker at field level than it is up here!"

With that he opens the throttle and levels off but then shakes the stick again for me to take over.

When we are past Red Brush and nearing the Pursley farm, he shakes the stick again, takes over and cuts back the throttle for our descent across the two-lane state highway. I can now see what he meant. It is much darker and autos coming in to Boonville have their lights on and the darkened hayfield ahead throws up a challenge to one's depth perception. I raise up and look back at Marty. He is practically standing on the pedals, his head and neck craned upward and over to the side peering ahead and downward, measuring our height as he lowered the tail in a perfect three-pointer when it was so dark I could hardly make out the cornstalks off to our right. Bumpity-Bump-Bump as the spring landing gear absorbed the Waco's weight. We roll up near the Ranger. Marty revved the engine up, swung the tail up and around, parked in front of the Ranger and our tie-down stakes, cut the switch.

"You did okay on those circles. Showed steady improvement. Next time we'll hook up your throttle with mine. Experience with your glider made a big difference. Way ahead of the new flying student who has never flown before." Then he added, "Well, let's have something we will call dinner. I had some sandwiches and a thermos of coffee brought down from the St. Charles. Your mosquitoes will be arriving any minute. Just as well get under the tent net and also kick around our trip. If you get your glider taken down and stored in town tomorrow, we will leave day after tomorrow. I'll spend tomorrow doing some up-keep work on the OX-5."

The cold hamburgers and lukewarm coffee is the best I ever tasted. My new barnstormer friend seems in a contemplative mood, his eyes looking at nothing, seeming to see nothing. They were thinking eyes. After several minutes I could stand the silence no longer. I break his unshared quiet with the first question that came to mind by asking him if he used maps on these barnstorming odysseys. He suddenly seemed startled, but more at the mere sound of my voice than at the substance of my question.

"Ah—waa— —? Maps? Yeah, sort of. Use just a road map to get compass headings more accurately than just the general direction that I remember. Many of these places I've been to before. Let's head up east generally along the Ohio River Valley. But we will be flying something of a zigzag route because all of our stops will not be in a strictly easterly line. There are some towns near the river and others will be north of those. Anything we do, no matter what, depends on the weather. As you know, growing up here in Boonville only ten miles from the Ohio, that very violent thunder storms roam up and down the river all summer long. Extremely high winds, zero visibility, extreme downpours of rain and bolt lightning. Planes like the Waco cannot ride out one of those storms. If we see one coming we turn and head the other way and then change our route north and circle around it. If worse comes to worst we land and stake down. Even then, if the wind speeds exceed the limit of our tie-down stakes it will turn the plane end over end for a mile and tear it all up. There will be times when we will have to fly in minor bad weather and rain but the cloud ceiling will be high enough so we can see the ground as our reference and make our way. But even then I will be looking for a landing spot and such shelter as we can seek for ourselves. In wet, rainy weather no one wants to take plane rides and landowners don't want airplanes taking off and landing all day on their wet fields. Another thing, we can't carry much baggage. No room for it. As it is you will have to share space in your cockpit with our very small duffel bags, a gas can, a funnel, wheel chocks, tie-down stakes and ropes and a mallet. I have fashioned a little spot behind my seat for my tool bag so that it cannot shift and interfere with control cables running to the tail. I have two light slickers, two helmets and two pair of goggles. Slickers of sorts are packed around my duffel bag. The maps will be in the map case in my cockpit along with the straightedge and protractor. I've talked to your dad about money. He can give or lend you thirty dollars. You will have to eat and sleep on that for six weeks. As I told you earlier the money I take in will mainly go for gas and oil. If I can I will pay you something, but the main, and maybe only, thing you will get out of the trip is fun and experience. For me I get to add hours into my logbook. Barnstorming is not a profitable business. It can even be an expensive business. Your main help will be to hold on to the waiting passengers and hold on to their money while I'm in the air and get them into and out of the airplane. There will only be the two of us to operate the plane. In starting the OX-5 you will be both cockpit switcher and chock puller. You will be doing a lot of that. There may be times when we are grounded for lack of funds to buy gas and oil. I've seen the time I've slept under the lower wing at night and lay under it for its shade all day for five days because I had no money for gas and no passengers to fly. Out in some lonely field that no one could seem to find or cared."

I only nodded my head in silent affirmation that despite the travails he had recounted I still wanted to go on the trip. He smiled, rolled over and went to sleep. I did the same because I had a lot of work to do the next day. Taking the Ranger apart so it would be ready to load when Mr. Roedel showed up with his dray and team of horses.

I woke to a sun well below the cornstalks on the east side of us. Marty was up lunching on something as he struggled with removing the top cowl of the Waco. I got up, taking down the "skeeter" netting and preparing to start un-rigging the Ranger. Marty looked down mischievously from his perch atop the OX-5,

"You slept good, kid! My God, how you snored! I don't know what I've got myself into here. When we sleep under the Waco you take the left wing and I'll take the right! Okay?"

He was kidding I hoped. Anyway I mumbled my embarrassingly shy assent, as I began loosening turnbuckles on the Ranger's flying and landing wires and unpinning the flying wires at the skid and wings. I will have to wait until dad and Mr. Roedel arrive to remove the wings. We will require three, one at each wingtip while I loose the landing wires and spar bolts at the fuselage frame. After that I remove the side brace wires, aileron cables and horizontal tail. Just as I am thinking it would be several hours before Roedel and dad would show up, I see the dray coming down into the field from the highway, drawn by two hefty draft horses, two men standing on the open platform of the heavy duty freight wagon, one holding the reins. I was embarrassed to have Marty see this operation. Already he was beginning to laugh as he saw the contraption making its way up the field toward us. It seems ridiculous to have such a crude outdated outfit hauling a knocked-down glider that weighs only 118 pounds! But Boonville had no other motor driven truck carriers in the business of hauling freight. Mr. Roedel has been the only one for years with a rig having a bed large enough to handle my glider. The Ranger is light and frail but it is large and bulky.

As they pull up I shout to them to halt before they get too close to the Waco. The way the big draft horses throw their heads around and stomp and kick, they could make short work of the Waco's wing tips. My action draws a look of relief from Marty. As I look up at him I see he is proceeding to remove the entire rocker arm assemblies from each OX-5 cylinder and is cleaning all the parts in a very meticulous fashion. I also notice he has re-moved both of the hoses from the radiator. I just hope he gets all of this stuff done properly, but on second thought I know he will because I trust him. We will be depending on this Waco a lot these next six weeks. I may be only sixteen in the eyes of older less knowledgeable folks but I know a real aviation expert when I see one. Not only that, I know that my dad has found out a lot from this barnstormer. This has been what dad has been doing with Marty when they did not see fit to have me in their company. Such as the breakfast at the St. Charles and the Essex rides to and from our field.

Dad and Roedel have contrived a wood A-frame on the dray's platform so that the Ranger wing panels can be carried on edge with the leading edges resting on the platform.

Dad says, "Well, we can't take your glider to Uncle John's tobacco barn warehouse on Division Street. He has a big group of men down there re-building the leaf hanging tiers to get ready for the tobacco harvest season. Your glider will be in the way during all that commotion. Besides, it is likely to get damaged. So let's take it further down Division Street to your friend Ray's barn where you stored it last winter."

In consternation I thought a moment. Dang it, I don't like surprises like this. Ray and his family will be away three more weeks. Then I recall I have a padlock key to Ray's barn. We have always stored it there before. So I tell dad, "Yeah. Okay. I have a key. The reason I wanted to use Uncle John's barn is that Ray and his dad are gone. But I guess it's okay. If not we can later move it to Uncle John's barn after tobacco harvest."

The long uncomfortable ride all the way across town is miserable. I worry about the Ranger's wings all the way. The iron tired wheels of the freight wagon give a rough vibratory ride that makes the taut fabric of the wings tremble and quiver. Just like every square inch of my own skin. A look of dismay and asinine humor on the faces of onlookers makes the trip even more distasteful. A trip in a truck or auto would have been smoother and taken only twenty minutes. The dray takes nearly two hours. And it's enough to fracture your teeth.

Roedel pulls up into the alley behind Ray's place as I unlock the barn doors. Dad drives up in the Essex, which he has picked up on the way past Uncle John's warehouse.

We rest the wing panels on two sawhorses, lean them against the wall along with the fuselage frame and tail surfaces. I lock the barn while dad pays Roedel his fee of three dollars. We drive home over to our nearby place at 420 Oak. Where has the day gone? It is dinnertime already and mother is fussing because it's ready and we are late.

At dinner I'm drawn to the sharp contrast between the spartan food and rigorous rest of my camp under the Ranger's wing and that of my mother's cooking. Mother is more drawn to dwell upon the vagaries of my upcoming flight into the skies of rural Hoosierdom, despite dad's assurances. He is brimming with enthusiastic confidence, saying,

"I not only questioned Marty but I know I have a way of knowing a man for his honesty and telling about it honestly. I told him we appreciated his giving Peyton this opportunity and that we believed he was not only an honest trustworthy gentleman, but a very capable licensed pilot. When I brought him here to see your mother he had his leather map case. He pulled out letters he said that testified to his ability, honesty and reliability. His log had several thousand hours he said showed he learned to fly in California in 1919, fourteen years ago. He even had a testimonial letter from either the Governor, Attorney General or other high officials after he participated in an aviation air tour. It was all impressive looking stuff. Your mother is very happy and relieved. So relieved that she got out all the drawings you made on your old glider and your detailed plane designs for light planes which you were saving to build someday and your collection of books and magazines on aircraft engineering and design and construction. She told him how you had been crazy about airplanes ever since Weyerbacher flew over town in the U.S. Navy ZR-1 airship in 1923 when you were six years old. He went over all your books and drawings and we could tell he was very impressed and very serious about you and your interest in aviation."

I blushed with both pride and anger. When I saw the pride in the faces of my parents, then the anger drained from my soul like water through a very large hole in a very small bucket.

My old bed feels very good tonight. No mosquitoes and the cool mattress are a far cry from the prickly alfalfa stubble. Even the old mosquito bites have healed into a tingling sensation of moderately pleasant softness. Slumber comes easily and quickly as a gentle cool breeze creeps through the screened window.

Dawn arrives seemingly in seconds, not minutes, much less hours. It arrives by a gentle shaking of the bed and the soft daylight of a low sunrise obscured by the neighboring house. Dad is standing aside, his thumb jerking over his shoulder, whispering, "Okay, aviator, time to take off!"

Soon I am up, packed and ready except for devouring mother's home made biscuits, honey, eggs and bacon. The wall phone rings and dad answers. Soon he appears in the kitchen laughing,

"That was Marty! Said he last night decided to sleep one more night at the St. Charles! Said he guessed sleeping on the stubble alone was a poor choice. He walked back to the St. Charles after dark last night. Said he thought the plane would be okay because no one could see him leave. Said he would walk the one block this morning down to Rudolph's station from the St. Charles and ride down with him to refuel the Waco. We are to meet him there."

I could see mother's eyes grow moist, busying herself with cleaning up the breakfast table. Dad sensed it too. I hugged her real good and told her not to worry. I told her the whole trip would just be a vacation breeze and I would be back and starting back to school before she knew it.

"Now you send us cards all along," she said in a stifled whimper, and "You promise to call us if you want dad to drive up and meet you wherever it is or however far away it is if you don't want to finish Mr. Marty's tour." With that she turned away to fuss with the dirty dishes. As I started to touch her shoulder it was dad's sober look that stopped me. He beckoned to the door angrily without a sound.

As we drive away I look back at 420 Oak in a way that has never even occurred to me ever before, thinking how happy mother would be in six weeks when I return. Dad drives down to Third Street, turns right for a mile to the Court Square, then left on Main past the St. Charles and down to Rudolph's station only to find that Marty and Rudolph have left for the field. When we turn down into the field I am surprised to find the Waco down next to the highway by Rudolph's red tank truck and Marty is busy up on the cowl with the gas hose. How did he get the OX-5 started so he could taxi down here? Only Marty and Rudolph were on hand and I could not visualize Marty allowing Rudolph to do my job of manning the rear cockpit switching. I feel a little hurt and embarrassed. I also feel more than a little guilty for not being here early enough to help start the OX-5. Had I failed on my very first job that was to last for six weeks? Marty seemed rather cool to us and did not even say good morning to me, which was hurting in a way I was scared to death he'd notice. It was dad who broke the ice, if in fact there was any ice. He called up cheerfully to Marty who was atop the engine cowling filling the tank.

"I see you taxied all the way down here from the north end of the field where you left it last night?" Then with a chuckle and a wink he added, "How in the world did you start the OX-5 without Peyton, the rear cockpit switching expert to help you? Pretty risky wasn't it?"

I am almost recoiling in my embarrassment as I watch anxiously for Marty's response.

Marty does not respond at all. He is busy capping the tank and handing the hose nozzle down to Rudolph. Then his frown breaks out into a laugh as he looks down at me.

"Nah! I knew Peyton had to get his reinforcements for this long trip at mother Autry's breakfast table. He had to chow down a dozen hot biscuits, honey, a pile of eggs and a slab of bacon before he could take off. It's important because it may have to last him six weeks even though I know some beaneries up the line that could only try but never could equal mother Autry's biscuits. Nah! It was hard but we made do starting the OX-5. I just had Mr. Rudolph here mind the chocks and I had to just run back and forth from the prop up front to the switch around in back!"

I smiled, I guess, because I am relieved he is not mad at me. But I feel a little miffed at the whole thing. Right now I know I could climb in that doggoned Waco and take-off all alone and not come back until the tank had just enough gas to make a landing. Yeah, sure I could! (Admit it, you are just hurt and mad because you are a kid. Dang it!)

I realize suddenly I am daydreaming thoughts something less than pious when I hear Rudolph's red truck grinding up the slope to the highway. And it finally sinks in to my consciousness that Marty has now been calling out to me for at least the second time.

"Are you ready? Or are you going to go back to Oak Street for more hot biscuits and honey?" It is obvious to me now that my dad for the past few days has been secretly and laughingly relating to Marty my fondness for mother's freshly baked biscuits—with honey, of course.

I drag out my drawstring denim homemade duffel bag and its meager contents. I feel the rubber band around the thirty one-dollar bills deep in my pocket that dad has given me. The front cockpit is already loaded with Marty's duffel, the gas can and funnel and barely room for me and my duffel plus the wheel chocks. The controls are still in place from our last flight. And I notice that Marty has connected up the forward throttle push rod. The ship is already facing north for our take-off and dad has set the chocks in front of the wheels. By now we have our engine starting routine down pat and we work more like automatons. I climb into the rear cockpit making sure the switch is off, magneto in "retard" and throttle at "idle" while Marty up front calls, "Switch off" and I call back "Switch is off." He pulls the prop half way through once and then once again. Then "Switch on" which I call back loud and clear. He gave it a good swing and the OX-5 is off and running at "idle." I climb out, let Marty climb in. I climb in the front and a minute later; dad is on the left lower wing step with the 2 chocks and ropes in his arms, dumping them in my lap. I get them in place on top of the duffel bags and strap up my safety belt. Dad reaches out and slaps my shoulder three or four times and then gives me a viselike handshake that I will still feel four hours later. Dad jumps down on the ground, reaches into the back cockpit and gives Marty another of those bone-crushing handshakes. He steps aside off the left wing tip to get out of the propeller blast as Marty opens the throttle and we move forward slowly as the tail rises off the ground. I look to the left and dad is waving with one arm while the other is uplifted with a skyward elevated thumb sign of good luck and good flight. We are rolling along over the stubble, a small bumpity-bump here, a small bumpity-bump there until the wings begin to lift enough of the weight of the airplane so that it is rolling ever so smoothly over the cut hay field and then the characteristically drop in noise level as we reach a few feet of altitude. I see my old empty glider niche in the cornfield go whizzing by at nearly 60 m.p.h. We are climbing north and I can see the big Boonville Fair down to the right and receding behind us. It looks as though the Fair is winding down to its last day soon. Not nearly so many parked cars in the green ring. Of course it's early. Then to my surprise Marty is banking sharply to the right until he is now headed south back over our field again. I had expected him to continue north for he had mentioned a plane-owning friend in Oakland City he'd like to see during our trip. But now we are over our field again. I knew dad would wait until we were almost out of sight before he drove home. The Essex was not there. Neither had he expected Marty to do a goodbye flyover if indeed that's what this was. There! Down there! I could see the Essex making its way into town going over Orphan's Home Hill on West Locust Street. We are still heading south over the highway and Marty throttles back and starts coming down in altitude and at the same time doing a gentle ninety degree turn until we are flying east at only 300 feet. Now! I can see what he is up to! He is flying the entire length of Oak Street from west to east but just a block south of Oak so I can look down to the left and see it all. First we pass over the farmland south of South Second Street where old Bill Koutz owned a beautiful long hay field that all the barnstormers loved. But all of their first visits were short lived, for old Bill, unlike Mr. Hart, hated barnstormers and their noisy "contraptions." Now we pass over South Third and I see Uncle John and Aunt Helen's new house to the left below us. Then we pass over Fourth and Oak and I see my classmate Jimmy Derr's and his dad Frank's place on the southwest corner, and across the street is Grandmother Hammond's great old brick house on the northeast corner. Now in a few seconds we pass over Fifth and Oak and down to the left I can see the Derr Brothers' Bottling Works run by brothers, Frank and Albert Derr, the fathers of my classmates, Jimmy and Charles Derr. Then we are over Sixth and Oak and the little corner home-owned grocery of elderly Mr. and Mrs. Varner. Mr. Varner is a long time deacon of the old Pigeon Creek Church at up east Lincoln City, where Abraham Lincoln and his parents were members in the early 1800's. Young Abe lived there between the ages of seven and twenty-one. His mother is buried there. Abe studied the law as a youth in Boonville in Judge Breckenridge's court. Mr. Varner was my persistently insistent Lincoln history tutor for now over six years, an inescapable obligation, which is another story.

Now we are passing over 420 Oak and Seventh Street and I do not see my mother in the front yard, which is no surprise. But she will hear our airplane and so will her highly conversant neighbors. In seconds I see the houses of my elderly German friends the Kirsches, and across the street my friend Helen Phillips and her parents Lester and Laura. Then across the street from them my friend Glenn (Bus) and Nial Fisher and their father Al who loved to tell night fox hound stories of years gone by on old Fisher's Knob (Mountain) in Spencer County. We are now whizzing past Forest Avenue and my old friend Carl Crowder's house and down to the right is the not so long hay field of Aunt Mary Johnson's where I tried to fly my Hocker monoplane. Now we are at the end of Oak Street where it joins Pelzer Road and we pass over Aunt Mary Johnson's old Victorian farmhouse, the only home at the end of Oak Street that faces west.

Now Marty is climbing back up to about 800 feet and seems to be indecisively mulling over the direction he wants to take to leave my hometown. We are still heading east and now flying along Highway 62, the main east-west route through Boonville. Below I can see the old County Poor Farm and the adjacent field, which had been visited by the unforgettable 35-plane air tour I had excitedly attended back in 1929. Up ahead four or five miles I can see where the road jogged north a mile to DeGonia Springs. It is the former site of the old DeGonia Springs Spa Hotel, a health resort of a by-gone era. The old brick gazebo and mineral springs pump still stands at the bend in the road. It brings back memories of Sunday afternoon drives when we would stop and drink the free mineral water from the pump from available tin cups, a rest stop always being a critical but awkward necessity within fifteen minutes.

CHAPTER III

M arty has heard me talk about DeGonia, the tiny place where my Autry grandparents lived and where my father and his siblings grew up in a bygone day. He cuts back the OX-5 into a sputtering mildly backfiring glide to about three hundred feet and we do a three sixty circle over DeGonia Springs, probably the first time in its hundred and fifty year existence that an airplane even passed over it to say nothing of buzzing it in a low altitude circle. Yes, there is the old brick gazebo at the ninety-degree turn in the highway next to the old shade tree park where the DeGonia Springs Spa once stood.

Now we are headed south, the old DeGonia cemetery off our left wingtip, the resting place of some American Revolutionary soldiers. A mile south we pass over the old country home of U.S. Senator James Hemenway, which was once the county's other spa, the former Ash Iron Springs. Senator Hemenway was an Indiana Senator in the U.S. Senate from 1905 to 1909. Off to the left I can see the meandering path of Pigeon Creek bordered by a mile-wide stretch of wooded bottomland on each side of the creek. The creek is a boundary between Warrick County on the west and Spencer County on the east. Below us now is the site of my Autry grandparents' early home-stead, now long since disappeared before the family moved to DeGonia Springs and later to Boonville. It brings back stories told by dad when he lived down there on the very edge of the Pigeon Creek deep woods when he was a small boy. One story will always remain indelible in my memory. Dad at age nine loved to roam the deep woods with their seasoned old hunting dog and his grandfather's ancient double-barreled shotgun with one barrel hammer broken and useless, essentially rendering the old fowling piece a single barrel gun. In that year of 1897 the men of the family, young and old, were hunters. Dad took to it like a duck to water. Even night hunting by oil lantern for raccoon, 'possum, muskrat and otter took him into the deep woods where the inexperienced could have easily gotten lost. But he knew every tree and landmark from his frequent explorations during summer days when he penetrated the wild deep woods to fish for catfish at a bend in the creek called Hoofer's Bend. Its name came from that of an early Hoosier pioneer who homesteaded in a long since bygone cabin. On one winter night dad had penetrated the woods to Hoofer's Bend, hunting up and down the creek for several miles. When his dog would tree a 'possum or raccoon he would bark and howl to bring his young hunter to the tree where the quarry had climbed in retreat. Suddenly on this night the dog began barking and howling in a highly unusual ferocious but clearly frightened fashion that he had never demonstrated before. And there was another new and frightening sound that sent chills up his spine such as he had also never heard before. The family had two tomcats that would on occasion get into ferocious fights, which could only be halted, with a pail of cold water. This sound up ahead was like a fighting tom cats except it was louder, much louder. And frighteningly more ferocious. His fearless old hunting dog had never barked, howled or growled like this before. It was completely obvious to dad that his dog was only holding his ground out of sheer panic and fear, knowing that if he bolted, that whatever it was that confronted him would tear him to bits before he could run a yard. The fear in the dog's voice turned his cold chills into ice. His fearless dog had always been his protection, giving him a confidence he had always taken for granted. Now that confidence deserted him. The broken old gun did little to console that icy chill when he heard the terror in the old dog's voice. As he approached the dog from the rear, the dim light of his lantern revealed his shoulder had been lacerated in a long bloody wound. Beyond the wounded dog, the howling, screeching thing's yellow eyes shone in the dark beyond, swaying back and forth as if to whirl around behind the dog to go for its flanks. Now the beast was confronted by the light of the lantern and the visage of a tall young lad holding a gun and who was scared to death. And the beast sensed his fear because it increased its fury, but only kept at bay by the lantern's light it did not lunge at the dog or its young hunter. Still scared to death but not quite out of his wits, dad slowly backed away but kept the scene in lantern light, speaking calmly to the dog, urging him to slowly retreat with him. The rest of the story is one of several hours of anxiety as he and dog slowly backed away from the creekside and through a mile of woods to the back of their house at the edge of the woods. When they reached the house the poor frightened old dog took protection under the back porch while dad sat on the steps with his lantern and gun as the panther slithered back and forth at the edge of the woods. Finally, dad's father (my grandfather) appeared at the back door aroused by all the commotion. He took one look at the yellow eyes slinking back and forth, emptied both barrels of his ten-gauge shotgun. The panther let forth a stinging cry and departed for the depths of the Hoofer's Bend woods. Dad and grandpa took the faithful old dog into the kitchen, bandaged his wound, bedded him down by the woodpile next to the stove and everybody went to bed. Just another hunt at Hoofer's Bend, but certainly one to remember and to tell a son someday when he had a son like me.

I have been daydreaming about Hoofer's Bend and now come to attention that off to our left is the very tiny hamlet of Midway. To me Midway is a historic place of rural Victorian times past on my mother's side of the family. The Whites and Bakers lived there. The Whites on a farm of half-productive fields and half of woods loaded with fat squirrels and hickory trees. Midway is a place where all humans yearn for, whether they know it or not. Midway is a place where time literally stands still. My childhood memories from three to seven go back to times when we visited the elderly Whites, two brothers Will and John, and two sisters Mary and Alice. One sister taught school in a country school. The brothers worked the farm and the sisters did the house chores and the flower and vegetable gardens. All four were well educated through a lifetime of devoted effort. The sisters had attended State Normal school for teachers. The brothers completed country school and high school at Rockport eight miles away on the Ohio River. All four spent their evenings together in the living room of the old whitewashed, two story beautiful old family home. Evenings were spent reading or listening to Mary or Alice play the organ. The living room walls were floor-to-ceiling bookshelves holding everything from World History to the classics. The only time they ever traveled was a trip to Washington, D.C. to attend a convention of Esperanto language devotees of which they were enthusiastic members. They carried on regular correspondence with devotees in other lands from Japan to the countries of Europe. Other than the D.C. trip their travels were limited to an annual trip to Boonville to visit my mother, my aunt and grandmother. My mother always said, and I agree, that this would be a perfect world if it were made up of the John, Will, Mary and Alice Whites. And here I am now flying over the old White place near Midway. My last mesmerizing trip there was eight years ago and they are gone. If some things should last forever, with God's will, it should be Midway and the White brothers and sisters.

We are now over the flat plain of beautiful farmland north of Richland and I keep wondering about this pilot Marty. I have no idea what he has in mind and I am beginning to wonder if he does. I thought we would be heading east and flying for several hours to one of his former barnstorming fields full of paying customers. Of course, we have only been in the air a good bit less than thirty minutes since we left Boonville. Why are we going down here heading south near Richland? Who knows about Marty? Then all of a sudden he turns north again. Soon up ahead I see tiny Richland's small row of houses and store, all stretched along the road south to the junction to Rockport and Owensboro. I get to thinking about the St. Louis son Roscoe of our neighbors the Popes on Oak Street in Boonville and how when they lived years ago in Richland and how Roscoe Pope had learned to fly down there near Richland. He had gotten acquainted with a visiting barnstormer in an old Standard World War I vintage ungainly biplane trainer and the guy had given him a few hours dual instruction.

Suddenly my thoughts are interrupted by the OX-5 being throttled down by my friend behind me and the Waco is nosing down and turning to the east. We are at about 1000 feet and coming down. A minute later the OX-5 revs up again and we are in a fairly steep banking turn, and after doing a one eighty, we straighten out and are gliding down westward back toward the Richland road. Then Marty throttles back a lot and noses down some more. Then it dawns on me. He is going to land! At Richland? Good gosh, we haven't been thirty minutes out of Boonville. Why? The chances of finding three people in Richland, let alone a flock of passengers with five dollars to spare is slim as hell. (Okay, mother, slim pickings.) I peer over the side in the slipstream, my hair whipping in the wind. The field he has chosen is a very long, freshly cut hayfield. Longer than the one we left near the Boonville Fair. Its west end abuts the road south through Richland. In fact, Richland is down the road south less than a mile.

Now he has cut back almost to "Idle" and kicking the rudder slowly back and forth to slow her down. Now he flares and I feel the wheels and tail skid touch almost at the same instant. The old Waco bounces gently and rumbles along until we have almost come to a full stop about two hundred yards from the road. He revs up the OX-5 and we trundle along in a little nudge of r.p.m. from the engine until we near the road. Then he blasts the tail off the ground, beautifully holding it level as he kicks the rudder and pivots the Waco around on the wheels for a full one hundred eighty degree arc, heading it back east, drops the tail down and cuts the switch to "Off." The OX-5 sputters and coughs, the prop swinging back and forth to a stop.

I unbuckle my seat belt, raise up grasping a center section strut to get out. I turn to an extricating Marty who is grinning from ear to ear.

"Why land here?" I shout incredulously. He pushes back his hair, chuckling.

"Yeah. I guess I didn't tell you. Three days ago at the St. Charles, I phoned a newspaper story to the Rockport paper announcing we would be here in Richland giving rides. The Rockport paper is taken by farmers all around here and people east, north and west of Rockport. Small towns like Richland, Grandview, Newtonville, Chrisney, Midway, Hatfield, Yankeetown and down to nearly Owensboro and places like Patronville and Enterprise."

I guess he could read some weak enthusiasm in my quizzical expression. What he didn't seem to realize is that dad and I had been to Richland many times before to rural baseball games played by players in denim overalls and barnyard shoes. I could not see it as a hotbed of aviation enthusiasts even if Roscoe Pope had flown an old precious antique of a Standard J-1 here in years gone by. We staked the Waco down securely in the warm sun of the open field. I thought back to Marty's remark about all the small towns along the Ohio and this nearby rural plain who read the Rockport newspaper. He had mentioned Enterprise, which was on the Indiana side of the Ohio across from the Kentucky town of Owensboro. My dad had been born in Enterprise just before my Grandfather Autry moved the family to Hoofer's Bend. On several occasions we had driven the dirt back road along the riverbank, the only access to Enterprise so my dad could view his birthplace. The only thing we could find at Enterprise was a one-room shack on river stilts (round post piling to keep the shack above flood stage). Not a soul at Enterprise. Only a muddy, rutted narrow road and the old stilted shack. Not a hotbed of airplane passengers.

A good woven wire fence ran along the field at the roadside so Marty concluded the plane would remain okay if we walked down the road to Richland. We had not seen a single automobile or horse-drawn farm wagon on the road since we landed, or for that matter, as we were flying along with the road from Midway.

We walked down along the fence for a hundred yards to a small opening, which we wired, closed securely after we passed through. Richland is small but rather strung out along the road. We passed 3 houses spread along each side of the road. The main part of the settlement seemed to be a small service and gas station next to an also small grocery and cafe. The cafe seemed to be the local gathering place for elderly coffee-sippers, also an eat stop for the few auto travelers who traversed the road.

Marty made some small mechanical talk with the service station mechanic and owner. Presently we amble into the cafe and immediately we are noticed and gawked at constantly as the strangers we are. We sit at a small table, order coffee and doughnuts. Five locals are on stools at the counter with their backs to us which is a decided inconvenience to all five of them since the stools are not of the pivoting variety. Our landing only a mile away was more silent than we expected for no one questioned us about it. I asked Marty if he told the elderly mechanic next door. He said he had not. I then asked Marty if the mechanic had asked if we were the immigrant aviators. No, he had not. Marty seemed amused at his lack of answers to my questions, then he seemed to take pity on my curiosity when he said,

"I would like to find out who owns our field. I like to ask permission even if it always must have to be after the fact. It's a bit unhandy to ask beforehand when you are aloft and saddled with a stall speed of fifty miles per hour."

That crack really amused me in its obvious but easily overlooked logic. So I break out laughing which is unusual for me because I have a reputation of being a young aviation nut who takes all things aeronautical very seriously and I am now seeing how Marty sometimes enjoys bringing me aground with something of a thud.

My laughter startles the stool five into turning around suddenly. The one on the end who is the lead gawker finally makes his bid. "We didn't see you fellas drive up. What kind of automobile you drivin' anyways? Must have a good muffler. Maybe a sleeve-valve Willys-Knight? They are very quiet, you know," he says.

Marty smiles, pushes his unruly hair back, strokes the tiny mustache, kicks my foot that I should keep silent while he replies.

"Well no, what we are driving sure is not quiet, in fact it's noisy as hell. What are we driving? Well, it's a Waco Model 10 with OX-5 engine."

All five looked puzzled, allowing as how they'd never heard of it, which I am one hundred percent sure they had not. Marty pays for the doughnuts and coffee and we visit the old mechanic next door who is surprised to learn we landed a plane a mile down the road without his knowing it. He tells Marty the field's owner resides in the last house on the east side of the road. As we stopped there on the way back to the Waco, Marty raps on the back door of the frame house. The front door seems never used, or for that matter never opened. Reminds me of the same practice I grew up to know all my life in Boonville with the older generation. Only time the front door was ever opened was for funerals. Two men open the door politely and in an air of hospitality. One is a farm weathered agile older man of over seventy. The other is about fifty, obviously the son.

Before Marty can speak, the older man says cheerfully,

"You fellas must be the pilots? Your plane sure is a pretty thing to look at. We saw in the paper we got in the box this morning where you will be giving rides. You're welcome to use the field. Just don't let your passengers drive their automobiles out there. They should park along the road and walk through the gate."

Marty thanked them very politely, told them his name, and introduced me. It was my chance to join the conversation with the one thing on my mind.

"I knew a man who used to live here. He learned to fly here in Richland with another barnstormer. He was our neighbor in Boonville. Lives in St. Louis now. Said the plane he flew was an old Standard with a water-cooled Hall-Scott engine used as a training plane during the World War in 1917. His parents and sisters lived here too. Their name was Pope. His name was Roscoe."

Both of the men came alert in response to my statement. The older man nodded his head in recognition.

"Why shore, we remember Elisha Pope and his family. They had a farm only a mile west of here. My son here went to school with Roscoe."

The younger man said, "Sure. We went to school in Midway, then here and then in Rockport. When that barnstormer came in that big old biplane,

Roscoe hung around it almost day and night until he persuaded the pilot to teach him to fly it. They used our field right over here where your plane is now parked. They had it here for nearly two months; flying passengers come over from Rockport and Owensboro. This barnstormer also taught several others in the area to fly it. Or at least he took them up and run them through the paces. But I think Roscoe was the only one who learned it well enough to make regular take-offs and landings. But the barnstormer pilot was always with him. He would not trust anyone around here to fly it solo, including Roscoe. Roscoe wanted to buy the old plane you call a Standard. I guess that's what it was. But Roscoe didn't have the money, he was just a farm boy."

As we talked to these friendly folks, Marty noticed an auto had parked down the road. Four people got out, stood at the fence ogling the bright red and silver Waco. We excused ourselves and made our way down the road, lest they might be paying passengers. The prospect of twenty dollars in twenty minutes of flying seemed to quicken Marty's pace. The four persons at the fence turned out to be two middle-aged couples. Marty, the polished entrepreneur, invited the neatly attired folks through the opening in the fence, taking care to direct the ladies to a path along the fence, bare of the prickly hay stubble on their slippers.

"Would you folks care to see the plane from a closer vantage point? If you would care to go for a ride I can take two of you at a time."

The ladies tittered happily about how the view aloft must be grand but how they regarded an airplane flight more as an act of heroic bravery than a cooler version of a Sunday auto ride along the Ohio River. But one of the gentlemen, the one in the sailor straw hat, spoke up with a more definitive inclination,

"Sir, we are from Rockport. My name is Stanley Murray. My wife Margery. Allow me to introduce Mr. and Mrs. Chester Shrode. Now, if we should fly with you, sir, what is your fee and where would you take us and for how long?"

Now, I thought, here was a man of inquisitive business acumen. Marty did not miss the point even for a second.

"Sir, it's five dollars per person. The flight usually is about fifteen minutes. But today there are no other passengers than the four of you so the flight can be made for between 15 and 30 minutes each. If you wish I can fly you over Rockport, down the river to Owensboro and back here. I suggest you gents leave your hats here with my young assistant. I suggest the ladies also leave their bonnets and replace them with tightly knotted scarves. Peyton here will help you into the forward cockpit and belt you in after we get the engine started and remove the forward dual controls to give you more room."

The two gentlemen held a brief conference, then quickly answering they would each take their wives on a flight and that the Murrays would go first. I take the cue quickly, run over to the Waco's forward cockpit, remove the stick, disconnect the rudder pedals and throttle, took out all of our gear and piled it neatly next to the fence and put the wheel chocks in place, helped the Murrays into the front cockpit, belted them in, then taking my place in the rear cockpit waiting for Marty to swing the prop.

The OX-5 ticking over in "Idle", Marty climbed in, revved up the engine to full power, lifted the tail off the ground, slowly gathering speed down the field eastward. I hustled the Shrodes down along the fence so Mrs. Shrode would escape the hay chaff laden propeller blast of the Waco. Otherwise her summer straw bonnet would surely be blown across the road and into the fields far beyond.

Now the Waco had climbed to five hundred feet, was heading southeast toward Rockport. I busied myself with needlessly rearranging our pile of gear and covering it with one of the yellow slickers. The Shrodes were obviously at odds with what to do with themselves for thirty minutes until the plane returns, so indulged their curiosity by engaging me in conversation. They ask me how old I am which makes me exceedingly uncomfortable. Then Mrs. Shrode asks if the pilot is my father. That really shakes me for a moment and I assure her that he is just a friend.

"Oh," she says sweetly, "How long have you known him?"

This line of questioning has gone way too far I decide. So I stop what I'm doing, raise up facing her, look her in the eye and reply,

"Only a week. But my dad, my mother and me feel we have known him for a lifetime. I am a glider pilot of my own glider. I have flown the Waco only the other day. Over the Ohio River. I live over in Boonville."

"My oh my, but you are an accomplished young man. I'm sure your parents are very proud of their handsome young and industrious son."

I can actually feel myself blush. Mrs. Shrode is old enough to be my mother but she makes the same sort of complimentary remarks that my mother makes when she embarrasses me in front of our neighbor friends. But Mrs. Shrode is obviously a nice lady and despite the awkwardness of her questions she seems genuinely interested in me and my personal agenda, as does Mr. Shrode.

At this point Mr. Shrode intercedes. It is mid-day on a clear hot August morning and we three are standing out in an open hayfield.

"How about joining us in the shade of our automobile? The windows are down and should be more comfortable." I nod silently and we make our way through the narrow gate to their brand new 1932 Ford sedan. They sit in front, me in the back. A gentle breeze after a few minutes relaxes all three of us. They are now even more talkative and I am more responsive and warm up to their obvious desire to be my friends. The conversation goes to my high school in Boonville, my teachers, my parents, people they know in Boonville and so forth. Mr. Shrode is intensely interested in my glider flying which appears to be a new thing to him, that an "airplane" can be towed into the air with an automobile. When I tell him it is not unlike towing a kite into the air on a string, he nods in assent and he sees the obvious principles now that I have put it that way.

They tell me they have lived in Spencer County all of their lives, mostly in Rockport. When they tell me they have known the White family in Midway for many years that fact alone forms an immediate bond between me and this friendly couple. Their sons have gone to school in Rockport, Mary White as their teacher. They had visited the White farm in Midway many times and had become interested in Esperanto as a result of their friendship. The Shrodes tell me more of Rockport's early history than I had ever heard before. My parents had taken me many times on Sunday drives to Rockport to view the old pioneer village and the antebellum homes on the bluffs overlooking the river. The Shrodes now tell me more of the old Rockport pioneer village than I ever knew before. All of the buildings are constructed of split logs, surrounded by split rail fences. All cut from local timber. Each building is furnished as in the days they were first built and occupied in the pre-Civil War days when flatboat commercial traffic plied the Ohio and Mississippi rivers between Pittsburg and New Orleans. It was from this area that Abe Lincoln as a youth made a flatboat trip to New Orleans for he lived at nearby Gentryville between the ages of 7 and 21.

"Do you suppose Mr. Marty would be interested in seeing Rockport in a more 'up close' fashion if we were to drive the two of you over there?"

The question surprised me so I was at a loss for a quick answer.

"I guess so. He might. I don't think he would go if there were other passengers waiting to fly. We have to earn money for gas and oil, you know."

"Oh, I'm sure that is so. But I'm afraid that piece in the Rockport paper was not large enough to bring a lot of folks over here. Not that it would not excite them enough to show up. I'm just afraid not many will notice it."

I hoped he was wrong. But the notion of being driven over to Rockport on a sightseeing trip, especially with Marty, was not at all unappealing, if the plane would be okay if left alone. Then I realized Marty would expect me to stay with it if he went to Rockport with the Shrodes.

I looked at my Pocket Ben to discover the amazing fact that thirty minutes had passed when at the same instant I could hear the barely audible sound of the OX-5 far to the south. We got out of the car and into the field again as Marty flew a wide turn coming in from the east, the Waco fishtailing back and forth, then in a long gentle touchdown that was really three gentle bumpity-bumps and a rumbling roll as the plane slowed down but the engine being revved up to the taxi speed of two miles per hour. I've always admired the way these three-place OX-5 powered biplanes fly and sound. I hold the Shrodes back from the prop blast as Marty revs the engine up, raises the tail and swings it around with the nose facing east for the next take-off. He cuts it back to "Idle." I have instructed the Shrodes to leave their hats in the Ford as the Murrays have done.

I climbed up on the wing and help the Murrays out. They hurry off to the side away from the idling windstream from the propeller, rush over to the Shrodes gushing their enthusiasm in a stream of excited commentary. I help the Shrodes into the cockpit, strap them in and wave Marty off. They go barreling down the field after the dusty baptism of chaff of Marty's take-off. They are in the air soon and headed back to Rockport for another 30-minute loop back to Richland.

"As we were coming in I could look down and see all three of you had taken shade in the Ford. Shall we go back to do the same?" Mr. Murray asked.

I follow them over to the sedan. Mr. Murray is telling me they live in the outskirts of Rockport. I find that remark a little unusual for Rockport is a small town and quite old. I mention that the Shrodes have invited Marty and I to return with them to see the river view from the bluff and also the pioneer village of old Rockport. But I have seen it several times before but that Marty has not. I say it might be of curious interest to him because earlier he told me that he grew up in Kansas and was born there in 1900. Somehow I had not thought of it before but that means he is 33 years old. Not as old as I had thought. He had barnstormed through Indiana and Illinois before but not in this area.

"Rockport is quite old. It pre-dates the Civil War as a habited bluff above the river," Mrs. Murray was telling me. Then she says, "There are stories that flatboat robbers lived under the bluff in caves and camps. According to the stories they would row out to intercept the flatboats coming down the river to rob and murder the occupants."

I did not tell her I had heard and read these stories too. My conversation with the Murrays was much the same as the one I had with the Shrodes. The Murrays also wanted to know all about my glider flying, my relationship with Marty, my parents' view of what seemed to them my premature adult-hood and all the rest of it. Like before, Marty's 30-minute flight was over before I realized it. I had warmed up to the Murrays. They were a likable and an interesting couple. Mr. Murray was a breeder of pointer dogs as was my dad. He urged me to urge my dad to visit them after my tour with Marty and to be sure and come along and to bring one or two of our pointers.

I could hear the OX-5 approaching from the south, making the same one eighty approach to come in from the east. I admired Marty's attention to a new field. This was his third landing here and he touched down in exactly the same spot. I am thinking to myself if I went out there in the east end of the field to look for the Waco's tire and tail skid marks there could only be one set! I'd bet money on it. They taxied up to near the fence, turned around to face east again and I run out to help the Shrodes de-plane. Marty switches off the OX-5 for there are no new passengers and the afternoon is soon upon us.

We all gather near the narrow gate in the fence and Shrode asks Marty,

"Would you and Peyton care to join us on a little ground level sight-seeing trip to Rockport? Of course we would bring you back here. It is only 15 miles."

Marty seemed a little surprised but thoughtful, and first looking at me, he replied politely, "Sure! That's a capital idea. However, we should remain here in case more passengers arrive. Also, it is a matter of leaving the plane unattended."

Immediately I blurt out, "No, that's okay. I can stay and watch the Waco and hang onto any passengers until you return."

Then I add, "I'll hang onto their advance money so they won't be inclined to leave."

Marty shows his embarrassment at my dumb but very truthful remark and the Shrodes and Murrays laugh loudly in appreciation. I felt like going around hiding behind the plane and kicking myself.

Then Mr. Murray suggests we all go down the road to the cafe for his sponsored lunch. Marty seems inclined to accept, but remarks that an aspiring passenger could drive by the plane and pass up paying for a ride because there was no pilot or attendant.

Again I blurt out, "You go ahead with them, Marty. I'll stay by the plane, it's my job."

He looks at me, lays a hand on my shoulder, "No, partner. I'm not going to lunch and leave you standing out here in the field hungry. We better stick to business. I suggest the folks here go down to the cafe and return here after lunch and then we'll see about going into Rockport with them."

The Murrays and Shrodes good-naturedly agree to return after lunch. It is now well after noon and still no more autos bearing five-dollar passengers. Over two hours pass as we loll about under the shade of the Waco's wings talking mostly about airplanes since I am the one steering the conversation. Marty seems more bent on taking a well-earned nap. Then we can hear an auto coming north from Richland. Our hopes are up for a load of passengers. But no, it is simply the Murrays and Shrodes returning. I'm thinking, 'Golly, they must have enjoyed the little Richland Cafe to spend over two hours there.'

They pull up near the narrow gate, and the two men get out and head up the field to the plane. Mr. Murray is carrying a large paper bag. He hands the bag to Marty, asking,

"We didn't see or hear you flying. No passengers yet, I gather?"

Marty shakes his head in reply. Peering into the sack he breaks into a broad grin and a loud laugh.

"This is really very thoughtful of you folks. Peyton, here, I am sure will appreciate his warm hamburger and bottle of soda pop as will I. Of course, as I mentioned before, he is more of a man for a dozen of Mother Autry's hot biscuits smothered with wild honey plus a good plate of eggs, bacon and fried potatoes. Of course, for the next six weeks he will do well to have hamburgers and ham sandwiches, when they are available."

I'm thinking Murray and Shrode laughed a little too uproariously. I know my face has become a shade redder than this hot August sun has given it. I find myself with head lowered and turning a toe into the ground—all of which makes me angrier with them and myself. Then I realize Marty is simply kidding me, so the only thing left to do is kid right back so I say rather loudly,

"Aw, that isn't so. Sure I like biscuits and honey. Marty here would jump at the chance for biscuits and honey. He's not fooling me!"

Marty looked at me in surprise like as if to say, 'Hey, he is finally showing he has a sense of humor. What took him so long?' Then he looks at Murray and Shrode quipping,

"If he had planned this right, he'd have had Mother Autry stationed all along our route with a portable kitchen, then I too could have had those biscuits and honey every morning!"

The men laughed again and Shrode changed the subject.

"Would you fellows like to go on a little sight-seeing tour of our little town of Rockport? Won't be long. We can bring you back well before dark."

"We would love to. But I don't want to miss any folks who want to take a plane ride. What do you folks think? Any chance other folks might show up?"

Murray and Shrode looked at each other, Murray pulling out his gold pocket watch, then answers,

"I doubt it very much. Not this late in the day. That article in the Rockport paper was small and back on page five and it came out yesterday afternoon."

I then blurted out in a dedicated fashion, "I've been to Rockport many times, so let me stay here and watch the plane while you go, Marty?"

He looks at me thoughtfully and appreciatively in a way that made my day. After a moment he says,

"Tell you what, even if someone else shows up, I don't think you, the super plane ride salesman, will be able to hold them here, much less their five bucks, until I get back this late in the day. No, you come along, it will be fun. We can stop up at the field's owners, the Gwaltneys. They can keep an eye on the plane just by looking out the north window of their house."

The six of us squeezed into the Ford, first stopping at the Gwaltneys, then down south turning left on the Rockport road.

Fifteen miles later we are coming into Rockport where the Murrays wanted to be dropped off at their place just west of town. Murray insisted that we stay a few moments so he could show me his kennel of English Pointer dogs, telling me to return this fall with my dad.

After many appreciative good-byes and thanks for their plane ride, we bid the Murrays farewell and continue on into Rockport and the Ohio River bluff overview. Marty seems real taken with the charm and antiquity of Rockport and its decided difference with his native Kansas. He seems very knowledgeable on the subject of early American architecture; seems to be talking to himself in terms like "revival this and that" as he views the old homes on the bluff and the block or two beyond the bluff. One place really intrigues him as it always did me when I first saw it. One of the homes has a rather spacious lawn on the bluff before the house. Near the edge of the bluff is a viewing gazebo—and what a view it has! The gazebo is literally the pilothouse of an old sternwheeler river steamer. The story goes that the steamer sank in full view of the home where the gazebo now sits. The pilothouse protruded fully above water level for some time until it was sawed away at water level from the superstructure beneath. It was taken to the lawn of the home on the bluff where it now reposes. Marty was exceedingly fascinated with not only the gazebo itself, but the story of its origin, life and demise. I think if he could have traded his Waco then and there for the old pilothouse he would certainly have done it—leaving me to get back to Boonville any way I could.

Our next stop was at the old Pioneer Village in a town park in the west edge of town. The buildings are of a period that pre-dates the Civil War. A small town that may have been Rockport in an earlier day. After all these trips here I forgot to count them, but the village has a half dozen houses, all built of hand-hewn split logs. Fireplace chimneys are on outside walls and made of uniform sized, unsplit tree limb sections laid atop each other and sealed with sod and clay. Several of the homes are two-level affairs. A typical larger design is two two-story structures separated by a covered breezeway and a common roof, a fireplace chimney at each end of the building. There are no iron nails used in these old houses. They are held together with wooden pegs driven into bored holes. All the houses have wooden floors, the first floors just above ground level. All are furnished with furniture obviously built by the same people who built the houses. Nearly every house has a homemade spinning wheel and often a loom for making their own fabrics from which their clothes were made. Cooking utensils and pots were iron and probably brought to Rockport by the flatboat trade from upriver.

The Shrodes were very proud of the Pioneer Village and the local volunteers who kept it in repair. I have, of course, seen it many times. My parents loved it and brought my grandparents who could remember their own parents and grandparents growing up and living in the same environment as Rockport's Pioneer Village.

Marty took it all in stride and asked many pertinent questions of the kindly Shrodes who in turn were exhilarated by his interest to the point that perhaps they misread his questions as an appeal for more detail and historical intrigue. Our tour had run its course when Marty peered into one of the furnished but uninhabited rooms for a long silent moment, then remarked,

"Without a doubt it is a great period of American history. And a period that should be preserved in memory for posterity. But the poor souls had never flown and never would, nor their children or grandchildren did not even conceive that some day hence there would be such a thing as an airplane. Poor, poor souls. Ground bound for generations. Not even an awareness of what they were missing. A blessing that they were not aware. If they had been aware they could not have lived with it. They would have died in despair. I guess it's really the essence of why history is vital to humanity. It teaches us how important it is not to know the future, but only to dream about it in one's own way."

Without much further commentary I could tell the Shrodes were deeply and spiritually impressed with this barnstormer's brand of philosophy. I know I was. We were all four silent, polite and highly respectful of each other as we drove back to the plane in the waning sunset of this August afternoon in the Ohio River valley.

The Shrodes let us out at the gate to our field, got out with us to walk to the plane, obviously reluctant to leave. It's getting late and we start unpacking our duffel bags and bedrolls, breaking away loose chaff under the wings. Mrs. Shrode reacted with honest but unnecessary remorse.

"Oh my, you are sleeping on the ground? Oh you poor dears. Oh, Chester, we can't allow it. Take them home to a clean bed with us. Oh, we didn't know. How thoughtless of us. Oh, my, oh my. Chester, how could you forget?"

Marty stood up quickly.

"Whoa! Whoa! It's our way of life. Aeronautical gypsies. In your cool sheets, my dear, we would only roll and toss. Not fit to fly the next day. If we did, we'd likely crash and kill ourselves from lack of proper sleep!"

I was not given to much humor but to this guy Marty I was growing more and more attached. It was all I could do to keep from breaking out into uncontrollable mirth when I compared her utterly serious expression compared to his cavalier remark.

Both the Shrodes were in an obvious stew as to what to do. Insist or desist on further insistence. Then a figure approached in the waning light. It was the younger Gwaltney. If he didn't resolve the situation for the Shrodes, he certainly changed it.

"Hey, you barnstormers! We have a north room for you and a couple of beds. You can keep an eye on the plane from there until dark."

Marty shook his head and laughed loudly, saying,

"Well, I was just telling these folks that we barnstorming gypsies don't know how to sleep in a bed. We are ground-bound for life. All we know is prickly hay stubble. On the other hand, my young friend here is new at this, so for his sake maybe we should accept your kind offer. And it will save the Shrodes from making a round trip once again to Rockport. So I'll leave it to Peyton. His last chance for a bed for six weeks?"

I shrugged my shoulders and nodded. Anything to resolve the tedium of decision. All four of us reluctantly say our good-byes and the Shrodes take their leave for Rockport. I hated to see these good folks leave and resolved that after my tour with Marty I would persuade my parents to drive over to Rockport with me to visit them. I am amused at the reaction that will occur when the Shrodes discover that my parents are dedicated Pioneer Village enthusiasts. When that happens I guess I can endure it because of my respect and admiration for the Shrodes.

The Gwaltneys are kind and hospitable, just like the Shrodes. Marty offers to fly them next day to show our appreciation for giving us beds for the night and for the use of their field. But they politely decline in a rather jocular manner. The fifty-year-old son relates that he and his father were given rides several years earlier by Roscoe Pope's visiting barnstormer instructor. It seems the old Standards' leaky water-cooled engine blew a radiator hose about three miles east of Midway.

The forced landing was something less than soft, but without serious mishap. It was made in standing corn and on exiting the field laden in 8-foot cornstalks, then proceeded to almost nose over in trying to pass through a barbed wire fence. So, no more plane rides even though Marty tried to assure them of the vast improvement of the 1928 Waco over the ancient 1916 Standard. Since that time they still loved planes and pilots but preferred to admire both on <u>terra</u> <u>firma</u>.

Our beds were cots in the same room on the north side of the house with a window view of our field and the Waco. As we unrolled our bedrolls on the cots, I queried Marty on his plans for tomorrow. For a few moments I thought he was ignoring me, then he said thoughtfully,

"I don't think our notice in the Rockport paper was big enough. It was not a paid advertisement and will be a week before the next one comes out even if we were given a new article. Let's get up leisurely tomorrow and amble down to the cafe for breakfast. If by that time no one shows, let's take off and head upriver. You know we flew only four passengers yesterday, that was twenty dollars, but you know Mr. Murray insisted on giving us an extra ten. He said it was worth it.

"By the way; Gwaltney Jr. told me he and his father would be up at 4 a.m. to drive their team and wagon up to Midway for the day for a load of feed corn. Said not to get up and to help ourselves to the kitchen and pantry if we wanted to make our own breakfast. And they said that if we took off before they returned for us to have a good journey. How about that? People out in these farm communities are good as gold. It's, I guess, the main reason I've always been addicted to this barnstorming. I hate to impose on them any more by using their kitchen tomorrow morning and eating food from their pantry. I tried to pay them some compensation but I backed off right away when I quickly saw that it would have been taken as a trivializing of their hospitality. We will hike down the road to the cafe after checking over the airplane."

My first night on this tour and I am sleeping in a bed.

I sure did not expect that. As I started to fall asleep, within minutes the opened but screened window welcomed a gentle breeze from the field. It seems every cricket in Spencer County is trying to out-cricket the entire army of crickets. Sure, a person can easily hear crickets but they can have a soothing, audible uniform level with relation to each other and even the other sounds of a rural night. I lay analyzing this intriguing situation. I can hear each and every cricket but I can also hear the cacophony of bullfrogs in the pond behind the house. A city bred person, if told about all this would immediately conclude that human sleep was impossible with all of nature's field musicians performing this monumental nocturnal symphony. But just the opposite is true. It is like a dose of morphine to a tired body and a resolute mind is rendered submissive beyond recall. In my case now, a mind consumed by a vision of an army of crickets examining every square inch of our Waco-10 in the performance of their duties as licensed airworthiness inspectors for the Bureau of Air Commerce. Not to worry. All ten million of them nod their bulgy-eyed heads in emphatic approval. They head back to the fields for more cricketing. I know no more, it's way too much effort.

I barely heard the Gwaltneys harnessing their team. Long after that I am conscious of low sunlight streaking the field and the glistening of sunlit dew reflected on the silver tail and maroon fuselage of the Waco and a dewy mist rising from the wings. My friend Marty was sleeping peacefully, his straight hair all which-away and snoring in a rhythmic rising and falling scale like a violinist testing his newly strung instrument. His snorting, gasping aberrations are like those he had accused me of doing under the Ranger's wing a few nights earlier. I'm thinking I'll risk ribbing him about his rasping snoring habits even if that is stretching the truth. In fact, his snoring is really rather harmonious. It had probably helped me sleep. But I would not tell him that, of course.

I got up, put on my trousers, put on my shoes, began to roll up my bedroll and neaten up the cot so it would be the way the Gwaltneys had turned it over to me last night. Marty gave a little snort, eyes wide awake, sitting up quickly.

"What! What you doin', kid? Good Lord! Morning already?

Feel like I slept for a week. Well, I guess you are telling me to be up and at 'em!" He peeped out the window with a look of satisfaction and a quiet remark.

"Good. Ship looks okay."

Out the back door, around the house to the road, we take a brisk walk down the road to Richland Cafe. "Gosh," I think, "what a beautiful morning it is!" The sun is low, only two or three big old white billowy cumulus clouds above the horizons. One to the east. One to the west and one to the north. A cool breeze floats in across the hayfields carrying with it the hundreds of fresh morning scents of a dew-laden countryside. In the past few mornings that I awoke in our Boonville field those scents of nature mixed with the exciting smells of doped fabric and cockpit furnishings of the Waco will indelibly impress my memory in the years to come. I just know it will.

The cafe is a-bustle with the local morning coffee sippers, mostly older gentry who lived nearby. A few of the young and middle-aged are just leaving, headed home for a day of farm labor. Two are riding horses, which by their equine conformation appear to undoubtedly do double duty as work animals. One man is driving a horse drawn open four-wheel buggy. The trucks are all Model T Fords of early twenties vintage.

We take our same little table. The "Stool-Five" are back on their same stools. Number Two turns to us as we both order bacon, eggs, biscuits and milk gravy.

"We seen you fellas flyin' yesterday. I didn't come down to the Gwaltney's field you're in, but I went by with my team yesterday. Seen your plane. I had to harvest on my peas. Herman, that just left, said your plane was a Travel Air. He rode in one once."

"No. That's close to the same type. Same engine. Ours is a Waco," replied Marty.

Marty made my day when he said the Waco was ours. He turned to me as Sam the cook plunked down our pile of breakfast and the blackest coffee in Spencer County. Marty was saying to me, slowly and thoughtfully,

"I don't see anyone here who will want a five buck ride. Those who could dig it up are too busy farming. The others who loaf in here could eat here for over a week on that much-if they had it. After breakfast, let's walk up to the ship and then head up the Ohio River for the Tell City-Cannelton area. It's only about 35 miles—as the crow flies as the old saying goes—or for us as the Waco flies. It will take about a half hour unless we wander around doing a bit of gawking which we probably will."

I break my first dollar bill for breakfast and coffee. I get back sixty-five cents in change.

We walk slowly for a mile because the day is warming up and we are in no hurry. Barnstormers never hurry leaving any place. If they do they may miss a passing motorist or a farmer who feels the sudden impulse to take a plane ride. We arrive at the narrow gate in the fence and wire it shut out of deference to the good Gwaltneys.

The Waco's silver and red surfaces are steaming as the rising sun strikes the dew-laden fabric. I untie the tie-down ropes from the lower wing struts and wrench the tie-down stakes out of the ground where we have driven them with the mallet. Marty is fussing around doing all of the sundry things he continually inspects on the OX-5. He both shakes and nods his head when I question him out of curiosity. His answer is that you must always look upon an airplane engine as a thing designed expressly to quit when you need it most. It does this, he says, by performing beautifully for hours on end until you are lulled into believing that it is dedicated to your lifelong salvation. It will give you some measure of that salvation but in return it wants you to dedicate your life to its constant care, feeding, watering, field surgery and outright coddling when it feels miserable and inclined to conk out over a paucity of landing fields. The most temperamental engine of all, he says, is the venerable good old OX-5. When I asked him why is it then that Waco, Travel Air, American Eagle, Eaglerock, Curtiss-Robin and many others all used OX-5 engines? He replies that its low cost made those airplanes possible—even made those companies possible. Waco-10 in 1928, he says, sold brand new for about $2500. The OX-5 made that possible. The same airplane equipped with the new Wright Whirlwind J-5 of 220 h.p. cost nearly $8000. The Whirlwind was more reliable and much more horsepower and horsepower per pound of weight and better plane performance. But what barnstormer could afford it? And his main point was this: If Waco and the others had not built their 3-place biplanes around the OX-5, then the total number of planes produced would have been enormously less and therefore the unit price of the Whirlwind versions would have been enormously greater than $8000—so much so that the surging commercial aviation of the roaring late twenties and early thirties would not have taken place. The OX-5 deserved to be coddled, he opined.

Marty's last act of Waco inspection on this fine August morning in 1933 was to carefully swab the crushed bugs from the propeller blades with a rag he had moistened on the dew-laden sides of the Waco's fuselage.

I checked the chocks and see that the duffel bags we have brought down from Gwaltneys and all the other gear are in the forward cockpit, after I have hooked up the front controls. By this time Marty has, for now at least, exhausted all of the fussing over the OX-5 that he can think of. He is standing alongside waiting for me to perform my ignition switching duties.

As I climb into the rear he walks out front, grasps the propeller blade, calling out,

"Switch off?"

"Switch is off," I reply.

He stands firmly on one leg, swinging the other to and fro as he then swings the prop. He repeats the process. Then a third time, and a more gentle fourth time. Then "Switch on?"

I carefully check the throttle at "Idle" and the magneto at "retard," throw the switch to "on" and call back, "Switch on!" He gives the prop a vigorous swing. There are a couple of loud, backfiring type of explosions, the prop seeming to kick back and forth, then the engine began to miss, then runs slowly and very unevenly, the exhaust stacks belching out blackish oil smoke. My cockpit is filling with the stuff and I am coughing my head off and my eyes are burning. I am wondering if Marty, despite all of his superior expertise, had overprimed the OX-5 cylinders with too much raw fuel before starting it.

After less than a minute, the OX-5 behaves more normally. The black smoke of the exhaust clears up and it is running more smoothly showing signs of steady improvement.

Now I am startled to note that Marty has been standing alongside the cockpit peering in at me. I look at him questioningly as if to ask over the noise of the idling OX-5, 'Are we going to go or do you want me to shut her down so you can again work on her?'

He merely grinned, giving me the jerked thumb over the shoulder signal to get out so he could get in. Which I hurriedly do. As I stand alongside he runs the engine up at higher r.p.m. and holds it there for several minutes, all the time with the stick back in his lap to hold the tail down as the Waco strains at the chocks. I stand away far enough so the stabilizer won't hit me if the plane jumps the chocks. I note that a passing farmer has reined up his team of horses pulling a wagon. Dust and hay chaff in a dense, high velocity stream blankets the road. Over in the field beyond still hovers a cloud of black oil smoke from the first hundred r.p.m.'s.

After a few minutes he cuts the engine back to 'Idle', thrusts his head out, yelling,

"Stow the chocks and climb in!"

I pile the chocks atop the duffel bags, strap up, then raise my arm high and yell, "Let's go!"

Log house of Pioneer Village, Rockport, Indiana, 1930.

Stern Wheeler Steamboat, Rockport, Indiana, 1930.

CHAPTER IV

The OX-5 comes to its full power and I can feel the tail rise up enough to get the tailskid off the ground and we are on our way headed east along the half-mile length of the Gwaltney's hay field. We lift off in a gentle climb as I look back and to the right at receding Richland. I can barely make out five small figures out in the road in front of the Richland Cafe. The 'Stool Five' no doubt. I can see Rockport up ahead and I am glad that this morning at breakfast I told Marty that I did not want to practice flying so I could concentrate on seeing the sights on the way to Tell City without distraction. I had been to Tell City and Cannelton many times with my dad's baseball team. But seeing it from the air would be a new experience I did not want to miss. The OX-5 was running along smoothly as though the rough, noisy toxic start a few moments earlier were the traits of some other engine far from Spencer County, Indiana. Bless the Lord! It is a wonderful day and I am extremely happy!

The meandering Ohio is sprawled out in the distance ahead of us. By air the straight-line distance to Rockport is only eight miles. We are over the small river town in less than a fourth of the time it took us to drive over there yesterday. It's not as easy to pick out familiar landmarks from the air the first time. Then I spot the highway and 'There!' I can see Stan Murray's home and his dog kennels out back. We are at about five hundred feet and Marty is climbing because I can tell by the sound of the OX-5's laboring. I have no altimeter in the front cockpit. That's only in the rear. Now I can see the Pioneer Village in the park and I amuse myself thinking of Marty's little philosophical dissertation on the poor deprived earlier generations' lack of airplanes.

We are now over the bluffs and antebellum homes on the bluff above the river. I can even see the home with the old pilothouse now used as a gazebo atop the bluff. Rockport is at a great bend in the Ohio River. At Rockport the river runs downstream due south. Upstream the river extends northeast. We now must be at about eight hundred feet and slowly circling Rockport. Up ahead around another great bend in the Ohio I think I can make out what I believe to be Tell City, Cannelton and Hawesville. The latter is in Kentucky and I think I can make out the Cannelton-Hawesville ferry crossing the Ohio. Looking south down the river I can see in the distance another great bend in the river at Owensboro, Kentucky where the river bends around to the northwest to Newburgh and Evansville.

Marty ends his circling over the Rockport bluff by straightening out and heading upriver. I could see that he could either keep above the river or he could take a "short cut." Good old Marty. He had remembered that I had asked him to fly along the river so I could see old familiar sites from the air for the first time. Sites I had seen eight years ago back when dad used to take me to Tell City with his baseball team. I could hear the OX-5 rev up and then the r.p.m. cut back and later pick up speed again and I knew he was slowly coming down so I could get a better look along the river.

Now we are nearing the bend in the Ohio and I could look down and ahead at the little town of Troy where we had stopped for cokes, coffee and beer with the baseball team. It was eight years ago and now that I have grown so much older at sixteen, my memory is not so good as it was back then, or at least that's what I hear my dad and his old cronies keep saying all the time so I guess it must be true. I remember that dad's team played both the Tell City and Cannelton teams but not on the same trip, of course.

We are now over Tell City, and Cannelton is just upriver and we have just completed the wide turn of the great stream.

I look for the rural baseball field, which I remember as being between Tell City and Cannelton. It never did have even the most rudimentary stands or bleachers for the fans, they just sat on grass chewing long stemmed weeds, rooting for their favorite players. I look down long and hard and Marty catches on for he begins slowly circling the area. I have to assume that the ball field has not been used for several years. The pitcher's mound, the home plate, the trampled path between bases, all of it seems to have gone back to grass. Dad will be disappointed when I tell him. Or maybe I have forgotten where it really is or was. North of Tell City or Cannelton? Or what? From this altitude I can see this whole area. I can't spot a baseball field or stands or backstops anywhere, but at the same time I know that this haven of baseball fans must have a team and a field somewhere down there. And it's August and it should surely show up if I could just spot it. So I guess it's something to ask the local folks if we land there as Marty indicated he planned to do.

We are now over the river and the ferry connecting Cannelton with Hawesville, Kentucky. I can remember us taking the ferry to Hawesville once to visit some of the Tell City/Cannelton team members who lived there. It's a tiny picturesque little place I'll always remember. Marty circles the ferry and the two river towns opposite each other for he knows I am fond of both Cannelton and Hawesville.

Then all of a sudden he straightens out heading south. Just as suddenly the engine r.p.m. drops to near "Idle" and I can see my throttle in the front cockpit move backward. Then he begins pounding on the cowling, shaking the stick and yelling,' "You fly her south down into Kentucky for a while!" Then he shoves the throttle forward and we are back up to our cruise speed of seventy-five.

I instantly recognize the Waco's old characteristics that I have been confronted with on that first training flight south of Boonville. It was docile enough even with a novice student like myself but it calmly insisted on being flown and cared for every second it is in the air. All very subtle. A gradual tendency to roll with engine torque and very slow habit of the nose to undulate very slowly. For a full minute the nose would gradually tilt down lower and lower, then halt for a short spell and then for another full minute start coming up gradually until it passed the level "neutral" but continue going slowly up until it tired of that, then back down slowly again. I could forestall all of that slow undulation by getting a fix on the horizon and holding it there. But if you became preoccupied with sightseeing or daydreaming it would persist. The roll was another thing. It can be compensated instinctively with a little lateral pressure on the stick, which only changes with throttle setting. If you let it have its way you could surely get into a diving sideslip, lose altitude quickly and maybe even get into a spin. The thought of a spin disturbs me. Marty could handle that if it could be handled but not me. I do a few slow turns to left and right flying a southerly zigzag course. Marty is letting me have my way and I am enjoying every second of it. Up ahead I see what I know to be the Blackford River picking its way to the Ohio. Once dad, his brother my Uncle George and my Cousin Conrad had gone fishing there and later had eaten a catfish dinner a few miles further south at Weberstown which I could also see up ahead. On that fishing trip we had driven Uncle George's Star touring car on to Knottsville, then up along the river and back to Hawesville.

Now we are practically over small Weberstown and I begin wondering if Marty doesn't want me to turn back? The very moment I am thinking about it I see the throttle being pulled way back, the OX-5's r.p.m. slows drastically. About all I hear is wind stream noise through the wings and struts. Marty whacks the cowling behind my head, yelling,

"Head back north!" At the same time he advances the throttle back to its cruise setting. I start a slow left turn, level off after doing a one eighty.

From this altitude at least, this area south of the Ohio in Kentucky appears to be flatter than the hill country of Perry County north of the Ohio. I get to thinking about how my dad's friend, Forrest "Diney" Davidson took me to his uncle's place deep in the hilly forest of Perry County. Several miles up in the hills from the Ohio River. His uncle's place was so far back up in the hills that we had to ford a creek in "Diney's" old Dodge. "Diney" was an ardent squirrel hunter. His stealth in the woods was phenomenal. A day's hunt was up at dawn in the cool of the day and back in time for noon lunch but called dinner because it was a full dinner. On a three-day hunt each day "Diney" would show up with a limit of ten squirrels. I was lucky to get two. One day I got none but I did get a five-foot Copperhead snake coiled six or eight feet ahead in my path. It was the best and truly real alibi I could have for not getting any squirrels. I could not bring my eyes up into the trees to look for squirrels any longer. They were glued to the ground all day looking for snakes. A Copperhead is very venomous like a rattlesnake. But that squirrel hunt was like a trip into the past of a hundred years earlier. "Diney's" Uncle Clarence made only one or two summer trips a year into Tell City for supplies. In winter it was out of the question. His old Model T sat in the barn on wooden blocks to keep the weight off the tires. In summer he'd take out the blocks, drive the old "flivver" through the creek to the winding narrow dirt road that found its way out of the forest to the gravel and eventually to Cannelton or Tell City. His farm comprised five hundred acres, but only forty of it was farmed, the rest being woods. That trip was six years ago but I will never forget it.

In a minute we will be over Hawesville. The old OX-5 is purring right along, although purring is the wrong word to describe it. It defies description. One you will never forget. The stick is shaking from side to side and the airplane is rolling a bit from side to side as a result. Marty wants his Waco returned to him, which I do.

Before we reach Hawesville he banks left, cuts back the throttle sharply and starts losing altitude faster than I had experienced before with him this past week. The river between Tell City and Cannelton runs almost north and south, about a line northwest by north and southeast by south. We are heading west and coming down fast. Then he banks steeply to the right at almost a one eighty. We now are heading almost due east or maybe northeast by east, approaching the Ohio at a right angle and soon will be crossing it. I can see Tell City off the left wingtip and Cannelton off the right wingtip; also I can see roads and trees running alongside the river on each side. I raise up in my seat as far as my loosened belt will let me and look back at Marty. His head is craned upward even higher than me, darting from side to side as he fishtails the Waco to get a better view of terrain across the river. We cross the river at about five hundred feet, then the Tell City/Cannelton road at about the halfway point between the two towns. We are passing over a long hayfield, which stretches beyond the road for a distance of probably a half-mile. On each side are low gradually sloping hillsides which are uncultivated and left to pasture, bounded by scattered trees and brushy areas of blackberries and a few eroded shallow gullies.

The gullies, this year, and the election of President Franklin Delano Roosevelt and inauguration of his New Deal are a subject of both political and agricultural contention. The president and his experts claim that the farmlands of America are eroding away from neglect. He intends to reclaim and rehabilitate gullies, like those below, with government paid work crews by putting the unemployed to work. He calls these work crews the W.P.A. or Works Project Administration. My dad and our new friend Marty have gotten along famously but I overheard them discussing President Roosevelt, the W.P.A., and reclamation of eroded farmland. Dad firmly believes the president has been sent to save us from the likes of past-President Herb Hoover and that reclaiming rundown farmland with the W.P.A. is a wonderful solution. But I was disturbed that Marty and Dad disagreed. They were very polite and friendly about it and the disagreement did not seem to mar their desire to be friends. Once they got it well out of their systems they dropped it from further discussion. Marty thought the election of Roosevelt wag a disaster for the country and that one day we'd regret it and that we would all become too reliant on the government to the point there would be no return to the basic tenets of freedom we have enjoyed since the Declaration of Independence and the American Revolution. As to reclaiming the land from the washed out gullies, Marty thought that should be left to the farmers themselves without imposing government intrusion upon them. I did not care about the question one way or another. I was supremely happy when they politely agreed to disagree in a humorous friendly way. I just wanted the subject to get back to one thing. Airplanes.

The end of the field we are over is bounded by a low fence. Beyond that is a field of corn. Further still is a mixture of various crops, pasture and woods. As we pass over the hayfield Marty has descended to less than two hundred feet until we reach the end and he climbs up and does what I thought was a one eighty turn too tight for this low altitude. Now we are heading back over the field again and in the opposite direction. I note a house and outbuildings on the road adjacent to the field and make a guess that this might be the field's owner.

Marty pulls up, climbs over the trees, making a wide turn over the river, and then descends in a shallow dive back toward the field. Except this time he veers to the left, passing directly over the supposed field owner's farmhouse and barn at an altitude of only a hundred feet. I cannot understand why Marty is doing this? If, in fact, the field's owner lives in the house we're buzzing he would be furious, let alone the possibility of letting us use the field. Besides, this low pass scared the living daylights out of me even though some of my Ranger flights were not too far short of hair-raising.

But as we pass over relatively slowly at about 65 m.p.h. I see figures behind the house waving their straw hats in what looked like enthusiastic welcome. At least they were not shaking their fists. But I did see two nervous horses in a corral behind the barn running in a circle and shaking their long manes and I suspect they are not merely playfully chasing each other.

Now Marty has drifted out into the center of the field has advanced the throttle and climbed back up and doing a one eighty lined up with the hayfield. A second later I see my throttle retarded a bit, the OX-5's r.p.m. wanes and we are nosed down. Looks like he is going to land. Or is he just setting up the farm folk for another low-level fly-by? If it's the latter there are going to be a couple of horses break through their fence. And maybe a couple of farmers are going to shake their clenched fists instead of a cheerful wave.

We are now over the corn, then the hayfield fence coming down fast and he is fishtailing the rudder, first right, then after a bit to the left. Our speed is dropping it seems too fast and he speeds up r.p.m. in a short burst, then back down, then up a little and holds her steady, straightens her up to give the wheels an in-line roll. We are down and stay down in one of Marty's neat three-pointers. As we slow down almost to a stop he runs the engine up to taxi speed, trundling along for two hundred yards until we come alongside the barn. The horses in the adjacent lot now seem not to be bothered by the taxiing airplane. I consider they must think it is just another piece of farm machinery. Flying low overhead with a "revved" up engine is something else. Marty swings around and switches off the engine. I'm not real sure what is going to be next, but I see two inevitably overall clad figures making their way to the plane. Marty climbs out to meet them and frankly I'm not sure whether to get out of the plane or not. But I figure I'd better crawl out if these locals are peeved about our landing, then Marty the old smoothie would want to introduce me in some eloquent manner that would encourage their welcome.

Both men looked about the same age, approaching seventy years. The one who seemed to be spokesman of the two held out his hand to Marty as he strode forward. "I'm Albert Veeck, an' this here is my hand, Henry Milhausen. We seed ye fly by more'n once an' figgered it was you."

Marty gives off with his most friendly warm handshake and eloquent manner, clearly effusing a hearty appreciation. "I of course know you received my letter and I surely want to thank you for your postcard mailed in care of my friends in Mt. Vernon. I sure appreciate your letting me use your field. Allow me to introduce my young associate, Peyton. He lives down in Boonville. He is something of a pilot himself. Built his own flying machine."

I couldn't help but blush as I shook the older man's weathered hand, but Marty's statement of my exploits seemed not to faze them. I guess it was so far out for them they didn't seem to get its significance.

Marty went on to reiterate what he had written to Mr. Veeck that we poor barnstormers could not afford to pay for the use of their field. And that our meager revenue all went for gas and oil. But he would be more than happy to fly he and Mr. Milhausen or members of his family.

"We'uns would shore appreciate seein' the river an' Cannelton from the air. I don't own the place here but just look after it. How did you know of the place here and to write me about it?"

Marty gave forth with his friendly grin, "The word gets around among barnstormers about the best and available fields all around the country. You must have had planes in here before?"

The older man's weathered face became thoughtful, "No, only once several years back. A feller from up around Jasper or maybe it was Vincennes was here one summer. Had a big old biplane he said was made in 1916. I took a ride in it. Darned near scared the livin' daylights out o' me. The feller that owned the place here flew in it. He claimed it was comin' apart while they wuz up an' they landed just in time. But this one here you got looks to be new?"

Marty sort of both nods and shakes his head. "It's a Waco Model 10 built in 1928 so it's not new. It's five years old but in good shape. If you would like a ride I can take you any time. No time like right now?"

Mr. Veeck was eager to go but Henry was a bit slow to make up his mind. As a hired hand I guess he figured he had to go if Mr. Veeck accepted.

I loaded them into the front cockpit after unloading our gear and disconnecting the front controls. I placed the chocks, then climbed in the rear to man the ignition switch while Marty swung the prop. The OX-5 was already warm so it started without any priming. I get out and stand aside as they taxi out a way and start their take-off. He climbs out to the east, turning slowly back toward the river to give the two old gents a look at the Cannelton/ Hawesville/Tell City area, while I move our gear back near the horse lot fence. With nothing else to do I take stock of this place where Marty has apparently decided to spend a day or two.

The field is plenty long enough for the Waco but it narrows at the upper end which I keep thinking is north but actually is almost directly east. It is slightly uphill and curved slightly and narrows at the east end but still plenty wide for the 30-foot wingspan of the Waco. From here it looks like the upper end of the field is about a hundred feet wide while down near the house it is three or four hundred. The field is in timothy hay, which has been recently cut. The farmhouse faces the road to Cannelton and Tell City with a narrow lane alongside the house leading to the barn. An opening in the fence leads to our hayfield through which Veeck moved his hay-mowing implements. The house is very small, as is the barn.

In piling our gear along the fence I notice a large brown envelope with the flap open. Some of Marty's gear I had not noticed before. It's open so I look inside. Yellow and red handbills reading in large black letters. "Take a plane ride! See your area from the air! Safe Waco plane flown by an aviator of much experience! only $3.00!"

Both the red and yellow handbills were identical. Then I noticed a big difference. The yellow charged "$3.00" but the red was "$5.00!" I'd better question Marty about this. In Boonville and Richland he charged five. People might come up to me wanting a plane ride while he was in the air. Was the yellow ones simply out of date?

With Veeck and Milhausen in the air no one seemed to be around the place. Just me, the chickens and two curious horses looking for attention. I amble over to the little barn and peer inside. Two old horse stalls alongside an aging dusty old Model T touring car with frazzled top. About a 1920 to 1922 vintage, I guessed. But looked to be occasionally used for the driver's seat seemed to have been kept clean by the occasional brushing by the seats of denim overalls worn by those climbing in and out.

Ahead of the Model T was a rusty but obviously serviceable horse-drawn mowing machine. It had been recently put in the barn because scraps of fresh hay still clung to the blades. Which meant the Model T had been moved out to put it in. Which also meant that the owner of the Model T wanted it more accessible than the mower. Then up ahead of the mower I discovered four old bicycles that had seen better days although not all that old. Probably ten or fifteen years old. Two have obviously been cannibalized to make the other two usable. The tires are up even though judging from their dusty saddles have not been ridden for several years. A ladder has been built onto the separation of the horse stalls ascending to a hole in the ceiling. The so-called hayloft, I guess. I climb up to find I am right. Except there is only a small pile of new hay just inside the loft door which overlooks the horse corral below. This barn is so small it could not begin to hold even a small fraction of the hayfield in which we have just landed. Obviously Mr. Veeck had just sold his recent crop as he cut and baled it. I am thinking that the loft and small haymow would be a dandy place for Marty and I to bed down for the night. I chuckled to myself a commentary an independent assessor might make: "A snoring good time was had by all!"

Then I look at my old dollar watch Pocket Ben. Thirty-five minutes have passed. Marty has been giving Veeck and Milhausen their money's worth. Then I hear the OX-5 approaching from across the river in a steadily increasing crescendo. Then all of a sudden they come loudly over the tree-tops and dive down to less than 50 feet. As they go roaring by the house and barn I see the bright-eyed mouth-agape expressions of the passengers who look over at the barn as though it is the last time they will ever see it. Then Marty slowly climbs to the east making a gentle turn to come in for a landing.

As they taxi up near the barn Marty switches off the engine and I climb up on the wing step to help out the passengers. Henry Milhausen tries to get up and out twice without unstrapping the lap belt, his face white as a sheet. Albert Veeck is all agog and bursting with bucolic delight.

"That was a regular thrill I'll never fergit! I'll go any time an' pay to do 'er! This Marty feller is a mighty fine plane driver! He sure knows how to handle this here airplane!"

Milhausen on the other hand, needed time to "ketch" his breathing before he could announce his approval or disapproval. Finally with his two feet firmly on the ground he grasped onto a wing strut, gasping, "It shore were somepin', that's fer shore. But I won't want to do 'er again!"

Marty climbed out and after a few cheerful compliments on what good fearless passengers they were, he then got down to polite business by milking important information from Mr. Veeck. Off aside I heard him mention gas, oil, Tell City, Cannelton, hotels, eateries and the handbills in that big Manila envelope. I did not want to appear the nosy eavesdropper so I stood aside but I heard Veeck mention the Model T and even the two old bicycles. I also heard the words "gas drum" and "hay loft." Presently the two older gents returned to their chores. Marty beckoned me over. As we staked down the Waco out of sight behind the barn, he filled me in.

"This is a good set-up. Veeck is going to take me in to Tell City tomorrow in the Model T. We will bring back a drum of gas with a spigot on back of the T. Set it on that sawhorse by the barn. And a large can of motor oil. Said he could use any we leave. Also he has two old bikes in the barn we can use to go into town and spread some handbills I brought. He offered to let us use the Ford but we are only two or three miles from town and don't need it unless we need a second load of gas which I doubt. He was apologetic as hell about our not sleeping in the house. Just no room. We will make out fine in the loft. I understand there's hay to sleep on." I nod and that makes him give me an inquisitive, mirthful look, saying, "You have checked all this out, every bit of it while we were in the air, didn't you?"

Sheepishly I reply, "Yeah, all except about the gas, but I did notice the homemade rack on the back of the Model T, wondered if it couldn't be used for hauling the gas."

Marty threw his head back laughing, and at the same time slapping my shoulder, quipping, "That's my old buddy! Thinking every minute of the day!" He couldn't know right then how much he had made my day. I'm liking this barnstormer more and more every day. Then he surprised me by producing a bag of sandwiches for our dinner. An undisclosed second bag he'd hidden, given yesterday by the Rockport couple from the Richland Cafe. Cold but very good. That night with our bedrolls in the haymow was the most blissful I'd spent in nearly two weeks. Sure we both snored loudly but snoring loudly means you are sleeping as soundly as a walnut log. No one to hear it but the nervous horses down below.

I woke a bit after break of day from the incessant crowing of a militant rooster out back of the barn sitting on the Waco's upper wing. Marty was intermittently snoring in a series of snorts and rolling over and over in the hay. Presently he sat up abruptly, his hair a tousled mess hanging over his face and ears. Then he vehemently voiced his complaint at being wakened so early. "Damn that damned rooster! My grandmother back in Kansas would have wrung his neck and had him for breakfast. Good Lord, what a noisy sucker he is! I've got some fine wire in the plane; we could wire the old sucker's beak shut. He would probably just blow up from too much bottled up compression."

It was the first time with Marty that I had laughed loudly and uncontrollably. He didn't seem to appreciate it, which made me laugh even more, but my laughing didn't seem to make him mad either. He just combed his hair, got up and pulled on his trousers and said,

"Let's ride the bikes down to Cannelton for some breakfast, then come back and take the flivver to Tell City for some gas and oil. Mr. Veeck will take us down."

The two-mile early ride down to Cannelton along the river was beautiful. I will never forget it and some day when I am an old man and not sixteen years old as I am now I will write a book about it. We meet very few local folk along the road. One in a flivver like Albert Veeck's. One in a horse-drawn buggy and another in a Studebaker farm wagon drawn by two sturdy horses with the biggest hooves I have ever seen. All three men nodded their heads in friendly "Howdy" greetings. We pull out in a little opening that seems to be a campground for local picnickers or fishermen where they can launch their skiffs. The Kentucky shore across the river is just as beautifully timeless as it is here. It is early as we ride into Cannelton but the general store is open with a goodly gathering of coffee drinkers on benches out front. There seems to be no cafe nearby where we can have a simple breakfast of eggs and bacon, to say nothing of a Mother Autry style breakfast. It only stirs unwanted hunger pains to entertain such a comparison. But the back of the store has hot coffee on a stove and homemade sweet rolls and cakes. We made do with 2 or 3 cups of black coffee and 3 or 4 rolls or cakes each. Total cost twenty-five cents.

Marty leaves several of the handbills on the counter and pins two on a local bulletin board in back of the store. An old cold pot-bellied stove stands in the corner, its service unneeded on this day in August. Marty also hands out the bills to each of the overall clad coffee-klatchers on the porch, raising several eyebrows and flustered comments when they realized we were the low-flying aviators of yesterday who had broken the tranquillity of Cannelton. Already the entire hamlet according to them were aware that we were the guests of Albert Veeck. Visibly they seemed not to understand why two such captains of aerial modernity would be riding two rusty old bicycles.

We pedal fast back to the farm to find Albert Veeck turning the Model T around in the barnyard, climb aboard and head up the road to Tell City a whopping distance of only three miles. Veeck stops at an old store near the river, very similar in age and style as the one in Cannelton, except this one has a gasoline pump. Veeck has his gas drum on the back of the flivver which is equipped with a spigot for filling smaller cans and a cap on top for filling the drum itself which has a capacity of fifty gallons. We fill it about two-thirds full so the weight is low enough that we can wrestle the drum off the Model T and onto the sawhorse back at the farm. Even then it weighs two hundred pounds. While Veeck and Marty fill the drum I look around in Tell City which I haven't seen for nine years. I ask an elderly bystander about the baseball field. He points up a side street with lengthy directions which don't mean much to me, then ends his instructions with the fact that the ball field no longer exists and wasn't more than a worn spot in the first place. It was now a small cornfield, he says. So much for the passage of time. At age sixteen I suddenly feel very old.

The men are now paying for the gas and oil and anxious to get back to the farm, but before we leave I leave more of the handbills at the store and hand more to customers and passersby on the street.

Back at the farm we roll the drum onto the sawhorse and Marty begins filling our own ten-gallon can. It is not a fast process for he is carefully straining the fuel both through his cheesecloth and chamois skin filters. We then carry it back to the Waco, climb up on the lower wing step and pour it through the filler neck into the 35-gallon tank of the airplane. A full can weighs 60 lbs. so it is no easy job. I quickly learn that it is better to not fill the can to the top and instead make more trips from drum to airplane. Marty did all the fuel straining. While I am pouring gas he is also adding oil to the crankcase and replenishing the radiator under the upper wing with water.

While I am running back and forth with a half-full can of fuel weighing thirty pounds I get to wondering how long all of this is going to take. I add up in my head that since leaving Boonville we flew first to Richland via DeGonia. Then Marty flew the Murrays and Shrodes about 35 minutes each, then flew to Tell City, then down to Weberstown and back. All told about two hours and twenty minutes. On the fourth trip the can almost fills the tank, within about a gallon. At five gallons per trip adds to twenty gallons, or about 8.6 gallons per flying hour. When I tell my analysis to Marty he gives me a look of amazement. "Gee, Kid. You have a keen sense of curiosity. That's good. Real good. Yeah, that's just about right on the nose for fuel consumption on the OX-5. While we have some time later on this trip I want to talk to you about the future."

Just as I start to ask him what he means by the future, we both notice some activity down on the road. Two autos were parking on the road. One was a brand new 1933 Ford Coupe, the other an earlier Chevrolet. No sooner than I noticed the autos an open horse-drawn buggy with four people hitched to the fence ahead of the autos. Then up the road from Cannelton I also noticed five pedestrians heading our way. In a few minutes, no less than fifteen people were strung out in the drive along the house making their way to the barnyard and the opening into the field and the Waco, its silver and red tail protruding from the area behind the barn.

Marty really comes to life, his eyes wide and lips in a broad smile.

He was even happier when I polled each of the 15 folks if they wished a plane ride? All fifteen nodded their heads enthusiastically and almost in unison. Then if this windfall were not enough, a half dozen more showed up asking if they could have a plane ride for three dollars. Both Marty and I came quickly alive. The first thing I am doing is collecting their money and their names and jotting down the order we would fly them. All told sixty-three bucks and maybe more to come. Marty unstaked the Waco and we lifted the tail and turned it around facing the center of the field. I chocked the wheels and climbed in and manned the ignition switch while Marty swung the prop. In a couple of minutes we had the OX-5 going and I loaded the first two passengers. Marty taxied down to the lower end of the field near the road and revved the engine up until the head temperature was high enough to take off. In the process the propeller blew hay chaff all across the road. The noise of the engine and propeller drew a great deal of attention from others passing on the road. It was good advertising too, because they all stopped, held onto their straw hats, making their way up to the lane to join the other passengers where I greeted them nicely and took their three dollars and their names. None of the crowd seemed to mind waiting their turn.

It became a social event for them. They all knew each other, looking upon the event as an impromptu church social or Grange picnic. I now had collected seventy-five dollars and twenty-five passengers. At fifteen minutes for each couple, over three hours of flying. Obviously, Marty and I have a busy day ahead of us. I figure I had better check with Marty first before I sell any more plane rides. With over three hours flying to handle what I had already sold, then it would be getting a bit uncomfortably close to having to re-fuel the Waco. We had used up all the gas in the barnyard drum, which meant going into Tell City again to replenish the drum. Even the most patient of the booked passengers would not wait for all of that to take place. They would rightfully want to leave and want their money back. The Waco should be good for another hour beyond my booked passengers at three hours flying time, I figure. But I must bear in mind that it probably would use a good deal more fuel when taking off every fifteen minutes as compared to one take-off and cruising for four hours. No, I must consult Marty before I sell any more rides. The last thing I want to happen is for Marty to have to make a forced landing over in Kentucky and then have the ignoble task of bringing them back to Cannelton on the Hawesville Ferry across the Ohio River! Horrible thought. Marty is too sharp to let that happen. He will be watching the gas gauge all the while he is hauling these twenty-five passengers. But also I don't want to take people's money and then have to give it back to them because we have run out of gasoline.

While Marty is in the air with each pair of passengers, I try to keep the passengers entertained as much as I can by at least quietly joining them in their visiting with each other. Some questioned me, dubiously wondering why a 16-year-old is a barnstormer. When they hear of my exploits with my Rhon Ranger glider down in Boonville, some of the more astute are enamored with my adventures. The others just don't comprehend even what a glider is, to say nothing of what it does. They are more interested in this year's crops versus last year's crops or the latest doings in Tell City or Cannelton or the tiny towns in the north of Perry County. When Marty lands I ask him if I should sell any more rides now that we have twenty-five. I tell him above the noise of the idling OX-5 my analysis of fuel consumption. His brow furrows in thought and he yells back at me, "Yeah, we use more gas making all of these take-offs and short flights. Just sell one more passenger. Twenty-five is an uneven number. It leaves one passenger flying alone. Thirteen flights. Get him a buddy." With that he takes off with the next load.

I go around asking if one more would like to fly with the odd man, a Mr. Schmidt. A lady steps up, says she is Mrs. Schmidt, and she has changed her mind and will fly with her husband after all. A few of the bystanders who know the Schmidts titter politely and compliment her on her marital commitment to fate, whatever it might hold.

I get to thinking that the Schmidts' flight, the last before we must refuel the Waco, will be flight number 13. If my Grandma Autry were here she would vigorously voice her superstitions and flight number 13 would be flown over her dead body. But she is not here and the Schmidts either don't know it's flight 13 or they don't care. I am sure it's the former and as Grandma's grandson I feel guilty for not telling them. But after all the Waco is safe and Marty is, in my mind at least, the best pilot in the world.

My fuel consumption analysis of three hours did not take into account the surprising amount of time it takes to taxi into and away from the fence and the time to load and unload the passengers. Consequently, after three hours, Marty has only flown eight flights. It's starting to get late but still a long time before dark on this August afternoon. The local people mostly eat their evening dinner by five o'clock and those who did not sign up for a ride are making their way down to the road to go home. Those who are still waiting to ride do so patiently and with obvious enthusiasm.

Another hour has passed when Marty landed with his twelfth load of passengers and one more to go. I unloaded number twelve and loaded number thirteen, the last before we shut down for the day. Marty beckoned me to come over alongside the rear cockpit as he cut back the OX-5 to the slowest idle without the engine quitting altogether. He motioned for me to put my ear close to his mouth so he could speak without the passengers up front hearing what he was telling me.

"She cut out on me while we were over on the other side of the river. It windmilled enough with a dead engine so I was finally able to get it going again. But we lost most of our altitude. Didn't re-start until we were down to two hundred feet. I had a field picked out just north of Weberstown. The passengers didn't catch on to what was happening. They just thought I was giving them a buzz at low level over Weberstown, which it turned out I did!"

I wondered why he was telling ME all this? His expression was very thoughtful as if he was thinking of shutting it down and apologizing to passengers No. 13, which I have just now loaded. I asked,

"Are you going to abort No. 13 and work on the engine?"

He remained silent for another moment, then replied,

"No. I'll taxi out and run it at over full power to 1500 for a minute and watch the tachometer. If it holds and sounds okay, we'll go. But after that we are done for the day. Don't sell any more rides today."

He taxis out to the inner end of the field, lines up for take-off, holds the stick back, and digs the tail skid into the sod, running full power at a standstill for over a minute.

The passengers look a little frightened at all the preparatory ruckus. After over a minute he cuts the r.p.m. back to 1400, lifts the tail and they go rolling down the field for a routine take-off. I think about what Marty has told me and I have read of the idiosyncrasies of the venerable OX-5.

The engine had been produced primarily for World War I trainers like the Curtiss JN-4, "Jenny" and the Standard J-1. Reportedly 15,000 engines were delivered to the U.S. Government, Britain and Canada between 1914 and 1918. Thousands of new OX-5 engines ended up in warehouses after the war, selling surplus for as low as $20 and as high as $300. Most were bought up by the booming industry of new airplane manufacturers as a result of the new Air Commerce Act of 1926, the majority going into new 3-place biplanes like the Waco-9 and Waco-10, American Eagle, Alexander Eaglerock, Travel Air 2000, and many others.

All in all, the OX-5 is a reliable and widely used engine, but has its idiosyncrasies. The consensus seems to be that the Curtiss V-8 cylinders, crankcase, crankshaft or "bottom end" of the engine is solid and reliable and able to stand several hundred hours between overhauls. The consensus, however, on the "top end" is another matter. The valve system mechanism suffers from poor lubrication, wear and general weakness, designed for a service life of only fifty hours before overhaul. Whether this is true or not, Marty says it is the skill, care and maintenance the owner and operator gives the engine. The valve mechanism is said to be primitive because it depends on hand greasing and oiling. A number of improvements have been devised by later airplane manufacturers such as Waco who used these war surplus engines; improvements such as roller-rockers and lubrication upgrading. The Dixie and Berling magnetos were used as a poor substitute to the more reliable pre-war German Bosche magnetos. The wartime Berlings and Dixies in OX-5s in the late 1920's with the more reliable Scintilla magneto. A much more reliable valve mechanism was available in a kit of improved parts produced by Miller. Another complaint over the years was water leakage of the cooling system. Still another was a temperamental fuel inlet and carburetor system. Much of these complaints, Marty says, came from barnstormers whose rural source of fuel was poor at best. Low octane gasoline stored under poor conditions and high in contaminants, mostly stored and used for farm tractors and early automobiles that ran inefficiently after a fashion on most anything. All of which was the reason Marty and other barnstormers filtered their gasoline to the point of obsessive extremism. Even then they had occasional stoppages and forced landings.

Then if the OX-5 had these idiosyncrasies, why did manufacturers like Waco use it in their airplanes in the late 20's and early 30's? As Marty had pointed out, its low cost made airplanes possible and affordable to the private pilot. The more exotic air-cooled radial engines in the same airplanes could increase the total cost of the airplane by as much as ten-fold. Instead of $2500, more likely $25,000. Considering that a brand new OX-5 in a brand-new Waco was not all that unreliable. What helped was a good respect and knowledge of owning and using the venerable engine. Most of the OX-5s used in the late 20's by factories like Waco were upgraded to the limit with all the available improved innovations up to that time. Also, when a full overhaul was necessary, after several hundred hours, an owner could replace the OX-5 with a brand new engine for as little as three hundred bucks instead of overhauling the original engine.

All of the bystanders have now taken their leave and I'm here all alone. I notice over the trees in the east a darkening cloud that seems to be getting not only darker but larger. Marty has wisely taken his passengers across the river into Kentucky instead of heading north farther up into Perry County. Perry County is mostly made up of forested rolling hills and in spite of its beauty, not the most hospitable place in the world for a forced landing. The Kentucky region south of the river is just the opposite. It is mostly flat farmland.

Then I hear two sounds almost simultaneously. One is the rumble and clap of thunder and bolt lightning over the wooded hills to the east. And it seems to be approaching even faster than I had at first thought. The other sound is the Waco coming in over the trees along the river. It is climbing as it passes over the upper end of our field, then at about a mile out makes a turn, heading back for a landing.

As Marty taxis up near the barn, I rush out to help the passengers deplane. They both look up at the approaching storm, thank Marty for the ride and take off for their auto parked down on the road. Marty guns the Waco around, swinging the tail up off the ground then back down into its stake-down location behind the barn, switches off the engine and climbs out.

"Kid, run up to the loft and get those bedroll covers. They also double up as cockpit covers!"

He covers and ties down the canvas cockpit covers while I lash the tie-down ropes to the front struts and the stakes. We also drive an extra stake and tie down for the tailskid. Before Marty covers the cockpits he lashes a cord around the stick and rudder pedals to keep the ailerons, rudder and elevator from being banged around in the high wind of the storm that is seconds away.

Then it hit. First a strong breeze and seconds later a gale force wind. A torrential downpour as we beat a hasty retreat for the barn. The horses out back had gotten the message early. They had already come in the side doors of their stalls, comfortably munching hay provided earlier by Mr. Milhausen.

We climb up into the loft to find the place dry and comfortable except for the wind-driven torrent impaling itself on the roof. Every few seconds a bright flash of lightning, followed by a horrendous clap of thunder.

Marty anxiously peered out the sheltered loft door down at the Waco, lurching and tugging at its tie-down ropes. At times the wind would lift the airplane almost up to the full extension of the springs and shock absorber struts of the landing gear. We certainly need to keep an eye on those stakes. They are long and deep with notched shafts, driven deep into the ground.

Marty is saying, "You as hungry as I am? We could ride up to Tell City and go to the old cafe on Front Street. One of the passengers told me the catfish dinners up there are out of this world. All the eight-inch fiddler cats you can eat for two bits and a dime, coffee and bread included. But in this storm we'd get not only soaking wet but be blown off the things more often than we'd be on them. Also I hate leaving the ship unattended. If those stakes should pull loose the wind could roll it over on its back and wreck the wings."

He had only uttered the words when we heard a shuffling sound down below. Albert Veeck appeared on the ladder wearing a rain soaked old felt hat and a black rubber slicker. He was carrying two old coats. Rather timidly he was saying,

"Me and Henry would be more'n glad ta have you and the young feller have supper with us. She is really comin' down hard out there. We ain't got nothin' fancy ta eat but we shore got plenty. Henry makes good biscuits an' we got mashed potatoes, corn-on-the-cob an' pork chops. They's room enough at our little kitchen table for all four of us. You'd need them coats to wear to run across the yard to the back door; she's pourin' so hard. An' looks like she's set in for the night."

Marty took one look at me, quickly detecting that I could not hide my watering mouth. He let forth in loud, uproarious laughter that turned my starving face crimson red and perplexed Mr. Veeck so much that he only stared in what appeared to be full surprise. Marty could not talk for laughing as he pointed at my face. Then he finally got his breath and told Mr. Veeck,

"Mr. Veeck, we already owe you a great deal, but with this storm and all, we would be absolutely honored to have supper with you and Mr. Milhausen!"

As we trooped quickly through the back door, Veeck hung up our wet coats on a series of wall nails inside the back door. We sat down at the table to welcome hot coffee and Henry began dishing out the biscuits, pork chops, corn and potatoes. Before I could snatch a knife and fork, Mr. Veeck without touching his ancient, tarnished silverware, clasped his palms together and gave thanks. He was just in time to save me from violating my puritan up-bringing in the name of hunger. I saw that Marty was closely watching me in amusement, but at least this time the doggoned son-of-a-gun said nothing embarrassing.

After dinner we remained at the table, drinking coffee, and eating Mr. Milhausen's apple pie. The storm still raged. Marty anxiously peered out the window where he could see the tip of the Waco's upper wing protruding behind the barn. It remained in its staked-down level position but rocked back and forth as much as the minimal slack of the stake ropes would allow.

Presently Marty rose and shook hands with the elderly Hoosier farmers.

"We sure do appreciate your sharing this wonderful dinner with us, and Peyton here and I insist that we do the dishes as I'm sure you both have still other evening chores to do before you retire. Even if the weather clears by tomorrow morning the field will be too wet to even taxi the airplane, as I'm sure you'll agree the tailskid and wheels would rut the field. Also, tomorrow I must remove the carburetor, disassemble and clean it thoroughly. Yesterday I experienced a temporary stoppage in the air but was able to get it started just in time to avoid a forced landing over in Kentucky near Weberstown. We do not wish to impose on you kind gentlemen any further, and especially the culinary favors of Mr. Milhausen here. Instead, would you join us for breakfast at our expense down in Cannelton? One of the passengers told Peyton of a nice little place down by the river not far from the Hawesville Ferry Landing."

Veeck replied, "Aw shucks, you fellers was more'n welcome to eat supper with us an' hear of all your plane flyin' experiences. We thank ye for invitin' us to breakfast. But me an' Henry promised to help do up-keep work tomorrow at St. Paul's up to Tell City. But you fellers make yourselves to home around here. They is a little workbench in the barn where you could take your carburetor apart an' clean it. We'll be back later in the afternoon tomorrow an' we can all take the gasoline drum back up to Tell City and fill it, because I know you'll want to fill up your plane afore you do any more flyin'.

After helping with the dishes, we thanked these kindly old gents again, donned our borrowed coats and dashed for the barn and up to our hayloft bed. The loft was warm and dry but the rain was still pounding incessantly on the roof. We peered out the loft door at the Waco, its waterproofed doped fabric wings draining like a waterfall. One good thing, the wind had died down to little more than a drenching breeze.

My belly is full, contented and warm. And the bedroll of blankets and canvas on the hay pile is nothing but slumbering contentment and the rain on the roof a lullaby to a tired, well-fed lad of sixteen.

Marty in these immediate respects, is just a more adult version of myself. I go to sleep almost instantly but still not fast enough to escape his magnus opus of snoring. But even it does not faze my retreat to the Sandman.

CHAPTER V

Completely oblivious to the pounding rain on the roof for eleven hours I am only awakened by a noise under the haymow floor. It is Mr. Veeck backing his Model T out of the barn, leaving for Tell City with Henry Milhausen. The flivver's rattling departure has no effect on the in-depth slumbering of Marty the intrepid, but weary barnstormer. No sooner has the flivver departed out of earshot when out back is the suddenly piercing "Cock-a-doodle-dee-do-do-do" of Marty's nemesis, the lordly militant rooster. Marty instantly jerks erect, hair a scraggly hay-laden mess—his eyes wide open and like two burned holes in a blanket. His utterance would have earned a stern reprimand from mother Autry had I been the one who uttered what he uttered.

"Geez, that old rooster cock son-of-a-bitch again! It must be 3:00 a.m., and that old bastard has started already! Peyton, go out there and grab that old son-of-a-bitch by the neck and wring it not once but two dozen times!"

I am taken aback by Marty's outburst. It's not like him, but that rooster really gets to him, like nothing or nobody else. I answer him carefully and cautiously. I look at my Pocket Ben watch. "No. It's not three o'clock. It's seven. Mr. Veeck and Mr. Milhausen have already left for Tell City. And the rain has stopped and the sun is out. See the sun creeping through the cracks between the boards in the walls here."

I peeked through the cracks, up and down, adding, "Not a cloud in the sky."

Marty sat in kind of a stupor, saying nothing for over a minute, then reluctantly, "Okay. Let's clean up in the wash pan down next to the barn and bike down to that old eatery we heard about in Cannelton. But I still think that damned old rooster belongs in old Veeck's oven, not out here scratching holes in the Waco's wing and ripping out people's ear drums at the break of day. The cock-a-doodle-doing old bastard!"

With that my fear of Marty's anger suddenly reverted to uncontrollable laughter. I could not stop. Marty just began combing his straight but tangled hair. Not saying a word, he gives me a rough but friendly shove head over heels into the haymow. I can't stop laughing. He just grabbed my arm, jerks me to my feet.

"Get cleaned up, you young laughing hyena, if you are going to breakfast with me!"

We wash up outside. Not a cloud is in the sky, the sun coming up just over the treetops east of the field. The barnyard is wet and muddy but drying fast. The wet hayfield stubble glistens in the early sun, its roots of timothy seeming to have soaked up the water. The slope of the field itself toward the river affording excellent drainage to the ditches down on the road flowing with water. Drains under the road allowed water from the fields and farms to find its way to the river. We ride our bikes out into the field; Marty concluding that after the field is exposed to sun all day we will be able to fly tomorrow.

We next inspect the Waco, removing the cockpit covers and draping them over the fence to dry out. Some of the wind-driven torrent had found its way under the covers and into the cockpits. The rear cockpit was the worst, not being protected by the upper wing as was the front cockpit. But Marty points out that the fabric covering of the fuselage has drain holes in the bottom surface near the tail to allow it to drain away onto the ground. The cockpit and entire airplane just needs to air-dry in the sun a few hours. The interior structure of the wings is well sealed inside their doped fabric coverings.

What a beautiful morning after the storm! We pedal down to Cannelton as I tell Marty that yesterday's passengers told me the very old restaurant that dates back to before the turn of the century is in a very old building on First Street near the Hawesville ferry landing. It is operated by an old couple who is the descendants of the early founders of the place. The fare abounds in good old fashioned breakfasts, lunches and dinners related to the area and the cultures of the emigrant settlers, Swiss and German. Lunches and dinners featured deep-fried catfish, the so-called "fiddler cats", ten inches long, filleted whole, minus the head. Not new to me for I had many such channel catfish dinners on the Ohio at Yankeetown and Newburgh near Boonville. But to Kansan Marty, it would be a special treat I knew he would enjoy. Perhaps we could come down here later for lunch or dinner or both.

We pedaled in to Cannelton along Front Street which runs along the Ohio River until Front becomes First Street. At First and Adams our hunger is forgotten for a moment when we encounter this mammoth structure on higher ground. We are told that it is the Cannelton Cotton Mill built prior to the Civil War. During the War it produced thousands of uniforms for Union soldiers during which time Confederate raiders from Kentucky attempted to burn it down. It rises three full floors above ground level. Each side of its long length comprises over a hundred windows or rooms and two separate six story towers and a two hundred foot brick smokestack at one end. Its depth or width is almost half its huge length. The double walls are three feet thick built of blocks of native sandstone outside and inside filled between with spall or rubble. The mill has been a source of employment continuously for many Cannelton residents since the days of the Civil War.

We go on down First almost a block and find the old restaurant we are seeking in a very ancient old brick building. The place has no name on the front or even on the door. Glass in the door or windows has not been washed in many years. But the inside of the place is surprisingly clean, as it is simple. The proprietor and cook are an elderly couple, the breakfast is out of this world, good staple fare of bacon, eggs, fried potatoes, hot fresh biscuits and coffee. $1.25 for the both of us. The breakfast and a sound night's sleep in a warm, dry haymow during a raging storm has elevated my spirits to the point I will never want to quit this barnstorming trip with Marty. I abhor the thought of it ending and going back to school after the six weeks duration we expect.

Marty has introduced us to the elderly proprietor and waiter. He tells us his name, but as I write this I have forgotten it precisely, but I know it is of German or Swiss origin. Let's say Mr. Weingarten, which I believe, is fairly close. He tells us that his father ran this same restaurant from the time he opened it when he was a young man, which would have put it back in an era shortly before, during or not long after the Civil War. Herr Weingarten has been an ardent Ohio River fisherman all of his life and he almost talks of nothing else. A collection of ancient faded photographs adorning the walls attest to his enthusiasm. All are replete with crudely printed notations with dates, lengths and types of fish. A huge catfish of 160 lbs. was caught just down the riverbank from the Weingarten eatery, by Herr Weingarten himself; the date on the photo is July 16, 1923. Another photo is of a 150-lb. sturgeon caught in a channel net on the other side of the river at Hawesville in 1918. other photos are of many typical Ohio River houseboats anchored along the shore at Cannelton, Tell City and Troy in which lived commercial fishermen who sold mostly live catfish from latticed fishboxes tied to their houseboats. Those houseboats are still very prevalent today in this modern year of 1933. I also remember them in earlier years as a boy with my folks at Yankeetown and Newburgh near Boonville in Warrick County. We bid the Weingartens farewell giving a certain impression we would be back for supper. Marty is anxious to get back to the Waco and clean the OX-5 carburetor. After we do that, he says we can bike into Tell City and soak up some more of the area's history.

Before we go back to Veeck's farm we bike down to watch the early morning passengers boarding the old ferry for Hawesville. Marty laughs at the ultra-low r.p.m. chugging of its laboring engine. I secretly wish we were going over to Hawesville to look around but I can tell the Waco carburetor is uppermost on Marty's mind for without a word he climbs on his bike and heads back up the hill through Cannelton, up and back to the farm. As we ride back through Cannelton I can not help but reflect on its tranquil, timeless quality.

Back at the farm the first thing Marty did was clean off the tiny work bench in the barn on which he arranged his tool kit from the Waco, then to the Waco to remove the cowl and then the carburetor, then back to the work bench where he very ceremoniously and delicately began dismantling it. Each part went into a small clean coffee tin of filtered gasoline after being brushed with a clean toothbrush. The filter was separately and religiously cleaned in a separate clean can of filtered gasoline. A few times Marty gave off with a knowing "Ah ha" as though he had found some obvious culprit as the cause of the OX-5's in-flight stoppage of yesterday afternoon. After a bit all the parts are spread on one of our clean handbills to dry by evaporation. Marty then carefully reassembles the carburetor as though he was a surgeon "closing" his learned procedure.

The next step was to install it and close up the cowl, then did our prop swinging, priming and starting procedure. Marty ran the OX-5 for several minutes at several different engine speeds, then shut it down and climbed out, saying, "Well, we have done all we can do. If she conks out again it won't be because the carb is clogged or otherwise malfunctioning. She is okay. Let's get on the bikes and go into Tell City and case the place. Do a little history trolling."

We bicycle down the lane to the road, turning right to Tell City working our way down to the Front Street road along the Ohio River. Front Street not only runs along the river but meanders along the Southern Railway, which also runs along the river through Troy, Tell City and Cannelton. After pedaling for nearly two miles, Front merges into Main Street and we are getting a look at the old River Central heart of Tell City. It is only three or four short blocks from Main to the river, depending on whether you are in the southern or central area of the town. In the south end the river is fronted only two blocks away by Seventh and Sixth streets, and further north by Fifth and Fourth streets. We coast down to those streets and ride along them noting the ancient buildings. Some of those along the shore of the Ohio River on Fifth and Fourth streets are very old, built of brick masonry or stone and date almost to the origin of the town in 1858. Marty, the intrepid aviator, is also the dedicated historian, especially history that is new to him is history that must be learned at all costs. He engages one of the elderly shopkeepers in one of the old buildings on Fourth Street, which faces the river only two hundred feet away. After a long discourse about the history of Cannelton, Tell City and Troy, the man urges us to the library back up the hill to Ninth and Franklin. This Marty is a good deal older than my sixteen, but he is still a very young man as men go, but biking around in these Tell City streets, some quite uphill, do not seem to tire him nearly as much as myself. I've always been interested in Hoosier history, especially Perry County, but Marty is obsessed with it.

The elderly spinster librarian strikes a real mutual chord with Marty. She seems not only imbued with their common interest in Perry County history but she can not help him enough when she learns that this handsome young man is also the heroic aviator who has been risking his life to give the local gentry a view of their fine city from the cockpit of his airplane.

Between the merchants down on Fourth Street and the dedication of this devoted librarian we learn many interesting facts about Tell City and its two companion towns. The very earliest history of Perry County, like others along the Ohio, are tied to the river. Steamboats were the start of progress in Perry County in the late 1700's and very early 1800's. Robert Fulton, the inventor of the steamboat, purchased one thousand acres between Cannelton and Tell City right where Albert Veeck's farm now is located, hoping to profit from a coalmine that had been established. Fulton died in 1815 in New York and his brother, Abraham Fulton, came from Louisville, Kentucky to oversee the land. Abraham died soon after in Troy where he had started construction of a log cabin. The tree he was cutting for the cabin fell, killing him. The hill where he cut the tree is known as Fulton Hill. Tell City was founded in March 1858 by a group of Swiss and German emigrants known as the Swiss Colonization Society. The Colonists originally intended to name their town Helvetia, the Latin name for Switzerland, but instead named it for legendary Swiss hero William Tell.

Marty literally devoured all this ancient Hoosier Ohio River history. I keep reminding him we had to get back to the farm to haul more gasoline for the thirsty Waco but he is obsessed with pumping all the information he can from the spinster librarian to such a degree that I stand ignobly ignored —a poor ground-bound, air-minded lad. He was learning that Cannelton was settled in 1837 by employees of the American Cannel Coal Company who came to the area to mine stone. It was then known as Coalhaven but most of it burned in 1839. A few residents held on and it was later replotted as Cannelburgh in 1841 and later as Cannelton in 1844.

In 1825 two famous Americans resided in the area; Abraham Lincoln who would later become president, and the famed Frenchman Marquis de LaFayette, hero of the American Revolution. Lincoln then in his youth operated a ferry across the mouth of the Anderson River, just downstream on the Ohio River from Troy. LaFayette visited the county when his steamboat "The Mechanic" struck a rock near Cannelton. The unhappy Revolutionary hero lost all of his possessions, but the records show he did not lose his sense of statesmanship and gave an impromptu speech to the group of settlers and enjoyed the warmth and comfort of their hospitality. The great American hero spent the first night in the log cabin of Perry County pioneer James Cavender. The next day he was visited by many farm families eager to meet or glimpse the famous General of the Revolutionary War. The General's visit is kept alive by a marker at LaFayette Springs near the Cavender cabin where the great man received his Perry County visitors.

The town of Troy is the smaller of these three small towns in this year 1933. The precise and studious spinster librarian tells us that its population is two hundred people but is the oldest of these Perry County river towns and became the first county seat in 1816. Legend has it that the town was named after an Indian maiden who reminded an early settler of the famous Helen of Troy. Marty really swallowed that romantic story whole, hook, line and sinker!—because he whipped out a paper and pencil and carefully wrote it down. All of which greatly impressed the spinster librarian who I'm sure dreamed for many evenings afterwards of the handsome, intrepid aviator who came to her as a free spirit in search of historical knowledge.

There are other smaller towns in Perry County further up the Ohio River. In the order of their distance upstream from Cannelton, they are Tobinsport, Lauer, Hardingrove, Rome, Derby and Magnet. The southern boundary of Perry County is the Ohio River and has nearly a dozen bends ranging from less than 45 degrees to over 180 degrees. Perry County stretches north to Dubois County and St. Meinrad on the west and Crawford County on the east. The western quarter of Perry County is a rural valley of agriculture stretching north while the eastern three-quarters of the county is beautiful forested hills. Most all of this geographical stuff I am familiar with because I am a native Hoosier who has been here many times with my parents when I was a kid and we were taught extensively in school about our home state of Indiana, especially the southern half. But Marty is devouring and retaining every fact and figure and I am literally fascinated with his fascination with this part of the county where I grew up. I figure if he likes it so much he must like me and I'd never let on to him but it is very important to me that he like me. And I think he does. older people would amusingly call it hero worship, which only would embarrass and anger me. It's something far deeper and more important than such a juvenile label born out of ignorance.

We bid the kind, helpful lady librarian farewell and I figure we must be heading back to the farm because there is yet the chore of coming back up in the Model T to refill our gasoline drum. But no, Marty wants to ride our bikes up into Troy and look around. Again we see old buildings, also a brick kiln, a coalmine and a small furniture factory. After an hour Marty asks me a question he has never asked before. He wants me to extricate my Pocket Ben and tell him what time it is. I quickly tell him it is 4:15 and I show him the watch to prove it. He gives me a rather bashful look that says I need not have shown him the watch to prove my verbal reply. Good old Marty. I really do think he likes me a lot. I smile and we head out of Troy and down through Tell City to Albert Veeck's farm and our precious old Waco, which we have not laid, eyes on since early this morning.

What luck! Veeck and Milhausen are driving the Model T in just ahead of us. Those two old fellows have been doing backbreaking carpenter work at the church in Tell City but they are just as lively and energetic as they were early this morning. I am tired and I get to wondering if I am going to be that full of steam as these old boys when I am 70 years old. At first the thought makes me more weary, then spurs me on to a renewed reserve strength I did not know I possessed, which in turn gave me pause to be more cautious on this point in the future. I had not been tired at all, only bored and lazy. In the future I'd have to be aware of that feeling and stop it in its tracks before it got another foothold. A man like Marty would not respect and befriend me if I let it happen. And I'm sure that men like Albert Veeck or Henry Milhausen certainly would not respect such a lazy lout. So, in the future it must be onward and upward with enthusiasm and diligence. There is only one time for laziness; bedtime and a good night's rest for a great day tomorrow.

While I am mulling over this moral philosophy the two old gentlemen and Marty are wrestling the gasoline drum up on the Ford and before I know it we are on our way to Tell City, have filled it and returned it to its sawhorse by the barn.

Marty interjects that Albert and Henry have worked hard all day and to show our appreciation for all they have done for us we take them to dinner by all of us loading into the Ford and have a heaping catfish dinner at the Weingarten's Cafe down in Cannelton. I am overjoyed that the old gents accept. But first they say we can all shower in the vacant stall in the barn where they have long ago rigged a gravity-fed shower from the water tank atop the barn.

I really live it up at the old Weingarten Cafe down on the river tonight. our plates are stacked high with ten-inch fiddler catfish fillets plus a hefty side dish of corn on the cob brushed with melted butter and salt. With Waco gas and oil at ten cents a gallon, Marty had plenty of cash left over for dinner for the four of us, even though it was $1.50 each, but what a feed! All the catfish and corn on the cob you could eat with heaping bowls of home made ice cream for dessert. And it literally put Marty on top of the world because his historical rewards extended beyond the bountiful feast, which he enjoyed as much or more than we Hoosiers. But the tales and discussions with the Weingartens, Veeck and Milhausen were a real treat for him especially, as it was with me as well. The three Perry County pioneers infatuated him with early day living on the river. They told of the emigrants who settled the region, the Swiss, the Germans. There were legendary tales of early flatboat crews who camped ashore on their long journeys from Pittsburgh to New Orleans. Then came the steamboats and even the inventor of steamboats, Robert Fulton who became a resident and large property owner in what is now Cannelton. Locals traced their Swiss and German lineage to ancestors who either arrived by flatboat or steamer the only means of transportation. Those who claimed flatboat ancestors distinguished themselves as the true pioneer settlers, even though those who arrived by steamer did so as long ago as one hundred years. After nearly three hours of eating catfish, corn on the cob and huge bowls of ice cream, we are off to the farm in the Model T and to bed in the comfy coziness of our dry haymow loft.

Next day we rise to another beautiful day. Down to the Weingartens to breakfast by bike, after which we return to filtering and loading gas into the Waco. While down in Cannelton for breakfast we had spread more hand-bills. Our two elderly patrons spread more handbills in Tell City on their way back to work.

People start showing up for plane rides by noon and continue on until 6 o'clock about the time when Veeck and Milhausen return from their church labors. Marty has been busy most of the day flying the locals around the area. He tells them the ride is twenty minutes and he will fly them anywhere he can go in that time. Some folks are from the small towns to the north and northeast flying over the Perry County heavily forested hills or Hoosier Mountains as Marty calls them. He flies some of them up as far as Lillydale and Gatchel and even Terry and Leopold, which means he stretched the twenty minutes round trip a bit in their favor. I worry about him flying passengers across the expanse of wooded hill country. If the OX-5 quit as it did the other day over Weberstown's flatter country, he would be into the tree tops and that would certainly be the end of our Waco and maybe even Marty and his passengers. But after he cleaned the carburetor he now seemed to have utmost confidence in the old Curtiss OX-5. I'm sure there may have been a clearing or two in places like Leopold and, knowing Marty, he'd keep track of every one while enroute in case he had to use them on the return flight.

He once told me very seriously, "When you're flying cross country you must continuously scan the country below every minute and every one of those minutes is a planned forced landing."

While he is in the air I spend my time talking to waiting passengers and in straining gas, which Marty cautiously and patiently showed me how to do. I can see why he is reluctant to let anyone else do it. It is not only slow and meticulously necessary but it is extremely critical to our safety. I was reminded of this because a couple of Boonville novice student solo pilots only last year had a series of OX-5 failures because they either failed to strain fuel or were unaware it was necessary. In one afternoon they made three forced landings, two from which they recovered to take off again after they got the OX-5 going again. On the third, the OX-5 failed on take-off and the Swallow TP they were flying nosed down into the roof of a farmhouse, totally demolished, but the pilot survived except for a smashed ego.

We fly passengers for about five or six hours a day out of the Veeck farm for the next three days and a regular routine of hauling in fuel from Tell City, taking meals at the Weingartens, showering and sleeping in the barn.

On the evening of the third day as we were taking our supper at the Weingartens, Marty set down his coffee cup in a rather contemplative mood.

"Well, Peyton, we have been on this trip a week now since Boonville. There are numerous places to go down here in southern Indiana and I think it's time we move on and bid our great friends Veeck and Milhausen goodbye, to say nothing of all the other fine folks of Perry County we have met or flown. It's a bucolic wonderland and I yearn to come back one of these days. Now—what say you that we gas up tomorrow and head north to St. Meinrad, Ferdinand, Mariah Hill, Huntingburg and Jasper? You and your parents have been to all those places before, haven't you?"

I tell him it's okay with me. He is the pilot. And yes, I've been to all of those towns on weekend drives and passing through on drives to Louisville and Madison. And of course, to Huntingburg and Jasper with dad's baseball team of which he was variously a catcher and an umpire. We tell the Weingartens we will be down for breakfast next day and that we will be off to the Hoosier towns a short ways to the north. They seem genuinely sad to see us go. They are old and they seem to dwell too long on the sad fact they may never see us again. We will return next summer Marty assures them and I'm sure he means it, which of course pleases me very much because this barnstorming could go on forever as far as I'm concerned.

The next morning we take Veeck and Milhausen to breakfast at Weingartens, then take the Ford up to the Tell City station for a load of gas. It is almost noon before we have the Waco gassed up and ready to go. The weather is still beautiful. Albert and Henry watch pensively as we load the Waco and start the OX-5. They give us warm handshakes and good-byes and urge us to use their field any time and to return soon. My face blushes as both the old gents give me a hug after a handshake. But I feel the well-meant warmth of it and it does not make me feel like a caressed child, but instead it makes me feel like a man. Marty looks over at me from the rear cockpit as this is taking place and the old look of amusement is not there as it usually is when he thinks I'm boyish. Instead it is a look of understanding and appreciation that I appreciate a great deal in return.

We taxi down near the road and swing around facing the field's length, wave our good-byes, blast the tail up and head up the field for a neat take-off over the upper fence and the farms to the northeast.

I had purchased my own multi-county road map at the old gas pump store in Tell City. Now I get it out and study it carefully while intermittently watching the terrain below. Off to our left and stretching out directly north is a long comparatively flat agricultural valley, but adjacent to it on the east and stretching north as well as east into the distance is the hilly Perry County forest. We are still heading northeast into the hill country. I guess that Marty wants me to see it from the air because I told him about my squirrel hunting stories here with "Diney" Davidson of several years ago. In fact, I'd related my impressions of the Perry County backcountry with "Diney" in the far back woods of his Uncle Clarence's secluded but forested "farm". I said I'd never forget it. Now Marty was showing me he would never forget it either. It was down there somewhere. All I could remember about its geographical location was that it was a long way back in the hills north of Cannelton. The torturous forested roads to the place had left me no clue how to finger it on a map. But it must be down there and to the right of the Waco's flight path, somewhere, probably further ahead and off the right wing tip. Anyway, I wondered if "Diney's" Uncle Clarence might be down there looking up at us. He probably had not seen a plane over his place more than once or twice before, perhaps never. Spending a week there was identical to going back in time one hundred years. Everything except his ancient Model T Ford. I see a small village nestled in the hills straight ahead and I deduce from my map it must be Lillydale. Then I am sure because beyond that and to the left I can see another village in the hills and conclude it is certainly Gatchel. In a few minutes, I then spot Terry, which is north of Gatchel a few miles. They are off to our left as we pass them. Flying at sixty-five miles per hour in a straight line, the Perry County "mountains" can be covered in a matter of minutes, but several hours would be required in a motor car in the winding roads. We are now deep into the Perry County forest over Leopold, which the nice spinster librarian lady told us was settled by Belgians in 1842. It was originally called Chapel Place and founded around the St. Augustine Catholic Church. At Leopold Marty swings left about forty-five degrees to due north and in a few minutes I see Bandon and Branchville up ahead. As we pass over Branchville, another of the small Perry County villages, Marty banks sharply ninety degrees to the left, heading due west. I know now that he is heading directly for St. Meinrad, which lies ahead just over the Perry County line into northeastern Spencer County.

As we pass over what I believe must now be Spencer County, Marty is swinging the Waco to the northwest and then I am certain of it when I see up ahead the imposing hilltop magnificence of the old St. Meinrad Abbey with its commanding view of the pastoral beauty of its surrounding parish. It immediately brings to mind my early trips here with my parents and one such trip in particular with dad and his baseball team. I was very small then but tagged along with dad and the team. I was only six years old and much of that ball game on a hot August afternoon is sharp in my memory. The young St. Meinrad divinity student players were dressed in black robes, bareheaded in the blazing sun. The ball field in a beautiful greensward bounded by shade trees. The imposing Arch Abbey on the hill above us a scene I will never forget.

We approach from the south, flying along the east side of the old Troy highway and just west of the Anderson River. St. Meinrad is only two miles ahead and Marty has already retarded the throttle and begins a descent. I'm guessing that we will pass over the Arch Abbey and the town at an altitude of just a few hundred feet to look over a possible landing spot. The bottoms about a mile south of the Abbey looked to be very flat, freshly mowed hayfields.

Up ahead I can see the twin towers of the Arch Abbey which I recall from a former tour with my parents that the priest guide said were 165 feet above floor level. We pass over the church at about 500 feet. The long thin spires of each tower are topped by a golden holy cross. A truly impressive sight whether from the ground or the air.

In less than a minute we are north of St. Meinrad and Marty is making a wide turn to the west. The rural countryside below is outstandingly beautiful. The neatness and precise layouts of the small farms attest to the self-discipline and devotional, of St. Meinrad parishioners. We are now heading back south along the area west of St. Meinrad about two miles until Marty then banks slowly to the east and then to the north. He is now approaching St. Meinrad once again from the south. I can see again the Arch Abbey looming up ahead and it seems so much higher now. This is because Marty has descended to under 200 feet and still coming down slowly. I rise up higher in the cockpit and crane my head out the left side of the windshield to see the field I know he has now selected for his landing. Off to the left and downward I can see the Troy/St. Meinrad road. In fact, I see two vehicles— an old automobile making its way north and a hay wagon heading south. In fact, the driver of the hay wagon is waving his bright yellow straw hat!

The throttle goes sharply back. The OX-5 coughs and sputters a bit as it adjusts to the much lower r.p.m. and at the same time Marty is fishtailing the Waco slowly back and forth, first a left sideslip, then a right. We come in over a fence and he straightens her up, aligning the wheels in the direction of our descending flight. We touch down gently and roll to a stop in the center of the field. We taxi over to the fence along the Troy road, swing the plane around to again face the field and switch off the engine. We are a mile south of the Arch Abbey and Monastery. From here it looms even larger, giving one a spiritual uplift by its imposing grace.

I hear Marty rustling about in the rear cockpit. I hear his seat belt drop on the floor and turn to see him getting up and poking around in the little storage area behind his seat. He rises, clutching a handful of our handbills. As I climb out on the wingstep, he is grinning mischievously, saying, "Well, let's nail a few of these on the fence posts over here so that they can be seen from the road."

He grinned even more when he saw the poorly concealed, quizzical apprehension on my face—frowning into his jovial, devil-may-care expression. I said,

"Yeah. But what is the owner of this field going to say or do? How come you landed here? I know it's a heck of a good field. Flat and plenty of room. Nice short cut hay. But hadn't we better find the owner? Then put up the signs if he will let us?"

Marty chuckled. "Oh Peyton. There you go. Worrying.

Don't you trust your pilot? Your friend Marty?"

"Sure," I answered. "But what's the point of tacking up signs if we have to leave?"

He laughed again, saying,

"Haven't I said before that an important part of barnstorming is planning ahead? Now we are right in the middle of the field that Henry Milhausen said was owned by the church and farmed by its parishioners. He also said that barnstormers have been welcome here for the past ten years. Let's just wait here until somebody shows up. Meantime nail up the posters. This is a fine church-going town with little more than five hundred people. Besides, we need to mark down these five-dollar posters. I'm now thinking it's too much."

As he spoke I noticed three bicyclists making their way down the road from the Abbey hill. All three were bareheaded and in black robes turned up discreetly at the bottom to avoid entanglement in the chain sprocket of their bikes. I immediately thought of the young monks who I had seen playing baseball here ten years ago when I was only six years old. These young fellows seemed to be about my age of sixteen, perhaps a bit older. Their dress and pleasant manner made it hard to tell.

All three carefully climbed the fence, making their way in friendly greeting to the eloquent, handshaking greeter, none other than my companion Marty. He with the dirty white cloth helmet and up-lifted goggles. For the young monks he was the obvious pilot. Like a clumsy lout I had left my tattered leather helmet and goggles in the cockpit. But Marty very graciously introduced me in a way that seemed to strike wonder and awe in the eyes of the young monks. I must admit I felt a surge of pride in my heart and when that seemed to turn to an urge of superiority I immediately stifled it—because their commitment to faith, church and the Almighty made my young aerial excursions seem so trivial by comparison.

All of this was another new phase, new people, so very different people and a new and different history to Marty. He invited us all to sit in the shade of the Waco's wing and talk. The young monks seemed quietly eager to question us as we were to question them. They introduced themselves by their first names or given names; Robert, Michael and Otto.

Marty asked if they had questions. They looked at each other as if to elect a spokesman. Otto spoke up.

"What type of plane is yours? We have had others here in this very field. A pilot from Jasper used this field several times. Also several different planes and pilots have landed here from O'Neills airport in Vincennes. I took two flights from here when I was in school and prior to the Order. Right over the Abbey towers! Will you be giving rides? How long will you be our visitors here in St. Meinrad?"

I could tell old Marty's interest was really piqued. He replied, "Our ship is a Waco 10 built in 1928 in Troy, Ohio (not Indiana). It is powered by a Curtiss OX-5 of 8 cylinders, 90 horsepower at 1400 r.p.m. It has separate cylinder casings and overhead valves. And yes, we will give rides at three dollars per passenger. We will stay as long as there are passengers or until we wear out our welcome." All three spoke at once at the word "welcome."

"You are most welcome to St. Meinrad," said Robert. "We were sent down expressly to welcome you by our prefect who also wishes us to convey the wishes of the Arch Abbey Abbot."

Marty is obviously very impressed and so am I. Presently he asked the three young monks, "Who owns the land we are on? We always like to thank them by giving them a free, extensive plane ride over their community. It is the only compensation we can offer. Financially speaking, barnstormers are really just aerial gypsies. The cost of fuel, oil and the maintenance costs to stem the deterioration of the plane and engine consumes all we take in from flying passengers."

Michael quickly replies, "This field belongs to the church, the Arch Abbey of St. Meinrad, as does much of the land around the Abbey. This field has been tended for several years by Mr. Streicher who has his home place farm three miles west of here. He has already cut the hay as you can see. He is a fine gentleman and I am sure he will rush over to welcome you if he has seen you flying around before you landed, as I am sure most everyone has. Planes landing here are fairly commonplace and widely accepted if the landings are after hay harvest. You are the first this summer. Last summer there were two flying together from Vincennes."

This only spurs old Marty on to more questions—Marty, the old history buff.

"The Abbey is a magnificent architectural work. What can you tell me of its history and construction?"

Three pairs of intelligent eyes come together for a brief moment and it is Robert who replies.

"In seminary school we learned that planning it in the 1890's under Abbot Mundwiler and excavation began in 1895 and the first cornerstone was laid and blessed by Bishop Donaghue on June 16, 1900. The actual construction required 8 years under Abbot Anthansius Schmitt. The church was under roof by 1904. The Abbey was designed by Dr. Adrian Werwer of St. Louis. On March 21st, 1907, the Feast of St. Benedict, the community entered the church in procession for the first time when Abbot Anthansius blessed the Abbey. The Abbey Church is the site for liturgies for the monks, local parishioners, and the students for the major and minor seminaries. The twin spires of the church are 164 feet in height. The church is 184 feet long and 64 feet wide. The spires are covered with copper and the rest of the roof is slate. The walls are 3 feet thick, made of hand-cut St. Meinrad sandstone, transported by mule from the quarry at Monte Cassino, which is one mile east of the Abbey. The stained glass windows in the crypt and along the roof were made in St. Louis. The lower windows depicting the Beatitudes and Benedictine Saints and the two in the apse came from Munich. The organ is one of which we are very proud. It has three manuals, 55 ranks and 3015 pipes. It was inaugurated on the first anniversary of the dedication of the Arch Abbey Church on March 21st, 1908. The initial cost of construction of the Abbey at the turn of the century was $50,000, not including the material and labor supplied by the Abbey."

For a change my friend and mentor Marty was wordless. His lower jaw dangling in admiration for this young man who knew his subject so well. All Marty could say was, "Wow!"

Then Robert reversed the interrogation. "Mr. Marty, ahem! As barnstormers, when you are not flying, how do you manage the other hours of a 24-hour day so that you at least have the bare necessities of food, drink, sleep and rest that you need for the following day?"

Even to me Marty seemed a bit embarrassed by Robert's question. Old Marty even squirmed quite a bit, which delighted me no end, but only in a joking way. "We-l-l," Marty says, "You need to understand that barnstorming is certainly not a financially rewarding endeavor. I guess we have to admit that we do it because we love it. We love it because the sky and billowy clouds is the place near our Maker where we love to lose ourselves in a sort of ethereal, spiritual, if you will, wanderlust. High above terra firma and its too frequent travails and trappings. In spite of the fact we must always return to earth for the simple reason that even Glenn Curtsiss OX-5 engines will eventually die for lack of gasoline. And we must descend and face our earthly responsibilities as humans. Much as we'd like, we are not birds and never will be. We always do barnstorm flying in summer when God's elements are more, but not one hundred percent, tolerant of our intrusions into His heavens. There is no point of my excursion of the fact that we are literally aerial gypsies. only our airplane is our covered wagon. We sleep on the ground under the shelter of the wing. If it rains we sleep under covers enshrouding the cockpits of the plane. occasionally we may treat ourselves to a bed in a cheap hotel. Our plane does not have the room or weight-lifting power to carry month-long caches of food, so we purchase that locally whenever or wherever we can with the money we have earned flying passengers. Another commodity of great necessity is hopefully getting gasoline near enough to our landing field that we can either transport it to the plane ourselves or have it done. At the moment our tank is essentially full from down in Cannelton, only a few miles from here. But if we will be flying a lot of passengers from here we will, of course, need fuel."

Three young expressions were not only of silent awe but abject sympathy. Realization of the latter almost caused me to burst forth in laughter, but I held a straight face and I'm glad I did. But old Marty, to me, made himself sound like not only an aerial gypsy but more like a boxcar rod-riding transient feeling out the heart cockles of unwary sympathizers. But as I dwelt on his eloquent passages describing our endeavor, I suddenly felt more compassionate about our self-inflicted flight and that so easily observed in the young eyes of Robert, Michael and Otto. I am now even prouder than before of my good fortune of being the flying companion of my hero, Marty.

It was Otto who injected, "Sir, if we can be of any service to you and your friend of which we are capable, I am sure our superiors will approve.

It did not take Marty long to "pick up" on the offer. But in his cagey way, without looking too eager.

"We surely do appreciate your kind offer of assistance. Our needs are rather simple, just the things I just mentioned. Being able to purchase food or the location of a restaurant to where we can walk. Location of a gasoline station or pump. And a way to notify your Mr. Streicher that we are impromptu visitors to his field."

I thought that covered a great deal, but crafty old Marty made it sound exceedingly trivial. When he talked of us walking to a restaurant, he did not mention who would guard the Waco. Then I thought he is very smart. To tell these young student monks that we were afraid to leave the plane unguarded would offend everything they and their entire community stood for. Yes, this field is the safest place in the world.

It was young Michael who suggested acquisition of food.

"Farther up this road into St. Meinrad is a German sausage and cheese shop that also bakes fine breads and other local foods, including fruit. We would be most happy to bring down your order this afternoon before vespers?"

The others nodded their agreement and Marty immediately seized the opportunity of the moment by extricating several dollars or denominations thereof from his trouser pocket, handing them to Michael.

"We are indeed indebted to you for your valuable offer. Peyton and I greatly appreciate your help. Please use all of this for whatever amount of bread, sausage, cheese and fruit it will bring. Also we could use some water. I'll give you our canteen from the plane."

Otto had something to add to the service. "We will likely see Mr. Streicher at church this evening. We will tell him of your concern that you have his permission to use the field even though we are certain that it is all right. As to gasoline, there is a fuel pump used by the parish community for their autos and tractors up near the store."

A church bell tolled somewhere up on the hill, either from the Abbey itself or from one of the other buildings in the church compound. At the bell, all three students hurriedly climbed the fence and pedaled their way back up the hill.

Marty said, "Well, I'm sure looking forward to that German sausage."

"Me too," I grinned back.

Marty handed me a hammer, tacks and posters without saying a word. While he fussed around the OX-5, I proceed to put up signs on the fence posts near the plane. While hanging posters, an auto appears coming from the south. A 1929 Chevrolet. An elderly gentleman doing the driving and one older gent not as old as the driver. They slowed from their normal speed of ten miles per hour so they could read my signs. Then they noticed the plane and came to an abrupt halt and switched off their engine to engage me in conversation.

"Good morning, young man. It certainly is a fine day," called out the younger of the two who must have been in his sixties.

"Uh huh," I managed to say, feeling rather awkward for I anticipated their next words to be a polite reprehension for littering the fence with these darn signs. But instead the old driver added,

"We recognize the signs as the same as those down at Tell City. You must be the same flyers of the past week stationed in Cannelton?"

"Yes, that's right. We were at the Veeck farm," I said.

"My brother in Troy flew with you down in Cannelton the other day. We didn't get the chance to go down there with my brother to go up with you."

Eagerly I replied, "We're going to stay here today. We would fly you now for three dollars apiece."

"We're glad we ran into you. I'm going to pull my auto down to the opening in the fence and we'll fly with you."

I nod with a "Yeah, okay," and run back over to Marty who had been listening from a distance. I cleaned out the front cockpit and removed the controls while Marty went to the propeller and the old gents made their way up the fence.

I led them up to the plane and aimlessly introduced them to Marty, helping them aboard and strapping them in, then mounted the rear cockpit and switch, then out to make room for Marty to take over. He taxied down to the south end, swung it around and took off to the north, passing over the east side of the Abbey so that at his moderate altitude the engine's laboring would not disturb the compound.

I go about my usual ground-bound tasks of stacking up the accoutrements from the front cockpit and laying plans to spend the night here. It is barely noon and hopefully we will be flying more passengers until dark. As I make work, another automobile is making its way down from the St. Meinrad hill. It is a Dodge truck with open bed and closed cab of 1930 vintage. He parks near the '29 Chevy, shuts off the motor and begins the usual local neighborly opening to the conversation. After the weather is duly commented upon with thankful appreciation, he asks, "Where are you airplane folks from?"

I tell him we just arrived from Cannelton but originated our tour of southern Indiana from Boonville down in Warrick County. He tells me he has a brother-in-law who lives near DeGonia Springs, so we talk about DeGonia for a few minutes. Then he asks, "There are two of you? The other man is now flying the plane?"

"Yes, two passengers just stopped by from Troy in the Chevrolet. My friend has them in the air now."

"Have you ever landed here before now?" the other asks. I tell him it is our first although I visited here several times in years past by automobile. I tell him Marty is from Kansas but has flown on barnstorming tours all over the Midwest in years past.

I get to wondering when he asks still more questions, but his questions are not at all offensive or intrusive. Anyway, I tell him about our visit by the three seminary students and how they answered our questions and helped us in several ways. I told him of our query of who owned or tended the field and how we were concerned about permission even though Henry Milhausen, a member of the church in Tell City, had recommended the field. I also told him that the students said our field was tended by a Mr. Streicher for the church. And further, the students would inform Mr. Streicher this very evening.

At this point the gentleman in the Dodge threw back his head in a hearty laugh. "Well, young man, thank you, but they won't have to do that now, but if they do, that will be very nice." With that he extended his handshake across the fence, announcing, "I am Herman Streicher."

He readily eased my blushing countenance with, "There is no permission required. In ten years we have had a dozen barnstormers. All we ask is that they not land before the hay is cut. If it is uncut there are many other fields around within a mile. If it is an emergency landing you can land even if the field is uncut. When your pilot returns I would like very much to meet him."

I then pointed off to the southwest. "Marty is coming in now. Will land from the south. If you will come around through the opening in the fence down there, you can meet Marty after we unload the passengers."

Marty was touching down with a couple of gentle bounces along the field. As he taxied up and swung around near the fence, I run around to the rear cockpit and yell at Marty.

"Don't switch off the engine. Mr. Streicher is here. Do you want to give him a ride? Wait till I unload the passengers."

Marty nodded emphatically. I unloaded the two gents from Troy and thanked them. Marty extended a hearty handshake from the cockpit. I then brought Streicher over for the same treatment.

Marty called out loudly. "Mr. Streicher, we wish to give you a free flight in appreciation for the use of the field."

The farmer did not hesitate a moment, Marty showing his delight in a broad smile, yelling, "Peyton, hook up your controls and you can show him how the ship is flown!"

This unconventional order coming from Marty startled me, but I hurried to do what he said because I am always eager to fly the Waco even alongside a passenger, which I have never done before. Suppose he panicked and seized the controls? If I were powerless, Marty would be equally powerless. Unless Marty had a blackjack hidden back there somewhere to knock the passenger out to free up the controls. I had heard the story that some instructors did resort to the use of a lead-laden sap on a new student they did not trust. The OX-5 was still idling away so I hurried to put the joystick in its socket and hook up the rudder cables in our front cockpit. I then got Streicher up into the cockpit ahead of me, he on the right, me on the left. I snapped shut the latch on the belt across our laps and waved to Marty to taxi out into the field and do the take-off.

I put my mouth to Streicher's ear as we swung around at the south end for a northerly take-off. "Keep your hands off the joy stick, feet off the rudder pedals and hands off the throttle at the side. I won't take over until after we get in the air. Marty will do the take-off and landing."

He nodded his head as though he'd done this before, or at least that he understood.

The OX-5 up to 1400, the stick went forward a moment, the tail came up and we were in an accelerated roll down the field, the Abbey hill dead ahead over a mile away beyond our flat hayfield. Marty climbs out above and to the east of the Arch Abbey. When he reaches about six hundred feet altitude, he shakes the stick and I take over. Herman Streicher watches my control movements intently; the stick in my left hand, my right hand on the throttle. I turn gradually to the north and in a half minute the turn has us heading north by northwest, then northwest until I straighten up to due west. Mr.

Streicher is looking in all directions. I call out to him, my lips near his left ear, "Where is your farm?" He leans over across my lap, pointing out and down to the left.

I bank the Waco slowly to the east until we are approaching the west side of St. Meinrad's hill, then I turn ninety degrees to the south, retard the throttle and start a moderate descent. Streicher immediately catches on and begins to gaze ahead and downward looking for his farm. In a moment he sees it, touching my arm with one hand, pointing ahead with the other. He turns his voice into my right ear. "There's my place. Between the two farm roads. Two story house. Two barns. Just to the left of my place my neighbor is threshing with a Keck-Gonnerman steam thresher!" he exclaims.

I shout back, "Yes, I see your place, beautiful farm. And I see the thresher puffing smoke. I know about the Keck-Gonnerman. My grandfather operated one for the Farmer's Co-op at DeGonia. I was water boy and fireman. The Keck-Gonnerman is manufactured at Mt. Vernon just west of Evansville!"

He nodded enthusiastically, apparently happy that I the young sixteen-year-old, steeped in aeronautical modernity would be so keenly interested and knowledgeable about locally built steam threshing engines or steam tractors as they are often called.

I level off and look below. We are at about four hundred feet and just west of the Troy road and by now about four miles south of St. Meinrad. I begin a mile wide one hundred eighty turn heading back north toward the Abbey and our field dead ahead. I give the stick an almost imperceptible shake. More of a question to Marty asking whether he wanted to land or go around St. Meinrad some more. For a moment no response, then a gentle lateral shake and I turn the controls over to Marty. The throttle comes back, the OX-5's r.p.m. wanes and we are coming down.

In less than two minutes we are taxiing back up to the fence and swinging around to park for the next take-off. The Chevy and the Troy couple have gone. Only Streicher's Dodge truck remains. And no anxious passengers standing by so Marty switches off the OX-5. As we climb out and sit down in the shade of the wing, Marty now has a chance to get acquainted with Herman Streicher. And, of course, Marty is full of local history questions. But it turns out Streicher is equally curious about Marty, and to my self-effaced pride, me as well, in fact, he beats old Marty to the draw, which amused me to the point I laughed out loud, which drew a blush and sheepish grin from old Marty.

III never realized anyone in Boonville was an aviator, much less owned his own plane. I go down there fairly often and know several people in Warrick County. My brother-in-law has a place near DeGonia."

Both Marty and I seize the moment to set him straight. I need not tell him my exploits as a pilot of my own home-built primary glider. Marty does that very well. So well, in fact, he won't let me tell it. Secretly it fills me with greater pride to hear him bragging me up than if I do it myself.

"Peyton here, he built his own glider, equal in fly-ability and conventional controls as this Waco in which you just had a ride. He has himself towed into the air on a six hundred-foot light cord with an automobile. We met only days ago when I spotted its brilliant orange 32-foot wing from the air." He literally gloated. I blushed but I ate it all up as if it were mother's apple pie.

"As for myself I was born and reared in Kansas, a real hide-bound aviation state with all its flat cultivated fields. I am 33 years old. I learned to fly when I was 19," Marty went on. "I've barnstormed most of those years throughout the Midwest from May until October. During the winter I do mechanical work on airplanes inside hangars whenever I can. Mostly back in Kansas. I have learned a priceless lot about America from barnstorming that you seldom find in newspapers and darn few books. Mr. Streicher, we live in a wonderful country. I know you know that, because idyllic places like St. Meinrad have made America the greatest nation on earth. How long have you lived here? Please tell us about yourself and about this beautiful place in which you and your fine neighbors live."

Streicher pursed his lips and his expression became one of thoughtful sobriety. "Well," he said, "I was born only a mile from my place. My father and mother came from Germany to Pittsburgh where they lived for two years. Then they came down the Ohio River to Troy. They had a small farm there for only a year, then moved to a new farm just four miles east of St. Meinrad."

The rest of Streicher's story about the history of St. Meinrad and the Arch Abbey paralleled almost exactly what the three seminary students had related to us.

Then Marty asked him about the aviation history of this St. Meinrad hayfield, which he apparently tended, for the church for many years.

"Well," he said, "this old field has seen a lot of early barnstormers. The one that stands out most in my memory is one who landed here most often. He was more of a local aviation hero. His name was Charlie Miller from Huntingburg. He was raised in St. Henry and moved with his family to Huntingburg in 1922. He learned to fly in 1923 in a Jenny from Bob Gast, a World War I pilot living in Louisville, Kentucky. By 1928 he bought his first airplane which, incidentally, he brought into this field many times. It was a Lincoln Standard powered, by an OX-5 motor just like in your Waco here. The OX-5 with the then new roller rocker arm was invented by his cousin Leslie Miller. I'm not a plane expert but this is what he told me and from others who knew him who flew in here. Charlie used the family farm one and a half miles south of St. Henry as an airstrip. He also used a field east of the Gossand factory building on old State Road. Besides Charlie Miller, there were others who landed here, such as Frank O'Neil from a good way north-west of here at Vincennes and Terre Haute. But mostly it was others over in that area of Vincennes, Petersburg, Princeton who learned to fly from O'Neil."

Marty was all ears and forthcoming with other questions about pilots and planes that landed here in years gone by, most of which Streicher could at least partially answer. Then Marty asked him about other fields that had been used in this area.

Such as Mariah Hill, Ferdinand, Huntingburg and Jasper, inferring that they were next on our barnstorming tour, which was news to me.

Mr. Streicher was even more helpful on that question. Yes, there were other fields and those in other nearby areas, which had a decade or more history of being understood as unofficially accepted landing fields for barn-stormers. He asked for paper and pencil to sketch some maps.

Marty leaped to action. He leaped to his cockpit, withdrawing his map case and pencils, the blank backs of one of the maps gave Streicher plenty of room to draw the location of the fields using county road intersections and outstanding farm landmarks as reference points. Not only locations of the fields but locations of the farm homes of the owners, most of whom he knew.

Marty was subtle but obviously thankful and carefully folded the map into its case and returned the whole thing to his cockpit. Then Streicher came up with another helpful surprise, saying almost apologetically,

"If you need to transport gas to your plane, I will be glad to help you bring it down in my truck from the gas pump up in St. Meinrad."

Marty was really impressed, expressing his thankful acceptance in his most gracious and eloquent manner. We were not low on gas now but if passengers began to show up in any number today and tomorrow, we would be in great need of his help.

Then Streicher came up with yet another surprise. "This afternoon I will return with some of my neighbors near my farm who will want a ride I'm sure. And I will invite our priest, Father John to come along."

With a friendly handshake Mr. Streicher took his leave, making his way back to his truck.

I said to Marty, "My, Mr. Streicher is a very helpful gentleman. And I have read about some of the barnstormers who used this field before in the Evansville papers as I was growing up, and I think I may have even talked to some of them when they barnstormed Boonville even though I didn't know their names. Now I wish I had!"

Marty was very thoughtful and almost wistful, saying slowly, "Mr. Streicher certainly is a fine man. And I believe his manner is typical of the people here. May all the peoples of the world become the same."

Before he had concluded this poignant remark, we both noticed movement on the road down from St. Meinrad. Our three seminary cyclists. As they rode through the gap in the fence I noticed each bike carried a bundle. They rode up to the plane in friendly greeting. It was Michael who spoke first, seemingly at the behest of the other two.

"We brought you some supplies for your stay this evening that we hope will help in the way that you have described as camping out with your plane."

Marty and I were nearly overcome at the aggregate size of the bundles. Far greater than the few dollars Marty had given them. Smoked German sausage, cheese, bread, dried fruit, bottled fruit juice, and our filled canteen. We thanked them at how bountifully our few dollars had reaped such a repast. It was patently apparent it would have been wrong to make up the difference with more dollars. Obviously the difference was in the good hearts of the people in this parish, the church, the shopkeeper and, of course, these three good Samaritans who viewed us as the wayfaring, wandering gypsies that we were. In addition, they had brought along a light canvas, one side of which could be tied to the lower end of the wing struts, the other staked to the ground to form a tent over our beds in case of rain!

Then Marty tries another tack to show our appreciation without the questionable taint of more dollars. He asked,

"We would like to show our appreciation of the valuable help you have given us. How about a free plane ride for the three of you?"

Otto began to reply as the three caught each other's wistful eyes. "We would be eager to accept but at the present time in our rule it is not possible to do so. But just the same we greatly value your offering even though we may not accept. Besides, we must return to our duties before the bell is rung with only minutes to spare."

Each of them gave each of us a warm handshake, then made their way back up the hill to the monastery.

We next packed up the bountiful cache of food with our other gear. But first we had cups of water, fruit juice and sausage sandwiches made with the Black Forest bread. We both crawled under the Waco's lower wing and proceeded to take a good afternoon nap to placate our stuffed bellies so aptly replenished by our heavenly host, St. Meinrad.

CHAPTER VI

We both pass out. Our full stomachs and the comfortable pleasure of a cool breeze under the shady wing were just too much. After some unknown number of minutes, I am startled awake. Oh! Good Lord! Forgive the vain outburst in this holy place, but old Marty is snorting and bellowing. When Marty snores it is like nothing else. I cannot for the life of me figure out how he can sleep **so** soundly when he is snoring likes this! How? How? It is a physically and medically defying paradox. How can this be? If I jab him he will suddenly awake. Or if I should loudly clap my hands together he would come awake with a start. But my loudest handclap could not begin to be louder than his routine snoring—which could go on almost endlessly without waking up. Is there some physiological reason for this?

For example, when he is sound asleep, is the sensory hearing nerves in his brain equipped with a switch to turn off the snoring noises which only he himself makes? If so, it is a miraculous contraption, at the same time allowing him to wake when I clap my hands or call out to him—or to poke him in the ribs—which is what he deserves when he snores like this. It is no wonder he brought a young, air-minded simpleton like me along on this trip. No one else would put up with his snoring.

But, I am for the moment saved. Two autos pull up along the road near the opening in the fence. So there you see? Old Marty wakes up. He can even feel the vibration of their motors through the ground two hundred feet away. The first auto is Streicher's Dodge truck, followed by another automobile, a 1928 Ford. Streicher has two men in his truck. The Ford is occupied by four other men. one of the men with Streicher is a priest, judging by his coatless but collared dark attire. Mr. Streicher introduces his friends all around. The priest is a man of about fifty who Streicher introduces first as Father John. They all are very amiable and extremely courteous and curious about we aeronautical gypsies. After chatting enthusiastically with each other for almost a half-hour, Streicher interjects that all his friends and neighbors would like to view Ferdinand and St. Meinrad from the air. Streicher says, "I have had my flight today. But my neighbors and Father John would like to view our parish from the air." With that he hands Marty eighteen dollars.

Marty thanks him in his eloquent manner, saying,, "Well, we would certainly be happy to fly you on this fine day over this wonderful parish. That would be three flights, two at a time. You can go in whatever order you wish."

Apparently they had already planned that order. One of the men from Streicher's truck steps forward first, followed by Father John. Since loading them on the plane is my first duty, I step forward and show them the step strip on the lower wing to enter the forward cockpit. The first man steps on the wing walkway and climbs into the cockpit. Then Father John next stands on the ground at the trailing edge of the wing. He is contemplating the wing-walk and looks up and ahead at his friend who is already in the cockpit. He closes his eyes, crosses himself vigorously, opens his eyes and bounds up on the wing, entering the cockpit alongside his friend. I strap them in and climb into the rear cockpit to man the ignition switch. Marty mans the propeller and in a minute we have the OX-5 ticking over and Marty replaces me in the rear cockpit. They taxi out and take off to the north and I set about "making do" by fussing with our gear over near the fence. I also do my other more awkward duty of making conversation with the other passengers. Except this time it is not like at Cannelton where I needed to keep them entertained while they waited for their turn to fly for fear they would get bored and leave before I had collected the three bucks. Mr. Streicher had brought this group and there was no way they would leave and embarrass him before we, the aeronautical gypsies. As in Cannelton all four men were very curious about both Marty and myself. They could not believe I had learned to fly by being "towed into the sky by an automobile on the end of a long rope." A couple of them, I believe, suspected I was not telling the truth until one of the younger farmers, a man about fifty, said that "No," he had read all about how it was done in a magazine. The picture he described in a magazine was a primary glider like my Rhon Ranger. Mr. Streicher politely listened to all of this. The magazine reader was his son-in-law, it turned out.

Time went fast for me when we talked of gliders versus airplanes. Before I knew it Marty had landed and was taxiing back to the fence. Without shutting down the OX-5, we unloaded the passengers and put on two more.

By the time Marty had landed the last load of passengers, it was approaching late afternoon. Mr. Streicher and his neighbors had to get back to do routine late-day chores at their farms. He approached Marty in his thoroughly helpful manner with genuine concern. "Now I understand you will be staying with your plane tonight and trust you will be comfortable. Now, will you be needing gasoline tomorrow? As I said before, I will be glad to take you to the fuel pump in St. Meinrad. I have a ten-gallon can and I see you have one too. We could bring down 20 gallons at a trip. If more is needed it is a short trip."

Marty shook his head and thanked him for bringing his neighbors to fly. Then he said, "Yes, I will surely appreciate your trucking our gas down here.

I think we will be moving on north tomorrow. There are several parish communities a short way north of here in neighboring Dubois County which we would like to visit or see from the air, Mariah Hill, Ferdinand, Huntingburg and Jasper."

Mr. Streicher assured us he would be down next morning to help us take on gasoline for the Waco. As they left, Marty said, "I hate to leave here but the passenger potential should be greater farther north. All of southern Indiana is rural. The area from Tell City on to Jasper north of here is all a rural, German Catholic farm community. So I figure it's best we don't spend too much time in one place and cover more of it by doing so. Then we'll head farther east and back up along the Ohio River. I know you don't want to miss the area up around Madison and Hanover where you used to go with your folks on vacation on paddle-wheel river steamers."

That sounded good to me but it would be a matter of weeks not days before we got to Hanover. But it made me happy if this barnstorming never ended. Of course, it would have to end by autumn. Barnstorming in winter would be unthinkable. It is definitely a summertime endeavor.

It is still early in terms of daylight hours. The sun is low but long before sunset, but too late for passengers to show up. Folks here are doing their milking and other late-day chores of farm life. But too early for barnstormers to lie down on the grass under the lower wings of our biplane.

The tarp shelter tied to the leading edge of the wing draped slantwise and outward forming a shelter from the early dew of a summer morning. or a nocturnal rain which hopefully would not come on summer days such as this. But we are still not far from the Ohio River and its regular routine of storms roaming up and down the river channel about twice a month. They often start in New Orleans, romping all the way to the mouth of the Ohio at Cairo, Illinois, and then all the way to Pittsburgh. Or they might be born in the Alleghenies brought in from a fractious Atlanta seaboard, then start their roaming romp down the Ohio in the other direction all the way back to New Orleans. Boonville was only ten miles from the Ohio so I've had plenty of experience with the violent summer raging storms that roam up and down the Ohio River Valley. When I view it from personal experience I'm glad the three young monks brought this tarp and I cross my fingers for thinking it cannot rain tonight, only the Lord knows.

Marty interrupts my thoughts as well as my tarp-anchoring program. "Well, Peyton, all of the good farm folk and all of the wonderful people of the Abbey and monastery have likely done their chores and are having their evening repast. We had a light but only tasty lunch. I suggest we spread out our St. Meinrad goodies on this bedroll cover of mine. Would you please do the honors of pouring water and grape juice into these tin cups from our canteen and from the bottle supplied by our friends Robert, Michael and

Otto? Let us spread out these handsome cuts of sausage, cheese and Black Forest bread. You say grace in conformance with your good Warrick County upbringing. once we have washed all the dishes, put them away and put out the cat, we will then retire into our respective top-floor bedrooms to put to rest our arduous toils of the day." That was the least of it. He did not quit his rambling eloquence for another fifteen minutes.

This guy Marty's humor absolutely tickled my sense of humor to the point it shattered my usual reserve. And I know he did it because he knew I was vulnerable. After he'd broken me down and had exhausted myself with laughter, I would then pout. But he knew I didn't hold it against him. But that was really the worst of it. He knew I'd break out into unconventional laughter (for me) but I was too weak. The urge was there but I was physically exhausted from the uncontrollable excess.

Now came the nightly inevitable test once again. He would wake me with his snoring. So to heck with it. I'll tell him he is keeping me awake and to try and control it for pet's sake. "Marty, you know you snore terribly and I cannot sleep. Can't you do something to keep it from happening? Can't you hear it? Doesn't it wake you up?" His answer put the whole thing in an impossible situation. That answer just left me speechless and hopeless. He just looked at me puzzled. "Hell, I don't snore. Whoever told you that? You are probably hearing yourself! Just go to sleep!" To my embarrassment it turned out he was right. At least this night. I slept soundly all night except for a short break at about one o'clock. I stuck my head out from under the wing and the stars were never brighter, in all the sixteen years I could remember. Another thing that I noticed was nothing short of a miracle. There were no mosquitoes! A far cry from Boonville. It was as though these satanic insects knew that the atmosphere in this godly place named St. Meinrad would have meant instant death to these creatures of Lucifer.

And was the godly purity of this place the reason Marty did not snore all night long? And was it the reason I slept so well? I don't know if its purity is why I slept so well but one thing I do know is that the reason I slept so well was the fact that Marty did not snore.

When I enthusiastically congratulated him the next morning I expected some kind of miraculous response from him. Instead, he groaned, pushed his hair back and said almost indistinctly, "I never snore." My exasperation was truly one of utter exasperation.

So we set about breakfast. And of course, a bountiful breakfast of grape juice, water, untoasted Black Forest bread, German smoked sausage and cheese.

Golly! It is another beautiful day. The low eastern sun bathes the awesome heights of the Arch Abbey in a heavenly glow. A sight I shall never, ever forget. Here a mile below the heights our bright red and silver biplane reflects that glow on the background of the bright green field on which it sits. An almost surreal but wonderfully real sight. I shall never forget or want to ever forget.

Old Marty sits there taking it all in and taking me all in as well. I can tell he is as overcome as I am. Presently he says,

"Those gracious, wonderful people up there. They are people who love everybody. You cannot, whoever you are, argue with that. They know that there is much more inside of us than the physical organs that give us bodily function. When you sit here and see this sight you know it is true beyond question. It is so obvious that we two airborne gypsies are being welcomed, even blessed, and shown the truth of it all."

I then and there made it a point to memorize forever what my friend Marty had just said. I will surely miss him when he flies his old Waco back to Kansas. We assumed it would be a while before Streicher showed up. But we had hardly "washed" and "put away" the breakfast dishes when the old Dodge truck pulled up to the hole in the fence. He came slowly down to the plane carrying an empty ten-gallon gas can.

Marty climbed up on the nose of the plane, reaching back to remove the tank filler cap, then thrusting down the dipstick, which he carried in home-made clamps alongside the cowl opening. He drew out the stick, put it back in its place, replaced the cap, jumped down on the ground.

"It has 19 gallons. We are down 16 gallons. I suggest we take both cans up and pump in 8 gallons in each. Then bring us back down here and I think I can put my filters in the filler and run it back in the tank that way. Mr. Streicher, I certainly appreciate your help. Peyton, you can come along with us. I'm sure you would like to see St. Meinrad first hand as I know I would too."

First we drove up to the Abbey and monastery where Streicher took us through the beautiful grounds. A most impressive place. I had been here before as a lad but it seemed even more impressive to me now. Marty said little but he was extremely absorbed, not merely noncommittal. More like speechless.

Back to the truck, we made our way along the road to the outskirts of this small town to a store with a single Crown gasoline pump with its large glass vial of gasoline. Pumped by hand.

After filling each can and Marty paying the storekeeper, Mr. Streicher suggested that we stop at his place on the way back. Obviously he was very proud of his place, wanted to show it to us. He is obviously proud of his association with we barnstormers and wants to introduce us to his wife and family. The drive to the Streicher place was three miles southwest of St. Meinrad. He said we would stop there a few minutes, then cut back east to the Troy road and the plane.

The countryside with its fastidiously neat farms can only be described as perfect. After making a series of right angle turns on the county roads, we arrive at Streicher's farm. it is the epitome of hands-on perfection in this neat, clean, perfectly arranged Germanic community. The common bond is honoring your neighbor and his place by making your own its equal. All in the name of God and the church.

Streicher's house is an ample two-story home built by his father before the turn of the century. Yet it appears to be only a few years old or even recently constructed. Two barns are the same. Built before 1900 yet they appear to be new. Painting, structure and functional upkeep seem to have been an obsession with the Streichers for all of three generations. We park in the shaded drive by the house and approach the screened back porch adjacent to the kitchen where Mrs. Streicher admits us and introductions are performed by Mr. Streicher. She is a woman that appears to be her husband's age, neatly braided hair, spic and span gingham long dress and apron. Her eyes are keenly intelligent and a courteous smile that seems to reveal a devout respect for strangers and especially for those she knows her kind husband has befriended. On the drive over, Mr. Streicher tells us that she was a schoolteacher for several years before and after they were married, until their first child was born. They have three grown sons and a daughter. Two sons are married with families, living on nearby farms. One son is still with his parents, now out in the fields working. All three still work sections of the "home" place as well as on church land. The daughter is married, lives in Warrick County.

Mrs. Streicher offers us all coffee which both Marty and I truly welcome having dined and breakfasted on grape juice and water. She has a real twinkle in her eyes when she says with a glance of admiration and amusement at her shy husband, "He always loves to bring the airplane pilots around to see our place when they land over in the Abbey field."

They both have a distinct German accent, even though they are a generation removed from their emigrant parents. In response to her remark, he says, "And more to have the pilots to meet my lovely wife of whom I am very proud."

It was very touching even for a lad of sixteen like me. And I could see Marty was very much moved. With thanks and well wishes to Mrs. Streicher, we take our leave, wending our way through the crisscross of county roads to the Troy road and back to our old beautiful Waco, gleaming red and silver in the sun. It seemed to say, "Where have you gypsies been? I cannot fly myself, you know!"

Mr. Streicher remained nobly by to help when Marty gassed up the Waco. Marty set up his filter funnel on the tank filler and between myself and Streicher, we helped him elevate and hold the awkward can as the fuel was poured through the strainer. The full can weighed nearly fifty pounds. I am thinking that this was not well thought out. A far cry from the way we did it down in Cannelton on Albert Veeck's farm. I guess I'm learning that barnstorming means mostly making do with a plain open field where there are no barns to sleep in, gasoline drums with spigots and home cooked meals in a country kitchen, cooked by someone else. The silent message I am getting from Marty is that St. Meinrad field is the typical barnstormer's landing field, not Cannelton.

By the time we have poured and strained the second can of gas our arms are so tired they are almost numb and incapable of lifting or holding anything.

So we get out the water canteen and share a drink with Streicher as we sit in the shade of the Waco's wings. After a while Marty gets up, stretches and rubs his arms. Streicher obviously dreads to see us leave. It makes me feel good and I know my pilot friend shares that feeling. I load all of our gear except the chocks into the forward cockpit and we set about firing up the OX-5, a procedure I have now grown so accustomed to that it seems second nature. As I crawl out of the cockpit the idling propeller's wake lifting the leather flaps of my old helmet, Marty comes around the plane lugging the chocks by their ropes. He climbs into the rear and I set about getting into the front to stash the chocks. I step down and shake hands with Streicher who has reached in to the cockpit to shake hands with Marty. As we taxi out into the field to take off, Streicher is resolutely standing by the old Dodge truck waving his hat.

I feel a bit forlorn as we climb out north past the 165-foot spires of St. Meinrad Arch Abbey. I will never forget this place of places where all who live here are born with a Sense of Place that I hope will pervade all of the communities of the world, be they small or large.

Marty has mentioned that we would fly first to Mariah Hill but did not say that we would land there. I know from past trips that Mariah Hill is west of St. Meinrad about five miles. It is on the meandering Indiana State Highway 62, which is on the main road from Evansville, Indiana to Louisville, Kentucky, both of which are on the Ohio River. North of St. Meinrad about a half mile, Marty starts a slow, wide turn to the west until we are flying parallel to 62 which is a narrow, two lane paved road. Even though Mariah Hill is only five miles distant, the area between it and St. Meinrad is the typical rural setting of all of this beautiful country. During times when we have been alone working on the Waco or after turning in at night waiting for our tired bones to be relieved by the blessings of slumber, I had told Marty of my trips with my family to this German Catholic community in upper Spencer or Perry and Dubois counties. On more than one occasion Dad and I came along with Uncle John, Uncle Ches and Cousin August to the church bazaar at Mariah Hill, which was held on the grassy grounds and slopes surrounding the church. The bazaar was made up of a series of exhibition stands displaying exciting crafts of the local parish as well as antiques, rare books and journals. My Uncles John and Ches were brothers and my uncles by marriage. They were Germans, their father and mother born in Germany. Their mother's family was staff members and servants in the old country to the Hohenzollern family for generations. They had many friends and relatives in and around Mariah Hill. So those excursions to the Mariah Hill bazaars are an annual summertime happening. Part of my story that delighted Marty was the occasion when my Cousin August (nicknamed Toots, Uncle Ches's son) became curious of the interest Dad, Uncle John and Ches displayed in a remote stand in a downhill far corner of the bazaar where homemade apple cider was being sold in gallon jugs, with the cork stoppers sealed with sealing wax. One of the portly German attendants of the stand was whispering to our menfolk and pointing to knife-like nicks in the sealing wax and I noticed that only some of the jugs had nicks. When customers distinctly requested cider they got jugs without the nicks. But if they asked for cider in a quiet voice and caught the eye of the portly seller in a certain way, their jugs then had the nicks. Because of this poorly veiled subtlety as well as its fringe location, Toots and I strongly guessed that this particular stand's connection to the church bazaar was highly suspect. Our three menfolks purchased a half dozen of the jugs with the nicks. On the way home Uncle John revealed the "cider" was the finest home distilled bourbon imported from near Hawesville, Kentucky just across the Ohio River from Cannelton. This story amused Marty very much. As we approached Mariah Hill he circled the church on the hill in a banking glide with the OX-5 at idle. He began pounding on the cowl behind my head, signaling me to raise up and turn around. He yelled, "is that it?" I nodded vigorously. He smiled broadly, looking kind of clownish behind his lowered goggles. Then he yelled again, "Which corner of the yard?" The question disoriented me. With the plane in a diving turn I kept losing the church. Besides, our heightened view from above seemed to flatten the hill. Finally in confusion I shouted back,

"The southwest corner of the yard!"

With that he burst out in laughter that I could hear above the noise of the slipstream, opened the throttle and leveled off. We circled this beautiful little town with its fond memories several times again. I looked back as we circled to see Marty's head bobbing back and forth. He was casing the place to find a field, or a field suggested by Streicher. We came in low along the clover fields along the highway near the town, then retreated out in a circle around town, then back across the fields again. It was a ploy Marty said he used to make the townspeople think he was going to land. If they began making their way to the nearby fields either by horseback, wagon or auto, it showed they had an interest and he would land. Those with interest were always prospective passengers. After thirty minutes and no sign of anyone hurrying to the field, we climbed out and headed north.

We are still heading north, chugging along with the OX-5 purring along like it has never purred before. I figure that we are heading to Huntingburg. Marty has said several times before that he was anxious to land in the area between Huntingburg and Jasper and also south of Huntingburg. He thought those two communities were larger and the potential of carrying passengers was much greater than we experienced at St. Meinrad, even though our trip to St. Meinrad and its small town atmosphere thrilled both of us for three days and we really hated to leave.

Now as we are cruising along, headed north toward Huntingburg, suddenly my premature conclusion is brought to a halt by Marty. He turns ninety degrees heading back toward St. Meinrad and I wondered, why is he doing this? We are headed straight east now and then I notice that we seem headed directly toward St. Meinrad. Then I notice that isn't quite accurate either because he is following a course about fifteen degrees north of east and ahead I can see St. Meinrad in the distance, but also I can see directly ahead the prominent hill of Ferdinand. Then I realize that all of the stories that I have told Marty these past weeks of Ferdinand, St. Meinrad, and Mariah Hill with their whole being and history are based central to the Catholic Church. In years past, my parents and I took many auto trips up to this area. While these places are new to Marty, they are not new to me at all although I have not been here for four years. This aerial trip, for me, is a whole new way of looking at these places. It appears now that my friend Marty is going to Ferdinand. He circles the Marian Heights Academy. Maybe he will even land and take a few passengers, so we shall see in a few moments.

Of particular interest is the church at Ferdinand, a monastery, rising majestically above the town of Ferdinand, and the Romanesque dome is the Monastery Immaculate Conception. It is home to the Sisters of St. Benedict of Ferdinand, one of the largest Benedictine communities of women in the United States. The monastery was founded in 1867 by four young German-speaking Sisters who arrived from a Covington, Kentucky monastery to teach the town's German settlers. Over the years several hundred women have entered the community in Ferdinand and their faith, spirit and energy have led to the establishment of other monasteries in the United States and even in Latin America. The Sisters minister throughout southern Indiana and many other states and several foreign countries in the areas of education, pastoral care, health care counseling, social services and mission work. The Sisters operate two ministries that are located on the monastery's two hundred acre Marian Heights Academy, a girls college preparatory, boarding and day school founded in 1870, educates students from across the United States and from other countries. And then there is the Kordes Enrichment Center, which is a part of this community also; it is a spiritual growth center providing a safe and sacred atmosphere for people of all faiths.

There is a main monastery building, St. Benedict Hall. What I remember most is the church, the infirmary and quarters of the Sisters. The Sisters are known for their hospitality, part of the Benedictine rule by which they live. The Sisters of St. Benedict of Ferdinand welcomed visitors who wished to share the peace and beauty of their facilities. Four years ago they took my parents and I on guided tours of the complex. And having told these things to Marty I gather that is the reason why we are headed there now. His historical curiosity seems never to be satisfied, so here we go.

As we approach, the hill on which Marian Heights Academy is located is very prominent. Marty swings around to the south and executes a complete circle around the town and the hilltop Academy. He circles to the area south of Ferdinand until we are coming in from the south to where we can see the town spread out before us. Beneath us is the road south to St. Meinrad. The road from St. Meinrad passing through Ferdinand to the north is the main street. I can remember driving through there four years ago then turning to the east after we entered the town to visit the Academy.

As we approach in the Waco, our minds are on where to land. The road south to St. Meinrad seems to be bordered by small farms with no fields large enough for landing. But over to the east, just south of Marian Heights Academy, there is another smaller road coming south, which has larger fields on its east side. Marty swings over and circles this area south of Marian Heights until he is approaching from the south, then I see the throttle move back and the engine r.p.m. comes down and we descend. Straight ahead lay a crossroad and a flatter field beyond. We pass low over the crossroad, touching down in a grassy field almost like a playing field. It's not a hayfield. Just grass and smooth turf. We gently bounce along, coming to a rolling stop. Marty taxis over to the road, which comes directly down from Marian Heights, shuts down the OX-5 and begins climbing out. Lifting the goggles up over his head, he is smiling at me very mischievously as though he knows "surprise" is written all over his face.

I think to myself without saying so to Marty that this location is beautiful but it is not on the main St. Meinrad route passing north and south through Ferdinand. Will anyone really know we're over here? They may have seen us flying around and seen us land, but we are definitely off the beaten track. In fact, this place looks almost as though it could have been used for baseball, football or other field sports. But there is no sign that this field has been used for those sports in several years. It is beautiful. Just a park-like atmosphere of flat neatly mowed grass. A good hard turf in which our Waco landing gear wheels did not even leave a furrow. Just a short way in front of our parked Waco is the road coming south from Marian Heights. There is no traffic on it. It is paved or partly paved. There isn't even a fence along the edge of the road as it was over in St. Meinrad. Just at the edge of the field, a ditch, then the road.

Marty is sitting on the edge of the cockpit grinning. "Well, I guess I surprised you. You know I got to thinking as we were leaving Mariah Hill, heck, we're not going to see Ferdinand unless we just go do it." He is still sitting on the edge of the cockpit with his goggles pushed back on top of his head, the flaps of his old dirty white cloth helmet turned up over his ears. I climb out, jump down on the ground and he does likewise. I ask, "Are we going to stay or go?"

Marty nods, "Seeing as how we have only been here less than a minute, wouldn't it be wise to wait around a while and see?" He walks around to the nose of the ship, checking over the tires, then he climbs up on the landing gear, then the lower wing and then on top loosening the engine cowl, handing it down to me, and begins tinkering around with the overhead valve rocker arms; pulled the feeler gauge out of his pocket and began checking the valve settings.

I asked him, "Isn't the engine running smooth enough to suit you?"

He smiled, looked down, and said, "Well, gotta do something, no passengers so far. I'll mess with the engine." I thought to myself, Well, don't mess it up, but I knew that was an improper thought because if anyone could fix the thing it would be Marty.

We did not have to wait too long. A Model T Ford and a Model A Ford both showed up, one behind the other parking directly in front of the airplane. Two youngish men climbed out of the Model A and one older gentleman from the Model T. They came ambling over with the usual slow curiosity, uneasily looking the airplane over and apparently too sheepish to ask questions. Then Marty blurts out: "Good day, Gentlemen. What can we do for you? Anyone for an airplane ride?"

The older man countered the question with: "Where you fellas from?" '

Marty quickly replied, "Not from very far away, St. Meinrad."

The older gent seemed puzzled. "Didn't know St. Meinrad had any aviators." I thought to myself, that's for sure.

Then Marty says, "Well no, as a matter of fact, we're on a barnstorming tour of southern Indiana. I started out over in southern Illinois. I picked up my friend Peyton here down in Warrick County in Boonville. We've been on the trip now for several days. Were down in Cannelton a couple of days, then up to St. Meinrad."

The younger men were a bit more antsy. They were digging their toes in the ground and whispering to each other, tentatively touching the taut fabric of the lower wing of the Waco and, of course, like all airplane newcomers, they couldn't resist the temptation to thump the wings and get that drum-like sound. Marty always said, "It's okay if they thump it, just as long as they don't run their fists and arms all the way through." Then one said, "How much does it cost for a flight?"

"Marty says, "Three dollars."

They looked at each other, ambled back over to the Model A and sat for a while in very earnest discussion, then they came back over. "How many can you take in one flight?"

Marty says, "Two."

Then one says rather sheepishly, "Then we'd like to go on one flight." Forthwith, plunging a hand into a side pocket pulling out six one-dollar bills.

Marty buckled down the cowling, hopped down on the ground, nodded at me; I crawled up in the cockpit, hauled all of our stuff out and piled it up on the ground, and we proceeded to swing the prop and get the airplane started and I load the two young gentlemen into the front cockpit, made sure the safety belt was fastened. Marty taxied down to the south end of the field near the crossroad, then took off coming by us and veering off into a climbing turn to the east of Marian Heights.

Here I was again, standing in an empty field with Marty in the air with passengers, me alone with the stranger would-be passenger—or hopeful passenger. I set about piling up our gear in one spot, ambled over to the older gentleman, introduced myself and asked him if he had lived here very long. He stated that his name was Mr. Heilman and that he had lived in the Ferdinand area all of his life. He was 72 years old. He looked at me very quizzically. "Is the pilot a friend of yours? Is he your father? Or perhaps your older brother? How does it happen that you are flying with him? You're not a passenger?"

I assure him no, I am not a passenger; I'm just an interested aviation enthusiast and I tell him about my glider flying down in Boonville. He looks at me very skeptically. I don't think he believes me. When I told him I was Marty's barnstormer helper he seemed to believe that. I asked him if he cared to take a ride?"

"Maybe," he said, "I been thinking about it."

This place is almost identical in many ways to St. Meinrad from where we just came. The field is south of Marian Heights Academy, a magnificent edifice on top of the hill is much like the spires of the church at St. M6inrad and our field is a couple of miles south of the church, just like it was in St. Meinrad.

Mr. Heilman came over as I rustled around in our baggage. He obviously had something to say, which seemed to be an event with him. "Young feller," he said, "My son lives over beyond the main road, the one that comes down out of Ferdinand to St. Meinrad. I'm going to drive over there and bring him over here and I guess maybe the two of us will take a plane ride as soon as your pilot friend returns."

I said, "Fine. You do just that and we will be all ready for you, sir."

He steps over, cranks up the Model T and takes off.

I'm left standing there looking to the north and marveling at the sight spread out before me. Marian Heights is a beautiful spot and the architecture of that Academy is something to behold. Every time I've been here I never cease to wonder at its beauty. The center is topped off by a high dome. one wing, the church, is topped by another dome extended to one side with another wing extending at a right angle. The domed extension is really two rounded domes, one higher than the other, the lower one extending even further.

Five minutes later I notice that Marty has circled Ferdinand and is coming south over to the west of me. He then makes a wide circle to approach from the south. As he skids back and forth, fishtailing first to the right, then to the left in his usual fashion to slow down the Waco, he comes in over the crossroad, touches down with a gentle bounce or two and rolls to a stop at the north end of the field. He raises up the tail, guns the engine and swings around back to where I am standing. He pulls up, parks, shuts it down and I jump up on the wing to help the young fellows out. They didn't need much help because they had already unfastened the safety belt, climbing out, making me feel a bit useless.

They gathered around the plane, talking up a storm to Marty. They had lost all of their previous shyness now that they had had a ride. They seemed a bit more outgoing than the usual farm lads around this German Catholic community. At first they had been shy enough, but now the closeness and the experience of riding in our airplane changed all of that. They look upon me now with an entirely new respect when Marty told them offhandedly that I, too, was a pilot and that I owned my own glider and had flown it many times down in Boonville. They bombarded me with questions as well as Marty. They stood around for a while, then sat down on the grass under the lower wing in the shade and became fast friends in a very short time. At least I felt so. It was a welcome change to the coldness of feeling I'd had toward them, and I thought them toward me, had now disappeared. Oh joy! It's a good feeling. Then when they saw that I had my old leather helmet and goggles laid out on the pile of duffel next to the plane, that really did it.

After over thirty minutes of banter and questions and answers and talking a blue streak among the four of us, Mr. Heilman's Model T pulled up along the road. There were two occupants in the back seat of the Model T. When they climbed out, obviously one of them, a younger man, perhaps thirty-five, was obviously his son. But the third person attracted the attention of all four of us, and especially myself. I could tell that the two young gentlemen with whom I had just sealed a friendship were also especially attracted to that person. As they came over, Mr. Heilman introduced the younger man as his son and the young lady as his granddaughter, his son's daughter. Her name is Katherine; she will be fifteen tomorrow, according to Mr. Heilman. A plane ride with her father will be a birthday present from Grandpa Heilman.

She is very slender, not tall; long straight blond hair to her waist. The Heilmans are a farm people but she seems so delicate, almost frail but outstandingly beautiful. Her little hands seemed to have endured no hard work at all. Perhaps, I thought, she is a little milkmaid, it fits her closely. With all my preoccupation with my glider, even at sixteen, I had no real girlfriends, although three in high school had given me warm feelings, not all at the same time. There was Dixie in the eighth grade, then Mary Frances as a freshman and Marjory now as a sophomore. No dates; we would spend recesses at school exclusively with each other and walk together part way home. I talked of nothing but my glider. They showed a disappointing lack of interest in it except Marjory showed real concern when I explained how high I would fly before releasing the tow line.

The two young guys hung around attempting to speak to Katherine but she clung to her father. They were at least three years older than me, about 19 or 20. They should not, even politely, be trying to get acquainted with Katherine. Don't know what is going on here! I don't know what is coming over me. I'm jealous. I had to counter their attentions to her. She would hold eye contact with me for a few seconds but she averted the looks of the other two. I hurried over to our pile of gear, pulled out my helmet, pushing the goggles to the top of the helmet, held up the earflaps. She now gave me a look of admiration and a smile that set my heart racing. I noticed that Marty noticed my helmet act and he burst out in a short laugh which he quickly stifled, but no one noticed. Bless him, he looked away to leave me to my desperate theatrics. The two young guys took my move as defeat; they hopped in the Model A and left quietly. I know that as local youths they will never forget Katherine and they will always be here to pursue her and I will be gone away which leaves me in a state of anticipatory frustration.

Then I begin to fantasize, yes, I won't be far away, I'll be down in Boonville; I can dream of borrowing my father's Essex and driving up here to see if somehow I can find Katherine and aspire to a friendship with her. She is so slim and beautiful, her blond hair streaming down almost to her hips; her face, neck, arms and legs are almost pale white. She seems so frail and delicate but so beautiful, but yet a healthy young farm lass and a smile and a twinkle of her blue eyes that seemed so shy and defenseless but so warm. All of this I've noticed in only the five or ten minutes that I've seen her here.

Then Marty and Mr. Heilman and Mr. Heilman's son break my trance when they begin to discuss their plane ride. Before I know it I am helping them into the forward cockpit and senior Mr. Heilman is worrying about Katherine's long hair blowing in the open cockpit breeze. He says, "You should have done it up in braids on your head in the same fashion as you do when you go to church." She nodded shyly; her father nodded his head understandingly. Then it was good old Marty who really broke the ice. He said, "Now, Peyton will not be flying with you, just the two of you and me. Why not borrow Peyton's helmet that will fit over her head and keep her hair from blowing around in the breeze."

Katherine's father looks at me questioningly, then at

Marty, then at Katherine. Katherine gives me a cute little smile and nods her head. Oh, that made me feel so good!

I stumble over awkwardly and hand her the helmet. She looks at it but she doesn't seem to know what to do with it, so I thought, now or never. I hold up the flaps, pull the goggles up on top, go gently around behind her, tuck her hair down her back, then I slip the helmet over her head and pull the flaps down, push the goggles up, then I confront her and I ask, "Would you like to have the flaps buckled under your chin, and do you want the goggles up or do you want the goggles down?" She didn't seem to know and I could tell from the way she tilted her head from side to side that she wanted me to decide. So I loosely buckled the flaps under her chin and then I pulled the goggles down just over her brow. I said, "Now, if the wind gets too strong on your eyes, just pull them down, they're nice and clear and you can see through them."

Then they climb aboard and her father takes over the helping of her into the cockpit. He puts her in first, then he follows. Then I hop back down on the ground, climb into the rear cockpit to do my switching duties while Marty swings the prop. He comes around and climbs in as I get out. As they swing around to taxi to the south end of the field for the take-off north, Katherine waves to me gingerly with her little hand and arm barely above the cockpit's rim. What a thrill it gives me, how cute she looks in my old leather helmet, the goggles upright and her eyes obviously looking at me as she waves. I will never forget it.

When they reach the south end Marty swings around and comes roaring by for the take-off. They climb out over the east side of Ferdinand and I'm sure that little Katherine and her father are getting a real good glimpse of Marian Heights.

Only Mr. Heilman and I are alone here now. It is hard for me to talk to Mr. Heilman, my thoughts will not stray from Katherine, then it occurs to me that that is not so smart. The last thing I should do is denigrate myself in the eyes of her grandfather. Someday I might want him to like me very much —enough to be looking forward to my return to Ferdinand. I try not to show my interest in Katherine, but he is a wise old man. He begins to question my telling of my glider flying, which earlier he seemed to me to lay to the bragging imagination of a sixteen-year-old. But now the questions he asked shows that he really did not know, did not doubt me so much as he did not know what a glider was. Flying was only done in a plane, only done in airplanes. What was this glider thing? The next thirty minutes was spent in my explaining all the details of glider flying. He listened carefully all this time and I really believe he understood. Occasionally he would ask such questions as: "How long was that rope you were towed with? How high did you get? How did you drop it? Why didn't the glider fall to the ground once you had dropped the tow line and you were no longer being towed by the automobile?" All of this took explanation and he listened very carefully. A very wise man indeed. After those thirty minutes, I feel I have now found a friend, or at least I had succeeded in repairing much of the earlier damage.

We were still talking when I notice suddenly that the Waco had touched down at the south end of the field and was rolling up to swing around and park next to where we stood. Marty cut the engine and I excused myself to Mr. Heilman and ran around the wing tip to the left side of the forward cockpit, jumped up on the step, swung open the door and unlatched the safety belt and swung it aside, hopped back down on the ground so that Katherine's father could extricate himself and Katherine. They both stood on the ground next to the plane and I was overwhelmed with little Katherine. There she was wearing my helmet with a beaming beautiful smile. She seemed rather helpless, stood looking at me, didn't seem to know how to take it off. I came up without looking her directly in the eye, and unbuckled the flaps on the helmet, pulled the flaps up and very gingerly lifted the helmet off which mussed up her long streaming hair and without thinking, just on impulse, I reached out and stroked her blond tresses out straight the way they belonged, and she tittered a little bit and hovered over next to her father, who I'm afraid gave me a rather suspicious but at the same time a kind of a warm look.

She then hurried over to her grandfather, gave him a warm hug, then she came primly back to Marty, held out her little white hand and thanked him for the airplane ride. The three of them gathered together, walked over to the Model T and unceremoniously the senior Mr. Heilman cranked up his Ford, climbed in while the other two climbed into the back. As they drove away my heart fell like it had never fallen before.

I sauntered back over to the plane; Marty was standing there leaning against the rear cockpit, pulled his helmet off, threw it down into the seat, turned around to me, winked, nodded his head and gave me a little sympathetic, very sincere smile. Then abruptly he said, "Well, kid, what do we do next?"

I said in feigned enthusiasm, "Gee, can you believe it? It's nearly five o'clock. We seem to have done so little and the time has gone by so fast. Where has the day gone?"

Marty looked at me quizzically as if to say, "Peyton, you are making conversation, this is not the sort of thing you usually comment upon."

"Oh," he said, "well, you know Mr. Heilman will be due back in about thirty minutes he told me. He had to take his son and granddaughter home but told me he would return." That really surprised me. I didn't know this but of course since I wasn't within earshot of everything he and Mr. Heilman discussed and I could not help but think: Is he really coming back alone? Not bringing his son and granddaughter back? No, that isn't what he said. He's coming back alone. I wonder why?

Marty laughed. He said, "Didn't you know? He's coming back to take us back up town. There are a lot of things here in Ferdinand I would like to see. I would like to go through that Marian Heights Academy, it's probably too late but he has invited us to stay with he and Mrs. Heilman."

I am amazed, "You mean we are going to stay in town with them? What about the plane?"

"Well, you know what we learned in St. Meinrad. No one is going to bother this airplane. What I told him I would do is taxi it back over to the far side of the field so we can stake it down there. I told him if by any chance a storm came up we would have to get back. He assured me he would drive us back here in no time at all. He'll probably be back down here in another twenty minutes. That will give us time to taxi the plane back over to the other side, then hike back over here to the road to meet him."

He gestures me into the rear cockpit, walks around to the front; we get the thing started; he comes around, climbs back in, and I hop up on the lower wing, hang onto a strut as he taxis back over to the east side of the field. It is quite a ways. About three or four hundred yards. We taxi back into a little niche, which is hidden behind some trees from the road. Marty shuts her down and we get out the stakes and other gear, proceed to put the ropes around the wing struts where they connect to the lower wing, drive the stakes into the ground and do the same thing back at the tail skid. Then we sort out the things we will take along with us and throw the rest back into the forward cockpit, heading back through the grassy field to the east road.

When we get within about three hundred feet of the road we can see Heilman coming down from the Marian Heights hill, chugging along in the old Model T. I can tell he is all alone. My heart sinks a little bit but when I think of going back up into town and the chances of perhaps seeing little Katherine may be somewhat enhanced. I immediately begin to wonder if she and her father and mother live with her grandparents? If so, we will have dinner together. On second (logical) thought that is just wishful thinking on my part. Katherine and her parents undoubtedly live out on a farm, but hopefully will come in to see her grandparents while I am there.

Peyton Autry and Waco Model 10, 1933.

The Swallow "TP," curtiss OX-5 powered 2-place trainer, owned by Wallace Whitcomb and Jarrett Roth of Boonville, Indiana.

Top: An airborne Johnson Monoplane. Bottom: Lou Johnson in a Johnson Monoplane, Terre Haute, Indiana, 1911. (Smithsonian photos)

JOHNSON BROS.
5c̄ −6°
~~90~~ Horse Power Steel
MONOPLANES

GREATEST OF ALL ATTRACTIONS
NOW BOOKING EXHIBITIONS
FLIGHTS GUARANTEED

ROSS L. SMITH, Aviator

For Information Write
Johnson Bros. Motor Co.
Terre Haute, Indiana

BUILDERS OF THE FIRST SUCCESSFUL AMERICAN MONOPLANE

Johnson Monoplane Advertising Circular, 1911

Lou Johnson at the controls of a Johnson Monoplane in Terre Haute, Indiana, 1911.

Smithsonian model of the 1911 Johnson Monoplane. (Smithsonian photos)

Shenandoah, ZR-1, somewhere along the Pacific Coast, October, 1924. (Smithsonian photo)

The ZR-1 being drawn from Lakehurst Hangar by her ground crew. (Smithsonian photo)

Waco GXE, 1935 (Livergood photo)

Waco Model 9 (Livergood photo)

Waco GXE, 1935 (Livergood photo)

Mead Rhon Ranger No. 12864 soon after receipt in Boonville, Indiana in the summer of 1935. Lloyd Gabriel shown seated in the glider in Sault Sainte Marie, Michigan (Lloyd R. Gabriel photo)

August 8, 1936. Mead Primary no. 12864, wind flipped it over and broke one strut.

Right panel of Mead primary glider no. 12864 after restoration and rounded leading edge modification of Durand 24 Airfoil to prevent stall buffet and "shake" in a towed climb. July 15, 1936. (Lloyd R. Gabriel photos)

Mead Glider and Whirlwind Travel Air at Soo Airport, August, 1936.

Bob McArthur and Stan Lyons, "Now flies 1000% better and doesn't shake anymore," after leading edge modification. August 22, 1936.

Soo, Michigan, August 17, 1936. Mead Rhon Ranger after restoration after being shipped from Boonville, Indiana. (Lloyd R. Gabriel photos)

The Lasley "Sport" designed by Peyton Autry in 1937. Powered by a 70 hp Velie 5-cylinder radial aircooled engine. (Lloyd R. Gabriel photo)

1950s modification of Lasley "Sport" designed for Lasley Tool and Machine Company in the 1930s, with Lambert engine. (Lloyd R. Gabriel photo)

Mead Primary Rhon Ranger in flight, towed to release altitude on 1800 feet of "piano" wire.

Clarence Bernier and Lloyd Gabriel, shortly after no. 12864 was received from Peyton Autry, August 8, 1935.

Preparing to glue and tack on 1/32 plywood leading edge cover of Rhon Ranger. (Lloyd R. Gabriel photos)

Back and side view of Waco Model 10, identical to the Waco flown by Marty and Peyton. Registration no. NC729E. (Lloyd R. Gabriel photos)

Lincoln-Standard LS-5, 5-place biplane powered by 180 hp Hispano-Suiza engine. (John Underwood collection)

Two views of Waco Model 10, registration NC904H. (Arthur F. Livergood)

An identical replication of Marty's Waco 10 with Peyton in the front cockpit and Marty in the rear (The Museum of Flight photo)

General view of the new Lincoln-Standard type LS5 commercial five-seater (180 hp Hispano-Suiza engine). (Antique Airplane News, 3rd Quarter 1974)

R.D. Weyerbacher at his desk in the Navy Department, September 1914. (U.S. Navy photo, National Archives)

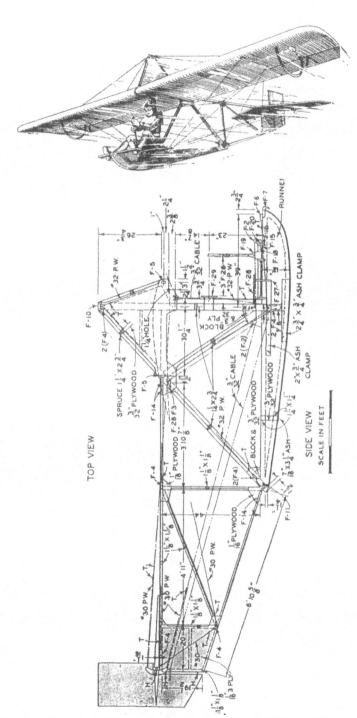

The Northrop Primary Glider as depicted by Douglas Rolfe in the Flying and Gliding Manual of Fawcett Publication, 1930.

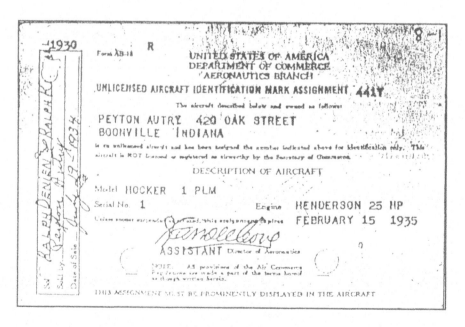

Hocker Monoplane owned and "flown" by Peyton Autry. Department of Aeronautics Branch Registration shows Peyton sold it to Ralph Denien on July 19, 1934. (1934 Flying and Glider Manual photo (top) and Federal Archives)

Department of Commerce, Aeronautics Branch Registration for Peyton Autry's Rhon Ranger Glider No. 12864, issued annually. (Federal Archives)

Early O'Neal advertisement of Frank O'Neal in Vincennes, Indiana. (Vincennes University)

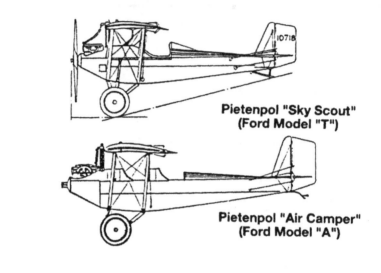

Pietenpol "Sky Scout"
(Ford Model "T")

Pietenpol "Air Camper"
(Ford Model "A")

Pietenpol Air Camper I inspected near Petersburg on the White River.

CHAPTER VII

M r. Heilman sees us coming across the field, turns the Model T around to head back into Ferdinand. I hop in the back seat, Marty in the front and we take off. Mr. Heilman is telling us that the road along our field is called Convent Road. He proceeds up to an intersection, which he says, is Fifth Street, turning left heading west. He tells us that he took this route rather than go up through the Convent because he will be taking us tomorrow morning for a tour of the Marian Heights Academy. He wants to proceed on Fifth over to Main Street, which is the highway into town from the south from Santa Claus and St. Meinrad. He wants to go up Main so that we can have a look at the downtown part of Ferdinand. He tells us that his home is on 11th Street.

At this point Marty says, "Oh, I thought you lived on a farm out southwest of town." Heilman replied, "Yes, I used to, that is the home place. My son Roy and his family live there now and work the farm. Two years ago my wife and I bought this place in Ferdinand."

I thought to myself, well, that takes care of little Katherine, but who knows, maybe she is still there at her grandparents' place awaiting the arrival of the daring aviators?

Presently we pull up before the Heilman house. A picket fence surrounded the front of the place. We pile out of the Model T, ambling up the steps to the front porch. Mr. Heilman opens the front door, calling inside. "Katie, we are here."

Katie Heilman is a tall slender woman, possibly Heilman's same age of 72, but her dress and hair are the epitome of neatness. Her hair is braided and done up in a bun atop an erect proud head; only a trace of gray showed in her blond, primly packaged locks, but the thing that struck me was how much she looked like little Katherine. She asked us to be seated in the living room having already prepared coffee and tea for us while explaining dinner would be in the adjoining dining room in just a few moments.

Marty is his old eloquent self. He began to expound on the beauties of Ferdinand and the Convent and Academy that we had seen from the air.

Heilman explained that he and Katie were blessed with three sons and a daughter. Two of the sons and the daughter lived in a neighboring county. When he had reached 70 years of age he decided it best to turn the farm place over to his younger son Roy and his family. He and Katie moved into town so that Roy and his family had the free run of the farm home and operation of the farm itself, and that he need not stick his nose into its operation or interfere in their family life, although they saw a great deal of each other and were very proud of all of their family.

On the mantel in the living room is an array of pictures.

The other two sons and the daughter and right behind them pictures of their families. Off to one end was Roy, who both Marty and myself recognized as the son to whom we gave a plane ride along with his daughter, little Katherine. And there, of course, next to his photograph and that of Roy's wife, was a picture of little Katherine. My heart did a few flip-flops. It was a beautiful photograph of her and it looked as though it had not been taken more than a year before today. I caught myself looking too long and I was afraid I would attract the attention of the Heilmans and old Marty himself. The photograph, as good as it was, did not do her justice in my heart. But it was Mrs. Katie Heilman who began to explain the thrill experienced by her son Roy and little Katherine in their plane ride this afternoon. It immediately aroused my attention.

Katie said that Katherine's plane ride today was her first, but that she was an enthusiastic follower of aviation and that her heroines were all famous women aviators. Marty named off a few of the famed aviatrix. Katie Heilman nodded her head, "Oh yes, she's read about those, all of them." Laughingly she said, "Probably many more." That really did my heart good. She would not be turned off by my glider flights and all of my enthusiasm for flying and planes. We had something in common besides what I felt in my heart for this little girl only a year younger than I who I had fallen for so completely in the last few hours.

Then Marty noticed that I was carrying a paper sack, rolled up with a string tied around it. He looked at me questioningly, then obviously thought better; he would not ask me what was in that package here before the Heilmans. It might be something private that I would not want to discuss in front of the others. He still had that puzzled look, then his expression turned to one of understanding.

Herman Heilman was saying, "Oh yes, she really enjoyed the flight. The young man here loaned his flying helmet; that leather cap thing with the ear flaps and buckle on the bottom with those big—what do you call them?— big glasses—those goggles, made her look just like the women heroes that she reads about in the books."

Then I clear up my throat and I said, "Well, I'm glad that she liked the helmet and goggles. They kept her hair from blowing around and spoiling her view from the plane if the hair got down into her eyes (Damn it—I'm beginning to stammer!) and—and—I have it here wrapped up in this paper sack and—and—I really don't use it much. In the summer time it's too warm, I think, and usually I don't wear it, it's just stuffed under the seat in the front cockpit and I was just wondering—if maybe Katherine would like to have it so she could use it the next time she goes for a plane ride."

Marty just smiled. Heilman seemed a little taken aback and he said, "But won't you need that thing? You know she won't be flying often. We only have a pilot come in here once in a great while. You are the first this summer."

Then Katie Heilman decided the whole thing right there on the spot. The final decision. She was a woman I really admired and respected. She said, "Katherine will be absolutely thrilled. Hand it to me and I will see that she gets your generous gift. Please take a piece of paper over there on the table and write your name and address so she can send you a thank you note when you return to Boonville in September. Thank you very much, I know she will be really thrilled. Thank you, Mr. Peyton."

I stammered, "Yes, my name is—my middle name is Peyton. Really, my first name is Charles but I go by Peyton. My last name is Autry."

"You just write your full name and address—"

We are led to the rear of the house. We clean up in Herman Heilman's washroom, his special addition just like he had out on the farm. Heilman had built this addition at the rear of his house when he first moved into this little town of Ferdinand two years ago. Even though it does not now serve the same purpose as out on the farm. He tells us the new house in town would not seem like home without it. These washrooms are typical of the farms here and are used when the men come in from the fields to wash up. Their soiled clothes, dirty boots and overalls, shirts, sox and underclothes are hung there on wall pegs and clean clothes are kept there by the lady of the house after she has done her washing. It is a first stage for the men in cleaning up from the fields, then the man goes to the normal bathroom after he has showered and put on clean clothes to shave or whatever. We revel in it. Our bedrooms are also in the rear of the house. The screened windows are open and I'm looking forward on this summer evening to having a good night's sleep in a bed, under sheets, the first now in many days.

After we are all tidied up, Katie Heilman calls us into the dining room. There are four places and four chairs, which means little Katherine and her family will not be here. I expected as much since we did not see her when we first arrived, but I am disappointed just the same. Dinner is wonderful! Pork chops, beef steaks, corn-on-the-cob, a special brew of cabbage and other vegetables. After grace is said by Herman Heilman, the food is passed from person to person in a polite and wonderful family manner.

Katie asks each of us to tell of our flying exploits. Marty and I look at each other and I nod toward him because his experiences far outdistance mine. He tells of his learning to fly back in 1919. He was 19 years old. In the early 1920s he had served as a flying cadet with the old Signal Corps of the Army. He told many of the stories that I had heard before, lying under the wings of the Waco, they were not new to me but were of his many experiences as a barnstormer. In all of his flying career he had never had a single accident; he had had numerous forced landings with engine trouble and that sort of thing but never a real serious crackup which had cost the lives of passengers or injured himself. Yet already at the age of 33 he had accumulated several thousand hours of logged flying time.

When it came my turn to tell of my flying exploits, it did not take too long since I am only 16 and they dated back about three years when I first started building and flying my gliders. And I told about the little monoplane that I owned at one time and tried to fly, which had a broken landing gear and I could never get off the ground properly because the left front wheel shimmied so bad at take-off speed that I could not control it.

Katie then goes on to tell of Katherine's recent fascination with women pilots. She said, "I bought her a small book and a magazine article telling of the flying records of women aviators. Names of those who flew in the 1929 Women's Air Derby. Names like Louise Thaden, Marvel Crosson, Amelia Earhart, Ruth Elder and Florence Barnes."

Then Herman Heilman cleared his throat and stated that he had reservations about Katherine's aerial fascinations. He thinks it will pass. Her place in the future is to raise her own family, keep alive the honorable tradition and greater family of the church. He not only thinks her fascination will pass but that it should pass. He does not say so but he has some difficulty hiding his suspicions that flying is more of a stunt than a life's dedication. Katie makes it very clear that she disagrees with her husband, which they both seem to cheerfully accept. She is as devoted to family, place and church as he, but to her that does not mean a member can not leave to pursue a rewarding and honorable career away from the place of their birth. This discussion between the two grandparents of the Heilman family prompts Katie to ask our opinion of aviation's future.

Marty looks at me and I look at Marty and I rather sheepishly nod my head toward him, but he could tell that I was eager to have my say also. He said, "This is the year 1933, and we are barnstormers, just vagabonds flying around over the country because we enjoy it, not because we are making a lot of money. It is a tradition of aviation in this fast time period but it's playing out. We are toward the end of the period where barnstormers are a familiar thing to people all over the USA. There have been great strides made in aviation far beyond we barnstormers or our airplanes that we fly as barnstormers. There are multi-engine airplanes that were even flown during the past war and versions of those are being designed and constructed for service as commercial transports. Air transportation of passengers and cargo is growing and growing fast. I believe that in the foreseeable future, not far off either, we will see multi-engine passenger transport planes flying frequently across the oceans. Some of this is already being done."

I follow Marty by reciting many of the numerous aviation magazine articles and the kinds of airplanes he just described by specific model number and manufacturer, size and numbers of passengers they carry and those that are being projected for the future, and how the sizes and reliability of aircraft engines are growing fast.

All of this seems to impress Herman Heilman very much. We fall silent when we realize that he has something to say and he is taking a bit of time to say it. Presently he says, "I've always wanted to take a trip back to Germany to visit my brothers and sisters and their families. Alas, my own parents are since passed away, the last of them my mother only three years ago. But I have many relatives in the old country, but the long trip by steamer and the expense and terrible trouble of all the travel has discouraged me."

I couldn't help but notice Katie's eyebrows lift and her headshake. Then Herman says, "If what you say is true, perhaps before long now, I could take one of your planes by simply taking the train up to Washington, DC or to New York City and flying to Berlin, from there I think I could find my way to my relatives. How long do you think it would take to make the trip?"

Marty says, "Well, from New York to Berlin, and let's say a fuel stop in London, you should be able to make it in less than two days very handily, including the time for refueling."

This really surprised Mr. Herman. He said very soberly, "I shall think about this. I really shall think about this. Shan't we, Katie? Would you do it?"

She replied, "You know I would."

With that we were off to bed, and what a good night's sleep we were to have. Looking forward to tomorrow and Katie's beautiful bountiful breakfast I knew it would be, and then the pleasurable trip over to Marian Heights Academy. Laying by the screened window, I think about the day's happenings. Beautiful little Katherine, these wonderful grandparents of hers, this bountiful feast they had just fed us and now with plans again for tomorrow. How wonderful it all is. I knew it all had to end and that did not make me feel too good, so best I go to sleep.

At sunrise the next day I am awakened by a little bird chirping away just outside the screened window. Then suddenly I am really awakened to a much greater extent by a loud rap on the bedroom door. Then the door opens quickly, in pops Marty's head. He says, "Rise and shine, kid. Can you just smell that beautiful breakfast? Get a whiff of that! Bacon, eggs, biscuits, milk gravy, fried potatoes. What a breakfast!" Then he comes in, closes the door, sits down on the bed while I hastily jerk on my trousers and rush about washing up and getting ready. It takes me about three minutes, including putting on my shoes. We make our way up the hall, into the kitchen and then to the dining room where Katie Heilman awaits us, gesturing to the chairs. Beyond her stands her husband, doing the same thing. Both greet us with, "Good morning, gentlemen," almost in unison. Herman Heilman says the grace and we then begin to enjoy this hunger quenching breakfast. How can I be hungry after last evening's dinner? But I am.

The conversation shifts centrally to Marty who is expressing our eternal gratitude for their gracious hospitality and he insists that we should reward them for their hospitality. Neither of them would think of it, and very curtly told us so. Marty, in his eloquent way, wormed his way around that by saying, "If not by monetary gratitude, I do insist on taking the two of you for a nice plane ride this afternoon, after we visit the Academy. I will fly you all around Ferdinand and its countryside. I suggest we make two or three low passes over your farm to give your son and his family a thrill."

When I hear that suggestion I think, 'Oh gee! I will not be there. I will not be in the plane, the three of them will be; Marty the pilot and the Heilmans in the forward cockpit. And lonely me back in the field waiting for them to return. How I would have loved to fly over little Katherine's farm, maybe wave to her. But perhaps another day. Besides, I feel I am becoming a little too obsessed with this beautiful little thing. I just do not feel like I am myself this past two days because of her. But I do not regret it, not for a moment.

Katie Heilman reacts to Marty's suggestion very quickly. She says, "Oh, we would be thrilled to fly with you and especially to fly over our son's farm. My husband has flown before. It was five years ago in an old rickety plane that was a far cry from your beautiful Waco plane. oh yes, by all means, we would be so happy to fly with you."

Marty smiles mischievously. "Yes, but no charge. Do not pay, this is free." Then everyone looks to Herman. He seems a bit cautious, not completely convinced, then he looks into his beautiful wife's face and he could see the longing, appealing expression and he caves in quickly. "Oh yes, I've flown before, I guess I can do it again."

When we have finished our coffee, Marty leaps up and he gives me a look that says, 'Get busy.' We start picking up plates and silverware and carrying them into the kitchen.

Katie frowns, "Oh never mind, that is my job." Marty smiles, "Not this morning, Lady, not this morning."

We set about washing and drying the breakfast dishes, while Katie busies herself getting ready to make the trip over to the church and the academy.

Finally, we file out through the picket fence gate to the street where reposes the Heilman's Model T. Herman climbs behind the wheel while Marty turns the crank in front to get the little flivver started. We all pile in, the Heilmans in front, Marty and I in back. We make our way back down Eleventh to what I notice is a turn to the left and later a turn to the right and we find our way out into the large spacious area of the convent and academy.

Katie is telling us that Ferdinand was established January 8, 1840 as a resting place for man and beast in traveling from Troy to Jasper. In those days Troy was the shipping point on the Ohio River for Dubois County. The town of Ferdinand is situated in the southwestern part of Dubois County and its land entry was the first made in Ferdinand Township. The original sale of the lots in the town plat was made in the city of Louisville, Kentucky, on the Ohio River. In 1845 a post office was established at Ferdinand. The town was incorporated in 1905 and was named in honor of Ferdinand, the then reigning emperor of Austria.

I have been here with my parents twice before, the last time only two years ago. Very little of this is news to me but Marty is hungrily eating it all up. He listens very carefully to what Katie tells us, as she goes on to explain the same things that I learned on the tour with my father, mother and my Uncle John and Aunt Helen only two years ago.

Katie Heilman says that the Sisters of Saint Benedict have enriched their religious cultural life in the locality since 1867. The Monastery Church is a most majestic and impressive piece of architecture. I can see that it has made a resounding impression upon Marty. It rises majestically above the town of Ferdinand, its Romanesque dome and its imposing title of The Monastery of Immaculate Conception. The Monastery is home to the Sisters of Saint Benedict of Ferdinand, one of the largest Benedictine communities of women in the USA.

Katie goes on to say again that the Monastery was founded in 1867 by four young German-speaking Sisters who arrived from a Covington, Kentucky Monastery to teach the town's German settlers. Over the years up to a thousand women have entered the community and Ferdinand, and their faith, spirit and energy led to the establishment of eight additional Monasteries in the United States. The Sisters minister throughout southern Indiana, in other states and even in foreign countries in areas of education, pastoral care, health care, counseling, social service and mission work. The Sisters operate two corporate ministries that are located on the Monastery's 200 acres, Marian Heights Academy, a girls college preparatory boarding and day school founded in 1870 educates students from across the United States and from seven other countries. Then there is the Kordes Enrichment Center. It is a spiritual growth center that provides a safe and sacred atmosphere for people of all faiths. Hospitality is one of the main tenets of the Benedictine rule by which the Sisters of Saint Benedict of Ferdinand live. They welcome visitors who wish to share the peace and duty of their facilities.

We arrive at the Monastery and two robed Sisters greet us very graciously to lead us through this churchly edifice. Before we entered, Marty asks to take several moments to walk around outside so he can view the imposing Roman architecture of the Monastery Church. A high dome occupies the center with long double tiered wings extending farther to either side. The ends of each wing and each tier were rounded in the dome-like design as the center. The two Sisters who greeted us at the entrance have eagerly given the equally eager Marty a thorough discourse on the Convent, the Academy and the Kordes Center as we proceed through the church. We spend a full hour in this most impressive center at Marian Heights Academy, walking about the grounds as well as driving the Model T. Even after three hours Marty seems almost too attached to this highly spiritual place to leave, but we board the little Model T and head south out of the grounds past the Academy and the long Convent road to the field where our old Waco is waiting for us, ambushed, as it were, behind a stand of large maple trees. After driving a little over a mile, we park alongside the road.

Marty and I get out of the Model T, leaving the Heilmans to wait for us as we hike across the field to the east to the large maple trees, behind which we have staked down the Waco. By this time in the morning, but almost noon, the grass is still wet on our trouser cuffs and shoes from the dew. As we reach the trees, behind them sits the old Waco waiting for us, its wings and fuselage gleaming in the sun, it still also a bit drenched but drying out from dew.

I untie the tie-down ropes, pull out the stakes, throw all the gear into the front cockpit, then climb into the rear cockpit to man my switching duties while Marty swings the prop. The first time the OX-5 coughs, backfires a time or two, the propeller kicking back and forth. Cold. Marty calls back, "Switch on." I repeat, "Switch on." He throws the prop again, the engine sputters a time or two and quits again. He lets it sit for a couple of minutes, then we repeat the process. This time the exhaust belches out a few clouds of smoke, gives a backfiring chattering noise as it usually does when cold. Marty comes running around, I climb out of the cockpit giving it over to him, then climb up on the lower wing step holding on to a wing strut. After letting the engine run for a while, he revs it up, raising the tail, whirls around, taxiing out into the open and heading back, slowly dragging along on the tail skid. A time or two he raises the tail off the ground with the elevators, gives the throttle a blast and I can see why he is doing this because the skid has gathered a lot of grass and turf which the prop blast blew away. After what seems a long while, we reached the road, swung around, dropping the tail down and letting the OX-5 idle. He motioned for me to go get the Heilmans and put them on board.

I explain to them that he doesn't want to shut the engine down; to keep it going to keep it warm. I usher them over to the lower wing step helping

Katie aboard. At that point I realized she had been carrying a package around. It was the same package I had given her last night, my helmet and goggles. She unwrapped the sack, stuffed it into a coat pocket, put on the helmet and buckled the strap under her chin, grinning mischievously at me, she said, "I will tell Katherine that I wore this helmet too."

I have now put them both aboard, strapped the seat belt, closed the little side door, jumped off the wing and gave Marty a "wave-off." Stepping aside I wait while he blasted the tail up, taxied down to the south, swung around again without stopping and opening the throttle. As they come roaring by me Katie gives me a big wave. Wearing my helmet, she looks exactly like little Katherine.

They are climbing out over Marian Heights Academy heading north, and then Marty will swing around town, heading back to the south, dropping down to the Heilman's son's farm and give little Katherine a buzz from probably about 100 foot altitude, if I know Marty, which I do. As they disappear into the distance beyond the hill I feel very alone.

Fifteen minutes pass and still no Waco. Then another fifteen minutes. They have now been in the air for 45 minutes. I begin to be a little concerned, then off to the south I can see a speck, then the two wings of the Waco coming lower and lower, closer and closer. They land and taxi up to where I stand; Marty swings the Waco around, cuts the throttle to idle, then shuts off the OX-5. I run up on the lower wing step, unlock the little door, unsnap the safety belt and help out Katie Heilman. She is absolutely beside herself, completely overjoyed, saturated with joy. "Oh, how I look forward to talking to little Katherine about this, and she will love this helmet." She was all agog, but I can tell that Herman Heilman shows some elation too, but growing rather tired.

We all gather around the plane, sitting on the grass for a while, enjoying each other. It is now just past one o'clock and Herman ventures that perhaps they should return home.

He asked, "Now, do you gentlemen intend to stay here and take up more passengers? I see no one arriving and I don't know if you will get any more passengers. But would you stay with us again this evening?"

Marty replies, "No, I have in mind flying up to the Huntingburg-Jasper area. There are some spots up there that we old barnstormers have staked out, passed around from mouth to mouth and letter by letter where we can expect to do a considerable passenger business. It will only take us a few minutes to get up there. We cruise along at about 75 mph so we can be there in no time. Our stay here is a memorable one and we truly, truly do hate to leave."

Looking back towards the Marian Heights, he said, "That place back there I shall never forget and some day I will return. it made a considerable impression on me that will last with me to the grave."

Katie Heilman surged forward, giving both of us a great huge hug. As she backed away, Herman Heilman came forward and shook both our hands, tears streaming down his cheeks. I could tell that Marty knew they wanted to be on hand to see us fly away, even though they hated for us to leave. They did not want to leave ahead of us. They want to see us depart when we did depart and Herman I suspect is very tired. Marty knew that better than I so he said, "Well, the time to go sometimes is just the time to go- He looked over at me and gave them another handshake. I did the same thing, then he nodded to me and I run back to the rear cockpit, climbed in, and waited for him to come around front to swing the prop.

The warm OX-5 started up the first crank. We both wave and taxi to the south end, swing around and come roaring past the Heilmans in their Model T, both of them waving vigorously, us waving back as we climb out over Ferdinand. Marty turns ninety degrees to the left, heading northwest for Huntingburg. We have climbed to only a few hundred feet, but dead ahead I can see Huntingburg in the distance. Southern Indiana is very rural and seems it has a timeless bucolic beauty. The towns are small, some very small, but they are surprisingly near each other at least as viewed and traveled by air. Much more so than by auto—at least in this year 1933 the roads are nicely paved, but narrow and winding. I hate to think that years far in the future will change all this. Anything that alters this rural distancing between these small towns and hamlets will be a shameful tragedy, but shamelessly achieved in the name of a rewardless progress.

Ahead and below I see a meandering creek snaking its way beneath us to the north and east of Huntingburg. I realize now that I am looking down on Hunley Creek. It brings back memories of endless, stories told by our old Boonville neighbor, Pete Miller, a talkative fellow who lived on Oak Street just a few doors east of us. Old Pete was quite a teller of what was termed 'tall tales' on Oak Street. Pete had grown up in Huntingburg and many of his tall tales had to do with his frequent fishing trips along Hunley Creek. He said he had caught any number of catfish along Hunley Creek weighing over 100 lbs. As I looked down on it now from an elevation of 500 feet, it would amaze me that a 100 lb. catfish would scarcely fit into Hunley Creek let alone being able to swim along its crooked channels and shady overhangs of willows and oaks.

Once Dad and another neighbor drove Pete to Huntingburg, taking in a Hunley Creek fishing trip. They spent the day and caught about fifty catfish, but all under ten inches long, tasty 'fiddler cats' my Dad called them. He said they fished along three miles of Hunley Creek and at the widest spot anywhere he could easily spit within ten feet of the opposite bank. That statement really infuriated old Pete. He said, "Well, you certainly ate your fill of those fifty fiddlers we caught. Now you are complaining. If you had done like I wanted, we could have stayed several days and we would have caught a few of them really big ones. But no, you had to hurry home so you could broadcast to the whole neighborhood that old Pete Miller is still just a liar, just like they all believe anyway."

Looking back to those days when I was maybe seven or eight years old, I recalled old Pete very vividly. He and his wife had no children and their marriage was a very hectic one indeed. Old Pete was quite a drinker. The story was that he made his own brew but never revealed that he did. He seldom appeared in public as a drunk but his sobriety was of a doubtful kind that was so compromised by his incessant braggadocio that you could not really tell if he was drunk or not. One incident in particular I remember vividly on a summer evening at two o'clock in the morning. Pete entered Oak Street in front of his home in his nightgown, preaching loudly and incessantly to the entire world of his marital troubles indoors. His poor portly and husky voiced wife stood in the door in her nightgown pleading for him to come inside and shut up. But he carried on for nearly a half-hour when Mr. Phillips joined in his nightgown, pleading with Pete to go to bed so the entire two blocks of neighbors could get some sleep. Mr. Phillips lived directly across the street from Pete Miller, but Pete still would not yield. He waved an old revolver, telling all that he wanted to kill himself but he had no bullets. Would someone please give him some bullets, he pleaded in a stream of tears. Mr. Phillips turned on his heels quickly, went into his own house. Two minutes later he came back out into the street and handed Pete five bullets. Pete refused the bullets, complaining his neighbors wanted him dead and immediately went back inside. Everyone along Oak Street then went back to sleep. The next morning Pete was up early, visiting his neighbors door to door as if nothing had ever happened.

As I look down on Hunley Creek now, I want to come here with Dad next summer and see if the locals had ever caught a catfish over ten inches long. And I'd like to see if I could spit across Hunley Creek within ten feet.

Suddenly I am jarred awake from my daydreams of Pete Miller. The OX-5's rpm suddenly drops from 1200 to 100. I immediately conclude the engine has quit and we are heading down for a forced landing. Then Marty is banging on the cowling behind my head and shouting. It is then that I realize he has suddenly retarded the throttle to idle speed. I turn my head to see him pointing off to the left. The hair on his bare head is streaming back in the windstream, his goggles are down around his neck. Old Marty, he likes the wind on his face on a beautiful summer day such as this. He shouts, "Dammit, look over there!" I peer off to the left. He shouts again, "No, dammit, Peyton, farther over. It's an airplane, dammit" Then I see it, bright yellow wings of a biplane and its tail a matching yellow and a black fuselage. Then Marty opens the throttle and banks sharply left and nosing down.

We pass over the big biplane at about one hundred feet. There are a half dozen people standing around it and I notice one wearing a soft white gabardine helmet with upturned goggles. obviously the pilot. I recognize the biplane as a Standard, but somehow it looks different, more modern than the old Standard **J-1** with the Hall-Scott engine, which I had taken a ride in eight years ago in 1925 when I was eight years old. The old Standard J-1 was built as a World War One trainer the same as the Curtiss JN-4 Jenny. In fact, they looked a lot alike, except the wings on the Standard J-1 seemed longer and larger. The upper wing on the Standard was higher than the Jenny. This biplane we had just passed over seemed to have the same size wings as the old J-1 but the A-frame cabanes atop the wing tips had been removed and their support cables replaced by struts that extended upward and outward from the lower wing tips to the upper wing tips. The forward cockpit was much larger than the old Standard **J-1.** Then I saw the round porthole windows at the sides of the forward cockpit, then I realized this was a Lincoln-Standard, the same Lincoln-Standard version like I had seen in September 1929 in the field next to the Poor Farm east of Boonville. I could never forget that big biplane and its Hoover-hating Democrat pilot, philosophizing on politics under the Catalpa tree next to the Boonville/DeGonia road, the big Lincoln-Standard parked nearby.

Now Marty is doing a mile-wide, slow banking turn heading back to the field where the Standard sits in the low sun. A nearby paved road bordered the field heading north into Huntingburg. Marty came in low, touching down at the west end of the field, the far end. We taxi up at a point about a hundred feet to the north side of the Standard, shut down the OX-5 and proceed to climb out. A few of the on-looking gawkers amble over to look over our Waco and perhaps to thump the fabric wings just like I am sure they had been doing to the Standard. It's a habit non-air-minded people have, kind of like kicking tires when the same types of people are looking over a new automobile.

As I approach the Standard, I quickly confirm it is identical to the one I inspected so closely in September 1929 at the Poor Farm at Boonville. But the pilot is not the same Hoover-hater of 1929. The airplane could be the same one. Damn, I wish I had memorized its Air Commerce registration number.

Marty immediately introduced himself to the pilot. They discuss at great length the genealogy of the Lincoln-Standard. It is virtually a built-from-scratch version of the old J-1 but with many improvements by the Lincoln-Standard Airplane Company of Lincoln, Nebraska. The old Standard J-1 was built by the Standard Airplane and Motor Company in New Jersey in 1916 for the U.S. Air Service as a training plane.

The fuselage of the Lincoln-Standard must be at least 18 inches wider than the old J-1 Standard because it seats four passengers in the front cockpit rather than the single passenger in the old J-1, which was originally intended to be a student pilot, not a passenger. This Lincoln version seats two facing forward and two facing rearward, facing each other. Portholes in the edge of the cockpit allowed passengers to look out without exposing so much of their heads into the windstream. The rear cockpit seats only the pilot. This Lincoln-Standard is powered by a 200 horsepower Hisso engine swinging an eight or nine foot propeller. The internal fuselage framework is trussed steel tubing, like our Waco. The old Standard J-1 fuselage was a wood framework braced with wire.

The Lincoln-Standard's pilot's name is Dave, but no one in this business seems to use last names unless they leave an address to correspond on trade secrets such as land owners throughout the Middlewest who allow barnstormers into their fields. I can see that Dave and Marty are already swapping information in highly animated conversation. Dave is a friendly fellow about Marty's age. They both hail from neighbor states, Kansas and Nebraska. They both spend summers in Illinois and Indiana where the farms are smaller and more populated with a greater passenger potential. Apparently Dave worked for Lincoln-Standard about the time his plane was built in Lincoln, Nebraska. I gather they are no longer in business of building the Lincoln-Standard. He says his was built in 1927 or 1928. He is the fourth owner. When I asked him if his Lincoln-Standard was ever flown to Boonville, Indiana in September 1929, he says he does not know but he tells me the name of the fellow who owned it then, but I never asked the Hoover-hater under the Catalpa tree his name. Dang it all, that's the trouble with being a twelve-year-old. You never mind the non-aviation details. it's just what excites you at the moment. It doesn't get much better when you are sixteen either. Like my not bringing Mother's box camera on this trip and my not taking notes and not asking questions when I should.

Dave has planned ahead in this Jasper/Huntingburg area. He has arranged with a local man for ground transportation and lodging in Huntingburg. He proposes that we join forces in flying passengers. On Saturday and Sunday we will keep both ships busy, he believes.

Even though I am only sixteen I don't feel like a juvenile and I consider myself a real expert on aviation history. Ever since I could read it has been on aviation, except for all the other subjects I had to read in school. Even Mr. Bennett, my teacher and fellow aviation compatriot, urged me to read aviation history and technology. He is my hero anyway, having been a pilot with the Royal Air Service from 1915 to 1918, starting flying training in Canada in his senior year at Purdue. I eagerly subscribed to aviation magazines like *Aviation* and *Aero Digest*. And I built my own glider with aeroplane controls and taught myself to fly. Not too bad for a 16-year-old.

For all of my expertise, I am amazed at Marty and his new friend pilot of the big 5-place Lincoln-Standard. As they talk they are expanding on the aviation history of Huntingburg, of all places. Here they are, hailing from way out in Kansas and Nebraska, and they seem to know more about Dubois County aviation history of Huntingburg and Jasper and smaller places of Dubois County than I do. Because I had read and heard of pilots and planes of this area, many others in Indiana and other states, but they know, it seems, more of the details. How can that be? As I listen it is now obvious, they have picked all of this up as barnstormers, from passengers and the few other pilots they meet. One of their great sources is O'Neil Airport over in Vincennes on the western edge of Indiana along the Wabash River. It is the usual Hoosier jumping off place for barnstormers from west of the Mississippi River heading east into Illinois and Indiana for a summer of barnstorming. They talk of Charlie Miller who they say was the first licensed pilot in Dubois County brought up in the little crossroads town of St. Henry a few miles south of this field; he moved with his family to Huntingburg in 1922. He learned to fly from Bob Gast, a veteran pilot of the great 1917-18 World War in a Curtiss Jenny. In 1928 they say he bought his first airplane, an OX-5 powered Standard. According to this Dave fellow, Charlie Miller was a cousin of Leslie Miller who invented the Miller roller rocker arm valve improvement for the OX-5 and I believe was the man who was big in racing car engine improvements for the Indianapolis 500 Memorial Day Race Cars.

Huntingburg and Jasper, even at my age of sixteen are not new places to me. It is my first time here in a plane, or anywhere else by plane for that matter. My plane rides have all been limited to rides with barnstormers circling Boonville, but I've done a dozen of those in almost as many different planes. My several trips to this area have been with Dad and the Boonville baseball team, traveling here by auto or train. Southern Indiana has always been awash in baseball teams, some very good teams and players, like Ed Rausch of Oakland City who someday will be honored in the Hall of Fame. Games where Dad and the Boonville team played the Huntingburg team was in the field at the Huntingburg Fairgrounds.

The sun is low and now it is Friday afternoon. We look forward tomorrow to a busy day of flying passengers. Most of the locals who have been hanging around the Lincoln-Standard have now dispersed and gone, leaving just Marty and I and Dave. Dave saunters over to the Waco and he says, "What are you fellows planning to do this evening? Have you made any arrangements to stay in Huntingburg overnight?" Marty kind of smiles, lowers his head and says, "Well, we spend most of our time in the sack under the wing, rolled up in our blankets."

Dave's eyebrows lifted and he seemed surprised. He says, "That's a rather hardy life, isn't it? I have plans all along the way where I can room and board, stay in hotels or whatever." Marty replies, "Well, that's admirable, but I don't see how you can afford it as a barnstormer."

Dave looks amused. "Of course I can carry twice as many passengers as your Waco. Of course, my engine burns twice the amount of fuel of your OX-5. I guess you could say I'm not really in this crazy business for money."

Marty nods vigorously in agreement. He says, "It does amount to a matter of economy. If you don't have money to buy gas, you are a little bit stranded out in these rural fields with no way to go on."

"Anyway," Dave says, "I have made arrangements with a gentleman here by the name of Henry Kornbrath. Mr. Kornbrath is an older gentleman who has his own auto and I have made arrangements through a friend, which I conducted by mail, that Mr. Kornbrath would carry us to and from and who has made arrangements with a fuel truck to bring out fuel and also arrangements to put me up for the night in the St. George Hotel. Are you familiar with it?" Marty says, "No, I'm not familiar with it. It's really the first time I've touched down in Huntingburg, but my young friend Peyton here has made several trips here. He lives down in Boonville, not too far away."

I answered the question with, "In fact, I have more than heard of it. My Dad has brought me up here several times in past summers with his baseball team. Once we stayed in the St. George, which is on Geiger Street, between Fifth and Fourth, I believe."

Dave looked a little surprised. "Yes, that's what Mr. Kornbrath tells me, it's on Geiger Street. He also tells me that the hotel is quite old and a number of the rooms have been closed off but there are portions of it in which rooms are still available for customers. The hotel dining room has long since closed and we will have to eat at one of the local eateries around near the hotel. I'm sure he can make arrangements for you two fellows to have a room, or he also tells me there are some rooms available and upstairs accommodations in some of the store buildings around in that area of the downtown part of Huntingburg. He should be here in about thirty minutes to check up on us. He tells me when he was out here yesterday that he'll bring his new Model A Ford touring car. He calls it new but it is one of the earliest models, about a 1930 or '31, I think. Large enough to carry us three, I'm sure."

Marty looks puzzled, "Well now wait a minute. One of the reasons why we sleep out with our plane is to guard it during the night. Now I know that southern Indiana does not abound with vandals who cruise around in the night tearing up aeroplanes, but at least it gives us a feeling of comfort if we are nearby to stand guard over our beautiful ship."

Dave's eyebrows lift again and he gives a little nod. "Well, here again it's a matter of planning ahead. Now Mr. Kornbrath has arranged for a young man to come out and stand guard over the Standard and the Waco, as well it turns out."

Marty says, "Great. Well then, Peyton, how about it, shall we go in and have a little bed rest for a change?" I reply, "Well, we did pretty well at Ferdinand with the Heilman folks."

No sooner had we spoken until a Model A Ford pulled up with two aboard. They came around the fence, walked over to the planes joining us. The older man introduced himself as Henry Kornbrath. The young man he introduced simply as Sam. Immediately after introductions, confirmation of our hotel rooms in Huntingburg with Mr. Kornbrath, Dave set about hauling out his stakes and tie-down ropes and we did the same with the Waco. After tying down the planes, we ambled over to the Model A, Dave climbed in beside Mr. Kornbrath and Marty and I climbed in the rear seat, leaving young Sam as night watchman. Mr. Kornbrath did a U-turn in the road heading north back to Huntingburg. I remembered this route when up here with my Dad two or three times before. The very first time was in our old Maxwell. As we drive up along Main Street, I see First Street, then Second Street, Third Street and Fourth. I thought back as we passed First Street that we used to turn right there and head east over to the old Fair grounds where the baseball park was located, a distance of about five blocks from Main Street. Now as we drive along, we get up to Fourth Street, turn left a block and we are on Geiger, and then up a ways on Geiger to the entrance of the hotel. I can remember it very clearly now. It looks very old. Even older than before.

Marty and I are dragging along our meager bags of belongings, changes of underwear, and he and his shaving kit. We take one room and Dave takes another. The room we take has two narrow beds and a window looking out on Geiger Street and over to the corner of Fifth and Geiger. Both our rooms are on the second floor. The manager tells us that the dining room is no longer operating and is closed off. We can see the old dining room door and some of the early menus on the door. The manager tells us of a few eateries along Fourth, one over on Fifth and another on Main Street. Common bathrooms are available on each floor. Marty and I take one and Dave takes the other. We shower and clean up a bit and meet him in the lobby about thirty minutes later. At that time we say we will have a little pow wow and decide where we are going to walk around to case the different cafes where we might partake of a little dinner.

As we walk down to Fourth Street, looking for a cafe, Dave tells us that he has gassed up his Standard earlier in the afternoon before we arrived and did we want Mr. Kornbrath to have the gas truck come out to fuel up our Waco? Marty tells him that we are probably okay up until the afternoon of the next day. When Kornbrath arrives the next morning to take us out to the planes Marty tells Dave that he would make an estimate of about when we would need some gas and to have the truck come out to fuel us up then.

The eatery we select is on Fourth Street. Very nice, like home cooked meals. We take our time sipping coffee and it is a great entertainment to me hearing Marty and Dave swapping stories and information about their barn-storming days. Dave says that he has flown several Huntingburg passengers in the last few days while we were in Ferdinand. He expects we will do a thriving business, because tomorrow is Saturday and then Sunday we will get even more passengers. He thinks we will have a very busy time of it. Monday he expects to take off for Bedford, Indiana and then from that point he expects to slowly make his way back to Nebraska across southern Indiana and Illinois. Marty tells him that we plan to head east from here, then work our way south again down to the Ohio River. We still have a few weeks ahead of us, Marty tells Dave as he gives me an amusing smile while I am having a kind of a worried look thinking maybe he is trying to speed up our trip too fast. It can last forever as far as I'm concerned. Marty expects his trip from Boonville through southern Illinois in September will be long flights with not much passenger flying on the way as we are doing now. He expects to hangar the Waco for the winter in Kansas, reaching there in late September or early October. Dave nods his head and shakes his head at the same time, saying, "Yes, when winter closes in it's not a good idea to be flying these biplanes around in snowstorms. We can get some real dandies in October, especially out in Kansas and Nebraska."

The next morning we all meet down on Geiger Street before the hotel and walk over to the eatery we had dinner in the evening before. We also meet Henry Kornbrath there and sit around a big table for our breakfast. Mr. Kornbrath tells us that he has already driven out to the planes and has talked to his watchman Sam. Sam told him that he had spent a comfortable night sleeping in the big cockpit of the Lincoln-Standard, everything was okay, no vandals had arrived, no problems had arisen at all. Once in a while he would get out of the plane and walk around, look things over, climb back up and go to sleep. Marty tells Mr. Kornbrath that he believes we have enough fuel in the Waco to fly passengers until about two or three o'clock in the afternoon. Kornbrath answers that he would be on hand before two p.m. He would drive into town and have the fuel truck come out to the plane.

Here again I am all ears listening to the stories from the mouths of Marty and Dave of their flying exploits. Their exploits were many and every one just as interesting as the last. Dave tells about how he had flown cargo in the Standard for farmers over in southern Illinois. There weren't many passengers to carry in some of the outlying districts in the prairie country, but that he got several jobs of ferrying farm tools from one farm to the other. Also he did quite a business just carrying freight from one little town to another.

Finishing breakfast we all filed out and into Henry Kornbrath's Model A heading south out to the planes. When we arrived young Sam was there to greet us. He seemed very cheerful and very much full of energy, having spent the night just sleeping in the plane, which must have been rather sporadic because he said that he arose four or five times during the night just to do a walk-around check for trouble. He was carrying a big flashlight. It amused me that he said he had examined every bush and fence row around the planes looking for hidden vandals and he had found none.

Marty and I pick up the tail of the Waco and swing it around to have it headed out into the field before we start the engine, then go through our usual procedure of him swinging the prop and me doing the switching off and switching on. We run the engine for about eight or ten minutes to warm it up, then shut it down again because no passengers have arrived. It is still early, the sun having only been up about thirty minutes. Then we walk over to the Standard and Dave and Mr. Kornbrath and Sam lifting up the tail of the Standard turning it around facing the field. I thought it would be rather interesting to see how they started it because the big Hisso was over twice the horsepower of the OX-5 and it swung a much heavier and longer propeller. In the last few days Dave had trained Mr. Kornbrath and Sam on how to pull the prop. It took two of them. Sam would grasp the propeller blade with his left hand and reach out with his right hand while Kornbrath grasped it. Then on command from Dave they would both pull together. Once it had passed through its arc at the bottom of its swing, they would throw themselves out of the way in case the engine started or the propeller recoiled backward from the compression of the engine. It seemed to me that Mr. Kornbrath was too old to be doing this hazardous task even though he was in the second position.

The two man propeller swinging crew was one my school teacher, Al Bennett, described the starting of the old 12-cylinder Liberty 400 horsepower engines for the DeHaviland 4's which he flew during the war when flying for the British. They had to be very careful. A really clumsy and rather awkward operation to say the least. But Dave had these two well trained. Once they started to turn the propeller they had to keep going. If the engine started and began to rotate even two or three rpm's, the propeller was really a killer, if a blade tip hit a person in the head or shoulders. So the propullers must lunge sideways and fall to the ground out of the way of the rotating blade tips.

On our OX-5 one man could grasp the propeller blade with both hands, and then swing down and run with the arc of rotation off to one side in much the same manner the two were doing here on the Standard. It was much easier to pull the OX-5 through, the torque of the engine being much less.

The big Hisso started reluctantly, belching out smoke, chugging along for several minutes, Dave letting it warm up. They had chocks in front of the wheels, Dave holding the tail down with the elevators.

Four young men came walking through the gap in the fence asking if we were carrying passengers. They came up to the Waco first; we said yes. They ambled over to Dave and he said yes. They asked Dave if he would carry all four of them or if he would be just as happy to let two of them fly in the Standard, then two in the Waco. Dave seemed a little hesitant to answer because it was much more economical for him to fly four at a time, but then he looked over at Marty and the Waco and he said, "Aw what the heck, two of you go with one plane, two with the other." Marty agreed with Dave that we would charge $3.00 a ride, the same that we had been doing recently on our trip. Marty took off first, then followed by Dave in the big Standard. With both planes in the air, at least two dozen prospective passengers had shown up within ten minutes. Flying passengers begets passengers. Having a plane or planes in the air is the best kind of advertising.

I found Mr. Kornbrath to be a very interesting man. He knew all about the county Fairgrounds and the County Fair of Dubois County and I told him about our visits to the Fairgrounds with my Dad and the baseball team. He knew all about the Boonville team and the Huntingburg teams, far more than I did. He knew all the players, some of whom I had never really bothered to remember their names.

He said he had been a brick mason and a carpenter most of his life. The airplanes were not a new thing to him, but were an infrequent thing. He only remembered the barnstormers that came through once or twice a year, but then one of the local businessmen had approached him with this letter that he had received from Dave asking for a contact man, so he thought he'd take the job. Sam was just a young fellow who had apprenticed for Mr. Kornbrath on brick laying and carpenter jobs.

I have told Kornbrath at great length of my flying exploits, my glider building and glider flying. His responses were all polite oohs and aahs. He wondered if I had a photograph I might be carrying around with me, which of course I did not, and I am afraid it cast a bit of a doubt in his mind about my stories, which I proceed to elaborate even more to take the place of the photographs that I did not have.

By now there were at least two dozen people standing around to be attended to while the planes were still in the air. So Mr. Kornbrath and I are going through the crowd one by one asking them if they wanted to buy a plane ride. We took their $3.00 and gave them a ticket off our ticket rolls.

Coming in from the east over the road was the big Standard. It touched down a few hundred yards the other side of the road, came to a stop down at the lower end of the field as Dave blasted the tail up high enough to swing around and taxi back up to the road and the gathering of potential passengers. In the meantime, Marty came in over the road, fishtailing back and forth, landed, turned around and taxied back up to the crowd.

Hot air balloon ascension by Captain Allen. "Cap" Allen did a successful triple drop on 3 parachutes. Peyton worked for Allen during the Warrick Fair in the early 1930s as an airminded lad.

CHAPTER VIII

The busiest barnstorming days I had ever seen were at the Warrick County annual fair. Barnstormers used the same field where I flew my gliders. On the busiest day the largest crowd waiting for a plane ride would be two dozen people. Many of those would tire of waiting and trudge back over to the Fair Grounds, spending their money on hamburgers, catfish sandwiches, pop, and the sideshows along the midway. A typical barnstormer at the Warrick Fair was one airplane and a lone pilot. Now, here at Huntingburg (and with no Fair in progress) there are two airplanes busy all day flying six passengers every fifteen minutes.

The crowd standing around on the field at the edge of the road numbers as many as a hundred. Some are onlookers while most bought tickets, waiting their turn to see the Huntingburg and Jasper area from the air. The onlookers reap a bounty in free entertainment. They can not only watch the planes landing, taking off, loading and unloading, but can carry on endless discussion with other onlookers, to gossip in a friendly way about who among friends or acquaintances were brave enough to fly. Such as: "Why there is old John Steinbrook climbing in that big plane. Why I'd never thought that old fellow would ever risk his life in an airplane. He's never owned or believed in automobiles or swore never to own or drive one. Always drives his horse and buggy. Why his sons are not even with him urging him into the plane. He is all alone, made the decision on his own. And he is tight-fisted with his money, too! Three dollars for a plane ride? Why he don't spend no more than three dollars a month and that's always at the store for something he can't grow on his farm. I tell you these plane pilots are making a fortune here."

The day wears on with the Waco and Standard flying passengers continually. At 3 o'clock, old faithful Henry Kornbrath shows up in his Model A, followed by his gasoline truck driver. Marty and I and the gas truck driver busy ourselves filling the Waco's fuel tank while fidgety ticket holders look on. When we are through gassing the Waco, the tank truck driver pulls over awaiting the returning Standard, its Hisso no doubt thirsty for a drink of gasoline. Before the Standard taxis up,

Marty has taken off with his two fidgety ticket holders, a couple of young, enthusiastic farm hands. As the Standard pilot shuts down the Hisso for the gassing up, its four passengers hurriedly extricate themselves from the big front cockpit. Henry Kornbrath and I observe this extrication with some amusement. Two of the passengers spotted me as Marty's assistant, running over almost in a panic, out of breath with an exciting message.

"We seen the little plane crash over yonder this side of Duff. Crashed into a barn up there." I couldn't believe it! Mr. Kornbrath immediately began to question the excited youth as to exactly where the Waco had gone down. I run over to the Standard's cockpit where Dave still sat, seemingly unperturbed.

"Dave, two of your passengers said Marty has just now been forced down and crashed into a barn up northwest of here. Did you see it?"

Dave looked surprised and began to lift himself up from the cockpit, then he called to Henry, and saying quickly to me, "Hell no, I didn't see the Waco go down. I saw him heading northwest about three miles out as we came in. I can't believe it. Sometimes these farm boys get all excited about airplanes like as if they are always supposed to crash." Henry tells us he knew exactly the location. He and I would drive up there the three or four miles.

Dave says, "Soon as I'm gassed up I'll swing over there and take a look but I cannot help from the air. You and Peyton drive on up there right now. If it's true I'll return here and get someone to drive me up and we will see what we can do to help Marty."

As Mr. Kornbrath and I enter Huntingburg from the south, I thought he must have heard the young observer wrong because we seem to be heading north all the way through town. I distinctly heard the boy say it was northwest of our field at a little place called Duff. In all the times I had been up here with Dad and his Boonville baseball team I had never heard of Duff, but Henry Kornbrath has lived here all of his life and he was over four times my age. Maybe that was the problem. Maybe he could not hear and even if he could hear he did not want to hear, as Dad used to say about Grandpa when they got into a political argument. I figured we would turn left off Main Street at about the cross street where we always turned right to go to the Dubois Fair grounds and its baseball field where Boonville played Huntingburg.

But Mr. Kornbrath keeps going through the center of town staying on Main Street. Finally, when we have almost left town, he turns left on Twelfth Street when I would have sworn he should have turned left at First Street much further back. At least we were now headed west and he could tell I was getting real nervous, so he presses the Model A up to 35 miles per hour, to him a breakneck speed. He must now feel like a real daredevil.

We are now out of town driving along some of the inner farms. The road is dusty and the Model A touring car has its top down. We pass a car heading in to Huntingburg and so encounter his clouds of dust for the next two miles because the air is windless and hot. Now we have turned gradually north and west and I note a weathered sign on a telephone pole announcing we are on Duff Road. Then Kornbrath points off to the right and up ahead. All I can see is a farmhouse, a barn and some smaller outbuildings. Then we turn off to the left on a side road. After a mile we can see beyond the barn, unobstructed by the house as it had been from the Duff Road. Then my heart skipped a real big beat. I can see the bright silver wing of the Waco. As I peer through the dust it at least appears the airplane is not on its back. If it were I could likely see the landing gear protruding above the wing. Soon Henry turns up a long lane into the farm. Now I can see that the silver winged biplane with its red fuselage is nosed up near the barn. Whether it has crashed into the barn and fallen back down I can not tell. Now I see figures walking around the plane. I pray to God that my friend Marty and his passengers bore no injury or worse heaven forbid.

Now at last we are pulling into the barnyard but the Waco is out of view behind the barn. I cannot contain myself as I leap from the car before it has stopped and before my elderly driver has switched off the engine. I am over-whelmed with confusion and joy as I round the corner of the barn. There sits our old Waco, apparently all in one undamaged piece, sitting on its landing gear and the old OX-5 softly ticking over, its undamaged propeller at the slowest idle rpm it would run without stopping. Marty and his two young passengers are back at the tail, lifting it up and turning the airplane around so that it is facing the hayfield behind the barn. The field in which the plane had apparently landed.

Then Marty spots me and his expression is of utter surprise and dismay, which he soon puts into full verbal expression. He erupts, "What in hell are you doing here? How in hell did you get here?" Then he sees Henry Kornbrath come around the corner. "Good Lord, what are you two doing out here?"

All I can stammer out in embarrassment was, "We thought you crashed into this here barn." My tongue is all twisted when I try to speak, on the verge of outright tears. Marty's face reddened, he strokes his moustache, comes over, grabs both my shoulders, looks me in the eye very seriously, gently raps my cheek with the knuckles of his right hand. Then he explains, "Not to worry but I'm sorry."

As he spoke the whole scene is enmeshed in a roar of loud noise. The Standard roars over at less than fifty feet above the barn, its passengers and pilot peering downward. it makes a wide turn to the north and back, takes a closer look, wagging its wings in salute. Dave now knows all is okay. Then Marty went on, "Gee, I'm sorry. I thought nothing of it. My passengers here are brothers. This is their place. The folks over there near the fence are their parents, brothers and sisters. They asked me over at the field if they paid me an extra $3.00 would I land on their home place for the family to see their aviator friend. I said I'd look it over from the air and if big enough I'd land. We came to a stop only 20 feet from the barn wall. There is a fence at the other end, which we passed over. Their Dad has now lowered seventy-five feet of it so we can stretch the take-off across the fence line and use the adjacent field in case we need it. The boys are staying. Peyton, you and Henry want to ride back with me?"

I said, "Sure, but Mr. Kornbrath has no way to get his Ford back over to the barnstormers' field at Huntingburg."

Kornbrath quickly agreed, "Ja, ja, I must take auto back for help to Sam and Mr. Dave." He seemed relieved that the Ford gave him an alibi. With that he expresses his gladness that no one has been hurt or the plane damaged and made his way back to the Model A.

But to me I was so happily relieved that I had no fear; I would fly anywhere with Marty. Heck, this take-off is nothing. We walk out to the end of the field making sure the uprooted fence posts were laid aside so the plane could pass through. The two young farmer passengers leveled the sod along the fence row, then laid nail-free planks over the top. I figure by the time we reach this point the wheels will be a couple feet off the ground anyway.

We make our way back to the Waco, its OX-5 still kicking over. The farm boys had placed old fence posts for chocks, which we withdrew. I climbed in the front, Marty in back; he opened the throttle wide, lifting the tail off the ground and sending a blast of hay chaff against the barn and we are on our way, gaining speed through the cut alfalfa. About 100 feet short of the laid fence and I feel the tail dip down and the nose go up and we are airborne, clearing the fence row by a good six feet. We climb out to about five hundred feet, banking to the east over Huntingburg, then southwest until we reach a point about two miles west of our field, then make a landing approach and touchdown. As we taxi up near the road I see that the crowd is still as big as ever. Autos and equine vehicles are parked all along the road. The Standard is in the air with four passengers no doubt. As we taxi up, Marty swings the Waco about for the next take-off, and I hop out, approaching the dozen or so waiting passengers who still stand by with Waco tickets I have sold them, get the first two aboard, strapped in and Marty takes off.

This routine goes on until 8:30 p.m. with both airplanes stopping only to exchange passengers. By this time most of the onlookers have left, no doubt with the conclusion that these airplane contraptions are here to stay after all. The remaining ticket holders faithfully stayed to the last man, child or woman, all exulting at the thrill of seeing a Dubois County sunset from the air.

We are all so tired but enthused, all of us, Marty, me, Dave, Sam and even Mr. Kornbrath who seemed more so. All the passengers have gone. With the engines shut down and the people all gone the silence is almost deafening as we stake down both planes and prepare to board the Model A for Huntingburg, a bath, dinner and bed. Young Sam seems very tired but pretending not to show it. None of us have eaten since breakfast. I remember that Sam had sat up all last night with the planes, just he and the crickets and the mosquitoes. Since I am the other barnstormer's handyman, I feel guilty as though it was now my turn, otherwise Sam would have to sleep out here again tonight. When I expressed the notion to Marty he frowned but gave me a very appreciative look. He said, "It's a hell of a nice gesture but you aren't obligated. We are on our own, but Dave and Sam and Kornbrath are a real asset to us. But you will be compensated, and so will Sam if I have anything to say about it. And I'm sure Dave will agree."

I said, "No, it's okay, we've both done it before, but maybe someone could bring me a hamburger or something." At that Marty laughs loudly. "You bet. I'll square it all with Dave." As they all drive away to the St. George and the Fourth Street eatery, I feel very lonely, but still very secure. In the big front cockpit of the Standard I can curl up just like in a bed.

Thirty minutes later, Henry Kornbrath returns with a big brown bag—two large hot hamburgers, a bottle of milk and other goodies for morning breakfast. As the old man drives away he says, "I'll see you early tomorrow, young man."

After the two burgers and a half a quart of milk, I get ever so sleepy, oh how so sleepy, even the sound of the crickets I have to strain to hear, and no mosquitoes, so far, in Huntingburg. A real blessing.

I rummage the gear of our Waco, using the duffel bag as a pillow and a blanket I convert the cockpit of the Standard into my old bedroom at 420 Oak in Boonville. I sleep like a log or a granite rock until two automobiles running along the road wake me up. I pull out the old Pocket Ben. It is daylight at 5 a.m. in the morning! I can not believe it! I hurry up cleaning up my bed and storing the bags over by the Waco, wolfed down the rolls, doughnuts and milk from the brown paper bag. Then I set about unstaking the airplanes and rejoicing at the beautiful day dawning. I think about Marty in our room at the St. George all by himself. Then I begin laughing uproariously out here all by myself when I think of the $64 question none of us had thought to ask last night: Who was going to wake up Marty from his cacophonic symphony of snoring?

By 8 o'clock I am getting bored and nervous. About a half dozen people have shown up and are standing around asking dumb questions and fingering the planes. Still no sign of Marty and Dave or even Henry and Sam. It is almost 9 o'clock before the Model A drives up with all four of them. Both Marty and Dave look very sleepy. It turns out that Henry and Sam had to wake them both by banging on their room doors. When Henry tells that so matter-of-factly I break out in a fit of laughter as I catch Marty's eye and sheepish expression. He says, "Aw, dammit, Peyton, knock it off." It just makes me laugh louder and longer. Kornbrath and Sam look perplexed by all of the laughter I am putting forth.

This is Sunday. The day starts off very slowly because everyone has gone to church except me, Marty and Dave, the barnstorming, vagabond heathens. Even Mr. Kornbrath leaves for church soon after he delivers Marty and Dave. He even takes Sam with him. He tells us they'd return before noon. They have even been to early mass before they woke up our two sleepy pilots at the St. George.

I wonder about my own folks back in Boonville on a beautiful Sunday morning such as this. I'm sure they miss me as much as I miss them. If I were there I'd also miss Marty and the old Waco and its smell of doped fabric.

At about 11 a.m. people start showing up. Dave is nervously prancing around, anxious to get in the air. He is taking the Standard up on a promotional flight over the Huntingburg and Jasper area to remind the populace of Dubois County that we are still at the field and anxious to carry passengers. So I proudly do the switching on the Standard while Marty and Dave pull the propeller through its priming and starting exercise. As the Hisso starts, Dave hurries around the lower wingtip, literally jerking me out while juggling the mag and throttle, fearful I have somehow deviated from his instructions, which I have not.

Dave takes off with his light, unloaded big yellow and black ship heading for a low flight over town, then on to Jasper to give them the same treatment. He is in the air for nearly a half-hour. By the time Sam and Henry return at noon the crowd has grown to the size of yesterday. By mid-afternoon it doubles and both airplanes are kept busy until almost nine o'clock. We are all very tired, but not so tired as yesterday for we had not really started real action on paying passengers until about 11:30 a.m. on Sunday. At 9 o'clock everyone has returned home to get a night's sleep and to begin the coming week on the farms of Dubois County, or their stores and shops in Huntingburg. We stake down the planes and Sam stays to watch over them for the night.

As Henry Kornbrath drives us in to the St. George he is saying to Marty, "Well, Mr. Marty, our friend Mr. Dave is leaving for Bedford tomorrow and you told me yesterday you and your friend would like to see some more of Dubois County and its history before you leave. I will be glad to drive you anywhere you want to go. Your young friend knows quite a bit of it for he has been here before. I have some odd jobs to do this week in town. You could use my car to look around while I'm at work."

Marty is elated beyond description and says so in his most eloquent fashion as he is wont to do whenever the occasion presents itself.

Henry leaves the three of us at the St. George saying he will pick us up tomorrow to take us out to the field to help Dave get on his way to Bedford.

After taking turns in the tiny shower of the St. George's common bathroom, the three of us make our way to the same eatery and saloon. In fact, the place is closed and the proprietor recognizes us as "the aviators," welcoming us in and locked the door. This is our last evening to enjoy a delightful repast with Dave. Hearing he and Marty talk planes and pilots in the years before 1933 leaves me all ears and my brain full of stories I'll never forget. We don't leave the place until midnight. Dave leaves the owner a $10 tip besides the $5 meal each of us had. I have turned over the Waco proceeds to Marty and between the two of them as they count it all out I have never seen so much money in all of my life. Mostly all in dollar bills. Between the two of them they must have taken in $500, most of which was Dave's because his plane carried twice as many passengers. Out of that they paid Mr. Kornbrath's gas tank truck man who runs a fuel supply business in Huntingburg. He delivers the fuel to the planes for twenty cents a gallon which did not sound like much to me.

In the morning we are met by Kornbrath at the eatery for a breakfast of ham and eggs, biscuits and coffee, heading out to the planes with a sack of hot rolls and milk for Sam who had the Standard all unstaked and ready to go. We stand around for a while to say our good-byes, which takes nearly two hours. I do the switching again on the Standard which pleases me very much for it meant Dave was satisfied with my brief test of yesterday doing the same thing. Dave and Marty pull the cold Hisso's propeller through its starting with billows of black smoke and coughing until it quickly warms up. Dave gives us a wave and takes off to the west, swinging around and flying low over us, rocking the wings back and forth in salute, then heads off to the northwest.

Sam and I have become good but brief friends in our duties as barnstormers' flunkies. When his father drives up to take him home I sure hate to see him go, promising to show him my glider if he comes to Boonville next summer.

I have told Marty of the Huntingburg Fair many times so as we head in to Huntingburg we turn right on First Street. He smiles and says, "Yes, I'm sure Henry here knows the way." I blush and stutter, "No, I know he knows how to get there," then teasing again, Marty quips, "Sure, I know. You just wanted to make sure we know that you know how to get there."

Turning off Main on First, we drive for five blocks until we see a large shady grove on our right and an entrance road. Adjacent to the grove stood the old grandstand facing the baseball field and grounds for all of the events of the big Dubois County Fair. It was for all the world like our Warrick County Fair on the Boonville Fair grounds. As at the Warrick Fair the Dubois annual week-long event had everything: all sorts of agricultural and craft exhibits, food stands, side shows, horse racing, balloonists' ascensions, acrobats, high dives, you name it. Along with a steady carnival atmosphere of Ferris Wheels, Merry-go-rounds, and small con games by traveling specialists in the art of relieving the rubes of their hard earned farm labor wages, but below the point where the local sheriff needed to intercede. We stand in the grove looking at the grandstand, Kornbrath tells many stories of the Fair's history and things he had remembered or had been told about at its beginning in 1887 up to the present day of 1933. The Dubois and Warrick fairs are typical of hundreds of counties throughout middle America. I hope the county fairs will always be with us. They are as much a true representation of America as apple pie, the flag and The Star Spangled Banner. I pray it will always be forever as it is now in this year of 1933.

Before we drive into Huntingburg, the problem of leaving the Waco unattended is discussed and solved. Henry suggested the same trick we had used at Ferdinand. We had taxied the ship far back into the long field; an old farm implement road bordering the field had been used by Henry to pick us up in the Model A.

Now we leave the Fair grounds, Henry driving to the northwest end of town where he is doing a remodeling job on a house, telling us to return at 5:30 this evening to pick him up. Marty insists we not only compensate him for the day's use of the auto but fill the gas tank as well. We then drive to the town hall down on Geiger Street. Marty is fascinated with the architecture of this big old style, brick, two-story building. It is very high for a two-story building, topped with a fancy, shuttered, clock tower. Henry had told us it was completed in 1886. It was originally intended and used as both a town hall and a fire engine house. But over the years has served as a courthouse, a school, an opera house on the upper floor, and as a theatre, and at one time, part of it as a jail. Marty thought its architecture was very similar to Independence Hall in Philadelphia.

As I look on the stately, timeless old building, I think back when I first saw it on my first Boonville baseball team trip here in 1925 when I was eight years old. This old building stands out in my memory. It is now 47 years old but in nice condition. Its style of architecture makes it appear older than it is. I am amazed that Dave knew so much of Huntingburg. He regularly does much advanced research on the towns he has visited or intends to visit in Illinois and Indiana on his barnstorming tours. It is he who tells Marty and I that Huntingburg was founded in 1837 by a Colonel Jacob Geiger, and of course, is the namesake of Geiger Street in Huntingburg where we stayed at the St. George Hotel.

Huntingburg is a town of many churches and the one that attracts Marty in his excursion about the city is Salem Church; it is one of the oldest in the area. The church we see as Salem Church, Henry Kornbrath tells us, is the third on this site with the same name. The first church on this site dates back to 1843 and was constructed of logs, replaced by a larger structure in 1859. The present church, a magnificent edifice, was dedicated on December 7, 1890. The dedication itself was a great event well known and well announced throughout southern Indiana. The old Airline Railway ran excursions from all points in southern Indiana and even over into Kentucky. These excursion trains were used for this occasion, some coming all the way from Evansville and Boonville and from Louisville, Kentucky over to the east and south. Each coach was crowded to its limit. The records tell us it was a gray, cold day of sleet and wind but, nevertheless, the great crowd of several hundreds of people awaited at the doors until it was announced they would enter and participate in the dedication ceremonies.

Besides Salem, there is the Methodist Church, St. Mary's Catholic Church, Central Christian Church, Church of the Nazarene, Calvary Baptist Church, and the Lutheran Church.

The Salem Church is most impressive in its architecture and that is what impressed Marty who has a hankering for great buildings. I think he must have been a frustrated architect, but airplanes and barnstorming won out long ago. The Salem Church is a tall edifice. It has pointed spires on each corner of the forefront, and a bell tower topped by a long spire, which reaches far up into the sky.

Next we drive out to the Uhl Pottery and Pressed Brick Company plant and kilns. Marty seemed interested in the Uhl Pottery process; to me it was very dull, all I could think about was getting back to the old Waco. But I did know something about Uhl Pottery. As I remembered, my parents and other older persons remembered that Uhl Pottery actually started out in Evansville and the story was that in years earlier the clay they used in the area around Evansville was inferior. They discovered the clay in Dubois County was more suitable and they had shipped it down on barges from Grandview, which was transported from Dubois County down to Grandview and thence down the Ohio River to Evansville. Later, this illogical process of transporting caused the company to move their plant to Huntingburg. This was many years ago. It has always been in Huntingburg in my young mind.

After visiting Uhl Pottery, we drive out to the Huntingburg Furniture Company, an old building strung along the railroad tracks. The furniture is manufactured by hand as well as with power machinery. Very fine furniture is turned out in Huntingburg as well as Jasper, a major local industry.

Going back to Main Street, we head north making our way to Jasper, a distance of about ten miles. After five miles Marty pulls off to the side of the road pointing out to the east. He says, "Gee, that is a nice looking field there, all freshly cut hay and must be over a half mile long. I wonder if we shouldn't bring the Waco up here in a day or two and see if we can't fly a few more passengers." I say, "Gee, that would be in the early part of the week. Today is Monday, we probably wouldn't get very many passengers. Most of the people back in Huntingburg have already flown or known about us."

He replies, "It's still a good field, I think maybe we ought to try it. Anyway, I'd like to make a landing and take-off here." So we continued on into Jasper.

In the last few days we'd flown over Jasper but had not actually driven in here. Henry Kornbrath had told us a lot about the place and for that matter, so had Dave the Standard pilot.

As we enter Jasper a landmark stands out very prominently; St. Joseph's Catholic Church, which immediately attracts Marty. It is a tall, large church much like Salem in Huntingburg. Jasper as well as Huntingburg is a first for Marty but I have been to Jasper several times before with my parents and my Dad's baseball team. St. Joseph's is on Kundek Street just a block west of Main. Marty, as usual, is very impressed. He walks all around the structure looking up at it, seeming to measure it in his mind's eye, holding up his fingers to sight over the tips of his fingers to measure its height, and many other contortions that I'm not sure I understand. According to Henry and Dave, early pioneers and settlers came to Jasper following the signing of the Treaty of Greenville, by which the Indians vacated much of Indiana and left it open for settlement. Archaeological evidence indicates that numerous Indian settlements existed in the area throughout several thousand years prior to the treaty. The last Indians to live in the area have descendants who still live here, according to Henry. Prior to the Indians' departure, pioneers visited the Jasper area from Vincennes, principally to hunt game in this heavily wooded area.

The first settlers had come to the area following two general overland routes: the Buffalo Trace which crossed the Ohio River at a place called The Falls of the Ohio in the Louisville-New Albany area. The old Troy Road which brought settlers northwest from the Ohio River. Many of these came down the Ohio on barges from Cincinnati or Pittsburgh debarking at New Albany or Troy, proceeding thence by road northward to Dubois County. The city of Jasper was named by Elander Enlow, the daughter of one of the first families to reside in the area. She is said to have rejected suggestions that the new city be given her name or a variation of it. She selected the name Jasper from the Book of Revelations (Chapter 21, Verse 19). According to Dave, this general area and the city of Jasper was first settled in about 1818. The county courthouse was moved to Jasper from Portersville in 1830 when Jasper was made the county seat.

I have never had so much fun in all my life. Here we are driving around with Marty at the wheel of Henry Kornbrath's old Model A, the top down. I had never looked upon Jasper in the way that I am looking upon it now. It just looks like a different town, doing different things in a different way. After looking at all of the churches and sizing up their architecture, Marty makes a few notes on that subject and then we cruise around looking at other buildings, stop at a few stores, acting like shoppers, then back out to the car again and drive another block or two. Finally, about noon, he heads out of Jasper to the northwest; we end up in the little town of Ireland. I can barely remember driving through there once for a short period with my Dad and some of his baseball team. Just a little crossroads place. We go into a little cafe, having lunch and coffee. After an hour of this relaxation, we head back to Jasper again, do some more driving around in Jasper, then head back south to Huntingburg. I notice the field up ahead which Marty had cased so thoroughly before. As we approach, I notice a farmer driving a horse-drawn cultivator coming along near the fence. No, it was a mowing machine, he was cutting weeds along the fence. I sure anticipate Marty's next move. As we approach, driving up near where the farmer rode his rig, Marty put on the brakes, shut off the engine saying. "Let's go talk to him." We trot across the road, Marty standing by the fence as the farmer moved up with his mowing outfit. Seeing that this odd couple wanted to talk to him he calls out, "Whoa," to his horse and we engaged him in conversation.

Marty says" "You know that is a beautiful field you have here. I won't keep you guessing, but we are the aviators with one of the planes that has been flying passengers this past weekend down around here."

The old fellow slowly answers, "oh yes, we went down there. No, I didn't take any plane ride. You had another fellow down there with a big yellow plane."

"Yes, that was our friend Dave. Well, sir, we were just wondering if you would allow us to land our plane here just for one day in this field and ride any passengers who might stop by. We would be glad to take you for a ride in payment for your kind permission."

He agreed, we chat some more, neighborly-like, then head off to Huntingburg, because we tell the old gentlemen we are driving a borrowed automobile which we must return, telling him we look forward to seeing him tomorrow and hoping he will fly with us.

We drive over to where Henry is doing his remodeling job on the house. He packs up some of his tools, puts them in the rear of the Model A, drives us over to the St. George.

"Mr. Marty," he says, "I understand you're leaving tomorrow. You will want to go down to your plane. I'll meet you over here at the restaurant for breakfast. Afterward we will drive down to the field."

"That will be fine," says Marty. "We will meet you at the restaurant at 8 o'clock and be sure not to have breakfast because we certainly want to buy your breakfast. We have gassed up your automobile and we also want you to think very seriously how much we owe you."

Henry replies, "We will discuss tomorrow, Mr. Marty. We will discuss tomorrow. It has been a real pleasure working with you and Mr. Dave. I have never been around airplanes much before, only saw a few who landed here to take passengers like you. Never up close or to know them. It has been a real pleasure, very worthwhile to me, a great change from my normal life."

After he leaves, we make our way to our town and to the bathroom down the hall to tidy up for dinner. Over at the eatery on Fourth Street, we settle down to enjoy a real good, "home cooked" restaurant dinner. Marty is given to reminiscing about his barnstorming, the building and flying of planes, stuff that I was just eating up, word by word. Some of it was things he had repeated before but I enjoyed hearing them again and again. I asked him how many forced landings he had ever experienced.

He thought for a moment and said, "Well, just offhand, I would say maybe two dozen times. I learned to fly in 1919, it's now 1933. In those 14 years about two dozen times. But about fifteen were deliberate for practice."

Then I said, "How many times in the Waco here?"

"Two," he said. He also noticed the worried look on my face.

"How long have you owned it?" I asked.

Quickly he answers, "Three years. It was just a little over a year old when I bought it."

"Has the OX-5 a reputation for conking out?" I asked him.

His eyebrows sort of went up and he cocked his head to one side,

"Oh yeah, it's been known to do it. A lot, in fact. A lot depends on the operator and how he keeps his engine up. I once knew two fellows who owned a surplus Jenny, who were very poor mechanics. One summer, flying passengers for three weeks they had a forced landing on an average of once a day. It was out in Kansas where fields abound so a forced landing didn't really amount to too much, except the inconvenience to passengers quite a bit."

After dinner we spend a full hour walking up and down Fourth Street for two or three blocks, looking into the store windows, most of them closed, getting a little exercise and satisfying Marty's unending curiosity about small Middle West towns. I dare say it satisfies a good bit of curiosity on my part too because most of my previous experiences here in Huntingburg was limited to just going to the ball park, sitting through baseball games, eating hotdogs and drinking Derr's pop. Derr's were the soda pop manufacturers in Boonville who sponsored the Boonville baseball team, bringing along all their own pop to sell in the stands as well as whet the thirsts of the team.

That night I sleep like a log as usual. And to say that Marty slept like a log is like saying that a cork floats. Even his snoring did not keep me awake this night. But I still had to arouse him the next morning. We tidied up, he making his shave at the "down hall" bathroom. Presently we rushed off to the eatery on Fourth to meet Henry Kornbrath. Sure enough he was there sitting at the table sipping a cup of coffee. "Good mornings" and handshakes all around between the three of us.

The restaurant owner addressed Henry with, "Well, Mr. Kornbrath, your friends have finally shown up." The owner chuckled. "Mr. Kornbrath has been here for 45 minutes. Either he is very early or you fellows are very late."

Marty and I look at each other, I smile and Marty frowns and his face reddens a bit. We snored in a little too much, I thought to myself as I chuckled. The other two didn't get it but Marty sure did.

After a good breakfast and conversation with Mr. Kornbrath, Marty anxiously got to the business of paying Henry Kornbrath for his good services and the use of his Model A Ford. We have filled the tank and after a great deal of Marty's eloquent persuasion, he finally accepted $10.00, then confessed that Dave had given him another $20.00 The old man seemed ashamed for accepting the money so here again Marty's eloquent persuasion finally convinced him that he had been indispensable to all of us. We bid the cheerful restaurant owner good-bye and load all of our belongings from the St. George, into the Model A, then head south to the field.

Presently Kornbrath turns off on a side road off to the west, then onto an old farm implement road running along the edge of the field inside the fence for nearly a half mile. Back in the distance and parked near an irrigation ditch is our faithful old Waco, untouched and unharmed but the dew gleaming on its wings and fuselage. Henry parks the Model A nearby after we get out and walk over to our dear old ship. I run my hands along the lower wing, the waterproof fabric is dripping wet, draining off the leading edges onto the fresh cut hay. We pull the chocks and stakes, me climbing into the back cockpit after we stow away the gear; Marty swings the prop in our usual fashion. The OX-5 catches, sputters a bit, begins to settle down and idle. Marty comes around, I climb out and give the cockpit over to him and he says, "First we'll say our good-byes to Henry here, then taxi up to the other end of the field for our take-off. By that time the engine ought to be warmed up enough without running at full throttle down here against the chocks."

We shake hands with dear old Henry and actually the poor old fellow's eyes are moist, tiny tears running down his cheeks. I shall never forget it. I climb up front, Marty giving the OX-5 a little gun and we start slowly taxiing, dragging the tailskid through the stubble, working our way the half-mile back to the other end of the field. When we get up near the road, he blasts the tail up, swings it around quickly dropping the tail back down on the ground, leaving us facing directly west. Off in the distance to the right we can see Henry making his way back up to the highway in the Model A. He stops and gets out, begins waving his arms. Marty gives the OX-5 the gun, lifts up the tail and we go roaring down the field and off, waving down at Henry as we leave the field.

Swinging around to the north and over Huntingburg, Marty makes three wide circles around the town, then heads north to the field he had selected yesterday. We fly well out to the east, way beyond some railroad tracks that run into Huntingburg. The highway we had driven on had telephone wires on tall poles. He is reluctant to fly in over those wires so we approach from the east over the tracks and touch down, rolling very slowly almost to a stop within several hundred yards of the highway, then slowly taxi up to the road. At about a hundred feet from the fence he gives the OX-5 the gun, raises the tail up, swung it around to the east, lets it down and switches off the engine.

About five minutes later, a Model T touring car pulls up and stops on the road near the plane. It is our farmer friend who owns the field. I recall his name as Herman Roth. Even though an old fellow he climbs over the wire fence very easily. He lives just up the road, saw us land, says he had made up his mind during the night he would fly with us since it was free. So without further ado, we load him into the front cockpit and Marty takes off to give him a ride around Jasper. He wanted to see Jasper from the air. I begin hanging two or three of our old signs we had buried under the seat in the front cockpit. I stand by while they are in the air with the two-fold purpose of killing time and spreading the signs on three or four of the fence posts along the road to attract passersby. While I wait several automobiles pass by. About half of those stop and question me, but everyone had seen the planes over the weekend and even half of them had already ridden in either the Waco or the Standard, most of them in the Standard which is what I would expect since it carried twice as many passengers.

Twenty-five minutes have gone by and Marty is still in the air. He has not flown for three days and is really anxious to get back into the air, a real pilot. I look all around; they are nowhere to be seen. I look along the skyline over Jasper, no planes in sight. I look to the east and west, still no airplane. I haul out my old Pocket Ben; gee, forty minutes has gone by. I hope he is not running low on fuel because we had flown quite a bit on that last day even though the fuel truck had filled our tank.

More motorists stopped by. All they had to say was that they had seen me, Marty, Dave, and Henry Kornbrath down south of Huntingburg. One of them had even flown with Dave. They went on after visiting a while. Then far off to the west I spotted the Waco making its way at about 1000 feet. They flew along for about three miles to the east, then make a wide, low, descending turn approaching over the railroad tracks, fishtailing back and forth just as though he were landing at a real short field. They touch down far back in the field, then taxi slowly up to the road, swinging the ship around with the tail high in the air, then drops it back down on the tailskid. I help Mr. Roth out of the front cockpit.

Marty waves me over. "Have you lined up any more passengers?"

I said, "No, only some visitors. Most of those have either flown with us or seen us before." He shook his head, reaches up to the switch and shuts off the engine.

Mr. Roth visits a while, then tells us he has many chores to do and must leave. Marty tells him we will probably leave late this afternoon or tomorrow morning and that he had asked the tank truck driver to come out and fuel us up. He nods to us, climbs over his fence post, cranks up the Model T and takes off.

It is now very late and we have already brought plane and gas truck together gassing up the Waco with a hose across the fence. Our dinner is in the sack brought from the Fourth Street eatery. Bedrolls under the wing, we sleep like babies.

Tuesday morning we take off to the east, munching on doughnuts. We are headed northeast for French Lick, West Baden Springs, Paoli, Salem and eventually to Hanover and Madison. I reminisce wistfully about this beautiful trip to Huntingburg and Jasper. What a great few days this has been this past weekend, with all those passengers and Dave and his big Standard. I will never forget this trip. And last but not least, dear old Henry Kornbrath and these dear old towns of yesteryear, Huntingburg and Jasper. And dear old Marty, forever measuring the height and architecture of churches! And, of course, our dear old Waco. What a beautiful ship she is, the OX-5 sputtering along. Now here we are in the air again and heading east.

As I munch my doughnuts down to the last sugary morsel, I gaze off to the southeast to the hill country along the north side of the Ohio River now visible in the distance. Ahead to the northeast the country is more flat and the farmlands are larger. The cool slipstream around the windshield and over my face makes me relaxed and happy with my lot in this beautiful world, a world complete with friends like Marty and his old Waco, and I give thanks to the Lord and everybody else for understanding and I especially give thanks for seemingly foolish parents who let me get away with all of this at the age of fifteen when other boys my age in Boonville are jealously ground-bound. I feel relaxed and begin to revel in all the things I've done and seen and all the wonderful people I've come to know in the past few weeks on this unusual trip. A trip my English teacher would have called an aerial odyssey. I think of the fine Hoosier folks on this trip, farmers and small town folk and all of the passengers to whom we gave rides and came to know through their enthusiasm as well as out own.

The one that stands out so vividly in my brain and ever so deeply in my heart is beautiful little Katherine Heilman of Ferdinand. oh how I miss her so much. I would never say out loud what I feel in my heart. I think that both Marty and Katherine's mother Katie knew that I was smitten with Katherine, but even they did not really know how much. But even I realize that the reality of life and the poetry of the heart more often than not, never become one. Perhaps some day in Heaven, but I also know that I am young and little Katherine is even younger and I can hope that some day I will return to Ferdinand to become her friend for life. And who knows from there. I feel guilty for having these feelings for her, she is so much younger than I, but as we both grow older that difference will diminish and along with it the guilt I would feel in the eyes of others. That thought inspires me to plan and hope the hope of fools in love to ride my bike all the way from Boonville to Ferdinand during our Thanksgiving school vacation. Then a depressing thought occurs to me: my arriving at the Heilman farm on a bicycle would be such a contrast to our recent arrival in the Waco might be such a shock to her that even I and my deep feeling for her could not afford to risk. I'd have to think of something more impressive. I could not afford even a small plane, and I did not have a pilot's license anyway, only a student glider pilot's certificate with the Bureau of Air Commerce, obtained by mail. Perhaps I could borrow Dad's 1926 Essex, not a very impressive con-veyance to impress the impressible Katherine, besides Dad would want to come along. He and the Heilmans would get along great but that would leave little Katherine and I to the adult devices of juvenility. Why are the beautiful inspirations of life so beset by reality's obstacles before fulfillment?

Oh my God! My heart has leaped into my throat! My cockpit rumina-tions of romance come to a sudden and frightening halt. Sudden silence in the air is far more frightening than the instantaneous surge of power from the engine. In all of our previous flights I have become thoroughly accus-tomed to the throttling back of the engine, even all the way back to Idle during a landing approach. At those times you can still hear the engine run-ning at a low r.p.m., but now all of a sudden the engine has abruptly stopped running. In one second it is turning over at 1200 r.p.m. but in the next sec-ond it has dropped to little more than 100. The propeller is simply windmilling slower and slower due to the forward but diminishing speed of the airplane until it has eventually completely stopped. The only sound is that made by a rapidly weakening airstream as it passes through the wings, struts and the windshield before my face. Almost as suddenly the Waco noses down sharply. I raise up in the cockpit, craning my head, gazing down ahead to see to what region of terra firma we are headed.

I look back to see Marty literally standing in his cockpit, head side to side and up and down. He yelled, "Get down, buckle up, I can't see a damn thing past your damned head."

As I drop down into the seat I can see by looking at the stick and rudder pedals what they really meant when pilots called this situation "a dead stick landing." As Marty managed the dual controls, his every move to keep the nose down or to bank or turn the airplane was done only with larger sweeping motions of the stick or rudder pedals than in normal flights. We are coming down steeply and fast.

I keep my head low but peek around the windshield. I can see what appears to be a hayfield bounded by one cornfield on the near side and another cornfield on the far side. The hayfield and far cornfield are separated by a barbed wire fence. But to my eye the hayfield looks so darn small! My God, we are losing altitude real fast! The standing uncut corn on the near side of the hayfield must be nearly ten feet high and Marty seems to be diving right into it. Good Gosh, the propeller has come to a complete stop in a horizontal position. The only noise is the slipstream of air through the wings, increasing as Marty noses the Waco down ever so steeply. We are going to crash nose down in the very center of the cornfield at an angle of about 45 degrees. Suddenly the stick in my cockpit is slammed all the way back, luckily past my legs for I have scooted over to the left of the two-place cockpit where I can peek out to see where we will hit ground. Sort of like a pet dog that cannot resist sticking his head out of a car window no matter how small the opening.

The nose of the Waco comes up sharply but still sinking rapidly at an angle now of only about 10 degrees. But the nose is still coming up and the stick is still all the way back. Then there is a loud rattling and snapping noise for all the world just like the cardboard noise clapper I have wired to the steering fork of my bicycle so that it intersects the wire spokes as they rotate.

Now I realize it is the landing gear threshing through the tops of the cornstalks, then I realize what soon must happen next. The leading edge of the 31-foot lower wing will soon be threshing through the cornstalks because we are now sinking ever deeper into the cornfield at about 50 m.p.h. But up ahead I can see the hayfield, but it seems so far away. Then all hell is breaking loose and I am more scared than I ever have been in my old Mead glider. The tops of the corn are threshing into the lower wings' leading edge all along the full length of its 31-foot span. The sound is deafening and tops of the corn stalks, leaves, silks, ears and all are breaking off and streaming back through the wings, struts and the tie-rod brace wires. Already the brace wires are filling up with the fragmented cornstalks. We are so low now the lower wing is cutting the stalks at their mid height. Then there is a moderate jolt as the wheels touch down in the corn rows, but thank God the light jolt results in the Waco bouncing up a few feet and the leading edge of the lower wing is now again only cutting off a foot or two off the tops of the cornstalks. Then just ahead I see the hayfield looming up fast before us. We break out into the open hayfield in a flared 3-point landing attitude. The Waco touches down rather gently, bounces a couple of times, and I can feel Marty as he yaws the ship about 30 degrees so as to head for the right forward fence corner to get the greatest landing roll distance he can get. We come to a halt less than 50 feet from the fence corner.

We both sit quietly for a while. I don't know about Marty but I am scared to death, but I now feel an immense sense of relief. Then I hear him stirring in the rear cockpit. I unbuckle, rise up and turn to find him standing on his seat. "What happened?" I stuttered. He looked at me like I was the stupidest kid in the world and literally shouted back at me. "The damned engine quit!" I was not satisfied to quit before I got an even more disdainful look so I gulp out the next question, "Why?"

He really shook his head this time. "Damn it anyway, Peyton, if I knew I would not have taken off in the first place." It finally sank in. What was needed now was quiet, and to wait for Marty to figure out what needed to be fixed.

I set about cleaning cornstalks off the leading edge of the lower wing as well as all the rest of it lodged in the brace wires, struts, and down in the landing gear struts and wheels. My galvanized action seemed to calm Marty as he set about removing the engine cowling.

I discovered that the wings' leading edges had not been damaged by mowing its way through all of those standing cornstalks at 50 miles per hour. The internal wood forward strip attached to the nose of 32 wing ribs had not given way to all of this corn lashing. Even the silver colored doped fabric covering over the leading edge had not even been scored or gouged, let alone torn away, but the corn had left dirty yellow streaks all along the leading edge for the full span of 31 feet. I wet a clean rag in the clear water of a nearby little ditch and set about cleaning the leading edge. I removed all the dirt but the smudgy streaks remained. Then I took the can of aluminum colored pigmented fabric dope from Marty's kit and touched up the leading edge until it looked just like it did before our faithful old OX-5 had re-tested that faith by stopping in mid-air.

Marty is on top of the engine, very busy removing things. I did not want to extend my luck with Marty's patience by releasing the restraints I had reluctantly imposed on my own percolating curiosity. Just then I looked up to see an old farmer making his way down the fence toward us. When abreast of the Waco, he took off a battered old straw hat and mopped his brow with a huge red bandanna handkerchief. He said not a word as he busily masticated a chew of tobacco.

CHAPTER IX

Marty looks down at the old gentleman, pushing back the hair, which always hung over his eyes whenever he worked on the OX-5. Raising his head he looks down squarely at the old farmer, "Good day to you, sir. Bit of a hot one today isn't it?"

The old fellow looks at both of us, puts his hat back on, leaning over to spat a spat of tobacco the likes of which I had never seen before. Even in Warrick County where tobacco chewing by some is something of an informal contest that has been going on for years. But this old fellow's single spat extends all the way from his mouth to the ground in one continuous solid stream with plenty to spare before the exercise is completed. He concludes the performance by drawing his sleeved right arm across his mouth. Then his blue eyes sharpen as he looks up at Marty, drawing out a sentence, which he had obviously been mulling over as he walked down the fence to confront us. "Don't you fellers realize you don't have permission to light your flyin' machine on my timothy field here, even if she's already cut now? And I seen you mowin' down all my corn there. Why you cut a swath through there 300 feet long and 50 feet wide. Why, I've a mind ta call the sheriff but I got no telyphone or I shore would. I want you fellers ta git right out o' here right now. If you don't I'm gonna go back ta the house and get my old 16 gauge so's you will, consarn it anyway."

Marty looked very tired all of a sudden. He climbed down off the Waco's nose, extending his hand and introducing us both to the old man. The old gent slowly and reluctantly took Marty's handshake at the same time taking a bite off a plug of tobacco he withdrew from the bib of his overalls.

Marty drew back his hair again and wiping his brow with a soiled white hanky he carries in a hip pocket, then said politely and painstakingly, "No sir, you are absolutely correct. We certainly do not have permission to land here, no permission whatever. But sir, may I ask you what you may take as a too personal question, but I assure you that once you hear my question you will agree it is absolutely necessary that I ask it of you. May I, sir?"

The old man looked taken aback and quite suspicious but he nodded, saying, "Shore, but I ain't got all day. I got work to do."

Marty said, "Okay, all I ask is this? Sir, are you a man who believes in the God Almighty? Are you a religious man? You go to church is my guess. A man looked up to by his neighbors, who lives by God's laws and actions?"

The old fellow's eyes came ablaze and his lower jaw jutted forth, the cud moved far to one side.

"Yer darn tootin' I believe in God and God's ways and sayin's in the Bible and I don't take to any flyin' machine drivers lightin' on my farm and tearin' it all up, then havin' the durn gall ta question my beliefs in the Almighty."

I could see the old fellow was really getting hot under the collar, until Marty holds up both arms like a preacher calling for the support of his flock in time of need.

"Sir, I know we landed here without your permission but that was not our decision. As a man of faith I know you will understand when I tell you that there is no doubt our landing in your fields here was purely an act of God. We are on our way peacefully to Paoli when the motor in this airplane suddenly quit. When the motor in a plane quits the Lord's force of gravity on all things brings the plane to earth over wherever it happens to be at the time. God chose your fields as the place we must land, including your standing corn which slowed us to a safe landing. Otherwise you would have had a couple of dead aviators on your hands. God saved you from that and saved us in the bargain. I assure you that as soon as God shows me how to fix this motor we will leave here as soon as we can. But we may have to ask you to lay the fence here so we won't risk crashing on it when we take off."

Marty's discourse set the old fellow to removing his straw hat and scratching his head. Presently he replied,

"Well, I guess I figgered it was God made you land fer I seen you fly over and yer motor quit all of a sudden. It didn't seem to throttle back and forth like other planes I've seen when they landed. But I didn't know for sure. But now as I've cogitated on it, it was God's doing all right. And he don't ask ner give permissions, that's fer dern sure. This here field is his'n, same as it is mine, but how long you think the Lord is given you to fix your motor anyways?"

Marty did some slow cogitating himself but finally said,

"I'm not sure yet. I'm guessing it's the magneto or distributor and they can be kind of complicated. I should know in another hour or so. But it's now well into the afternoon and we cannot take-off in the dark, or even late afternoon, because we would be caught in the dark before we landed at our planned destination east of here. We might have to sleep here tonight as we sometimes do under the plane's wing."

The old fellow cogitated some more, then spat again, clearing his throat.

"Well I got lots of work to do. If you can't leave today you can sleep in my barn loft up yonder. They's plenty of hay to bed down for the night. They's a lantern down below hanging on the stalls. But don't take it to the loft for I don't want my barn burned to the ground by aviators who don't know nothin' about kerosene lanterns. In the morning if you get your motor fixed I'll lay the fence down fer yer take-off."

Marty says, "Thank you sir. We are extremely grateful to you." With that the old man made his way back up to the fence to his house and barn.

I look up at Marty still on top of the Waco's nose. He has the distributor cap removed and working inside it very intently and very carefully. Presently he climbs down, making his way around the lower wing to the rear cockpit, begins rummaging around behind the seat. He carries his tool kit back there but he already has it spread out on the ground under the engine. But I also know he carries a few critical spare parts back there, neatly bundled up in cardboard parts boxes. He seems to notice I have completed my cornstalk damage repair and seems more relaxed and not so likely to abruptly fend off my curiosity as to what caused the OX-5 to quit running so suddenly. He offers no clue or solution, only giving a sly grin to salve my burning desire to know and help. Like tossing a hungry pup a small, dry, meatless bone.

I haul out my pocket Ben. Time has passed suddenly and swiftly in the same way the OX-5 had conked out without even uttering a cough. The old dollar watch is running as always and it reveals it to be nearly six o'clock in the evening. Finally I conclude that I must strike up some oral communication with Marty. I clear my throat and these seemingly strange words came forth: "Marty, it's six o'clock. I guess if we are going to stay here tonight I'll get the ship all staked down for the night while you are working on the engine."

Marty let on for a moment like he doesn't hear me and then he says rather absentmindedly,

"Yeah, you better stake her down good. Too late to get up to Paoli. Besides, we need to get that old farmer gent to help us lay down the fence. You say it's six o'clock already? Let's see that dollar watch of yours again. Is that thing running? Where did you get that, out of a Crackerjack box?"

"No," I said seriously, "it's an Ingersol Pocket Ben but they are good watches. They call 'em dollar watches, but this one cost me a dollar ninety-five, and that was four years ago."

I could see that Marty was actually planning in his head about how he was going to take off. Also, he was now his old relaxed self again. The super-concentration and tension were gone. That meant one thing: he had found the problem, and furthermore, he knew how to fix it fairly quickly. Then I begin to get mad, or shall I say flustered. Doggoned it, I'm his partner and helper. I got a right to know what went wrong and how he's going to fix it. It bothers me that we are stuck here in the middle of nowhere with an airplane that won't fly, sitting in a field where our welcome is very much in doubt. Finally I get up nerve enough to blurt out,

"Marty, what caused the OX-5 to stop, and do you know for sure how to fix it?"

Marty threw his head back and laughing loudly, which only makes me feel like a dumb kid who does not need to know because he will not understand anyway. Then Marty's manner changed and he put his hand on my shoulder.

"That's okay, Peyton. I wasn't sure myself until just a few minutes ago. You finish your stake-down of the ship and I'll show you exactly what went wrong and the easy fix. Be sure to stake her down good like you always do. Storms come up over night in this country."

I drive stakes at each wing tip and another near the tailskid. The usual procedure is always to loop the tie-down ropes to the lower ends of the front inter-wing struts. Same thing on the tailskid. For good measure this time I run a rope from each front lower wing strut attachment over to individual fence posts, which same posts I lean on vigorously to test their affinity with the ground. All of which I could see quietly amused Marty. He climbs down off the Waco's nose and I help him put the cowl back on to keep the engine covered during the night. I noticed that the electrical leads to the distributor were dangling loosely, but the distributor was missing. Then I notice it on the ground along with his tool kit and a small parts box as well as a paper sack which I recognize as the sandwiches which our old friend and driver at Huntingburg had given us.

Marty heaves a long sigh, then says, "Well partner, guess we better head up to the barn, look over our straw bed and eat these stale Huntingburg hamburgers. Also we can work on this distributor outside the barn while there is still some daylight and maybe use the lantern if we have to."

The barn is nearly a quarter mile up along the fence line. The old two-story farmhouse is still another three hundred yards beyond the barn. our less-than-hospitable host is the owner of a very large farm. Marty looks all around us as we stride along. He surmises the place must be between three hundred and four hundred acres. I look back at the airplane. The poor old Waco stands forlornly in the distant fence corner back there. It looks for all the world like a big poor old bird, wounded by some amateur hunter whose marksmanship bordered on recklessness.

Marty says the barn is one of the neatest he has ever seen, going on to say that he grew up on a Kansas farm where barns vied for cleanliness with the farm houses. The haymow in the loft is reached by ladder nailed to the livestock stalls. The area below has some benches and stools. The owner has set out the lantern like he'd promised. He also has laid out two clean canvas tarps, which we could lay in the haymow for our beds.

Marty says, "Let's take the stools and bench outside where there is still some daylight where we can work on the distributor." He sits on a stool with the bench in front of him on which he lays the tools, distributor and the small box. Then he looks up at me and begins to laugh, handing me the sandwich sack. "I'd better give you this before you pin me down and take it away from me. Your eyes have the look of some kind of a starving heathen who's just come out of the African jungle."

It embarrasses me and I can feel my face blush, then we laugh together. I gave it right back to him, blurting, "Well, you made me hungry by your just keeping me in the dark about what made the OX-5 quit."

He retorts, "Well, okay, pull up your stool on the other side of this bench and munch your dinner and listen and look. Here," he said, "see, I have removed the distributor head so you can see the eight points for each cylinder and the distributor finger which rotates to make contact with each of the points as it passes by. The tip of this finger is sometimes called a brush."

I can not refrain from showing off my own knowledge, blurting out, "Yeah, I know how distributors work. I've even helped Dad work on the one in his 1926 Essex. It's a lot like this one, the same principle."

Marty's lips pressed together impatiently. "Well, since you are an expert on these things, maybe you can tell me precisely what's wrong with it."

Cagey son-of-a-gun, he had me. All eight points looked clean and the brush finger looked okay and intact. Sheepishly, I said, "I don't know. It looks okay."

"All right," Marty says, then he reaches to one side, picking up a little speck of something or other that I had hardly noticed except to assume that it was a small rock or piece of dirt that had been on the bench all along.

Marty says, "This afternoon when I took the head off the distributor I found this laying loose and slipping around inside attached to nothing."

Then he deftly reaches down with forefinger and thumb, pulling the distributor finger and its shaft out of the distributor. He turns it over, pointing to the under side of the tip of the finger, the area designed to brush across the points as it rotates. He then takes the small piece, laying it over the underside of the tip. It fits perfectly in the area from which it had broken off. The piece had fallen into the open area between the circle of eight points and the shaft in the center. This meant that the underside of the tip of the rotating finger had broken off, leaving a huge gap between the rotating finger and each point as it passed by. The result was no ignition to all eight of the OX-5 cylinders. As Marty put it, "Dead in the water," and as I thought to myself, 'Dead in the air'.

Marty opens the little cardboard box and from it withdraws a brand new spare part, a distributor shaft with its integral finger and brush tip. He simply inserts it into the distributor, putting the head cover back on and the broken finger and its shaft back into the little cardboard box. He gives a long sigh saying,

"Now all we have to do is connect it back up on the leads in the morning and fire up the ship for a take-off. Now, let's eat these sandwiches and then go up and make our beds before it gets too dark. We can't take that lantern up in the loft."

Then he says with a look of late recognition, "My gosh, you've already eaten your sandwich. Guess I'll have to eat alone. After we make our beds in the loft, we'll take the lantern, go to the house and tell our friend we can take-off in the morning, but we'll need to lay a section of fence."

We mount the ladder and spread our tarps out on the hay which takes all of less than five minutes, then Marty says, "You want to go up to the house with me?"

Just as we leave the barn we are suddenly confronted by our host, he also carrying a lantern.

"I didn't tell you fellers my name is Tom Sherman. You said today you had your dinner in a sack, I guess you've eat it by now. My woman said we should have you'ns for supper, but you fellers come to breakfast in the mornin', at the dinner bell ringin' on the back porch at six o'clock."

Marty extended his handshake, saying, "We would be pleased to have breakfast. You folks are very kind. By the way, I've fixed the distributor on the plane and if you can oversee our laying the fence down, we can take off and trouble you no more."

Mr. Sherman spat his usual spat of tobacco, replying, "That's dern good ta hear. I was afeared you was a-goin' ta have ta leave it or have trucks or teams ta come in and haul her off, tearin' up the fields gittin' it out. We have ta be real keerful layin' the fence so's I don't have ta do a new fence." Marty assures him we will help him exactly as he wanted as long as we had enough clearance for a safe take-off.

With that said Tom Sherman spat another spat of tobacco, then turned around and headed for the house. Marty turns down the wick on the lantern saying he was going to leave it outside, saying he did not trust kerosene lanterns in barns full of hay and straw on hot summer nights, even on cool nights.

I said, "How are we going to find our way into the loft? I can't even find the door, let alone the ladder, it is now so dark."

Suddenly Marty switches on his flashlight, which I had entirely forgotten back with the plane's tool kit. "How come you didn't use it instead of the lantern?" I asked Marty.

He replied, "Well, you didn't ask and I could save some batteries."

The haymow is softer than others we had tried, like those down at Cannelton, and in a few minutes I am sound asleep, but twice I was awakened by good old Marty snoring like a foghorn.

Something woke me very early before sunup the next morning, but early dawn was barely showing in the cracks between the board walls. I peer over the edge of the loft. It is old Tom down there doing his chores. He is turning some stock out of the stalls below into the adjacent fields. Soon he is gone. Last evening he told us to wash up in the morning in the small shed behind the house.

I lay there for a while not able to sleep any more. I look at the old pocket Ben, suddenly finding it is by now five thirty. By the time we walk up to the house and wash up the dinner bell will be ringing. In a panic, I wake up Marty. Actually I wake Marty up three times. We dress and go down the ladder and start the 300 yard "walk" to the wash shed in a trot. Mrs. Sherman is not yet to be seen but a strong smoke emanates from the kitchen chimney. As we hurriedly wash up the cold water on our faces and arms put new life in both of us. Marty's eyes are alight and ready for action. Suddenly the bell rang and a portly, elderly lady holds the screen door open for us without much adieu except to say she is Maggie Sherman and that Tom has already had his breakfast.

The breakfast is great, even as good as that one in Cannelton and Huntingburg. We each have enough eggs, bacon, biscuits, gravy and coffee to tide us over for a good while. The best part is that Maggie Sherman is happiest when we are eagerly accepting seconds, thirds or fourths. Then she tells us Tom always breakfasts at four-thirty and has already done his stock chores and gone on down to the plane to lay the fence.

Marty gathers up his distributor and small pack of tools and parts and we head down toward the plane at a fast walk. Marty says so we can get there "before old Tom Sherman takes a pitchfork to our venerable and precious old Waco." I can not believe that Marty really meant it that way but is likely more concerned that the old fellow might lay the fence is such a way that he, Marty, would have to change it after we got there and that would surely provoke an argument with the old fellow which is the last thing we wanted.

As we near the airplane we can see that old Tom has pulled up five of the fence posts, laid the fence down with posts attached for a distance of about sixty feet, all directly facing and symmetrically distributed, facing the 31 foot swath we had cut through the cornfield. I can see that Marty is impressed that old Tom is really using his head showing he understood what Marty had been planning for his take-off all along without ever having told the old fellow. But just out of earshot Marty mumbled to me, "Why that cagey old bastard got up before the crack of dawn just to prove to us he knows more about getting our airplane out of here than we do. Rooting those fence posts took a lot of muscle and digging around them, not breaking a one and not cutting the fence wire from them."

Marty strode up to the old gent, saying, "Mr. Sherman, you've done a fine job, but I wish you had woke us up to come along. We expected to do all the labor on this, with your supervision, of course."

The old fellow took a long spat of tobacco carefully to one side, simply saying, "I allus get up early and do my own work."

Then Marty said, "You sure got the fence down exactly where I had in mind to go through on my take-off, because the best place to clear the corn is the passage through where we landed." I noted that old diplomat Marty used the word "passage" through the corn instead of referring to it as the swath that it was. Then Marty explains that it would be necessary to cut the downed fence wire at one end and roll the wire and posts up carefully. Otherwise the plane's wheels could tangle in the wire as they rolled across it. The barbed wire could easily puncture a tire as well. Also with the ten foot spacing of the posts the plane would have to be steered to miss them with considerable difficulty lest a wheel or propeller tip hit them, making the plane nose over on its back. In which case Mr. Sherman would have a wrecked plane and a couple of dead aviators on his hands.

Mr. Sherman replied that he had, "Already figgered ta roll up the fence and posts." The old fellow already had a pair of wire cutters in his overall pocket. The fence, posts and all were rolled up in a six-foot roll leaving a sixty-foot gap for the Waco to pass through on its take-off.

Now Marty took his attention to the Waco. We take the cowling off, get ready to re-affix the distributor.

While Marty busies himself hooking up the electrical leads to the distributor, I set about looking over the fence line where the fence formerly lay. I trample down grass and weeds that had grown under the wire. Mr. Sherman quickly reprimanded me. "She's all right, young feller. I cleared her all off after I rolled up my fence. Leave 'er be. Don't make me more work, none of it I needed in the first place 'fore you fellers lit your plane here."

I take the not-so-gentle hint, wandering up through the hayfield which lays beyond the fence we just removed. It is all flat, freshly cut alfalfa, much like the field in which we had landed. It extends several hundred yards to the east where it ends in another cornfield. I walk all the way to the corn and look back to the west. The two fields now, plus the swath in the west cornfield would give us plenty of room to take-off, judging by the other fields we had been using, if we taxi up to this end and swing the tail around for a take-off to the west.

It occurs to me we should hang our red bandanna handkerchiefs on the roll of fence wire on one side of the gap down there, and another on that side where the fence was still standing. From this distance the gap in the fence is not easy to see. The red flags would help Marty hit the gap dead center as we pass through. The gap is sixty feet wide and the wingspan of the Waco is 31 feet, leaving only about 15 feet of clearance on each side. I had two big bandannas so I started walking back intent on hanging these red flags. Just as I started back I could hear Marty loudly calling out, "Hey, let's go!" so I started running. I panted up to the gap, tied the bandannas to the fence wire, then rush over to the plane. Marty has the cowling all on and fastened down while Mr. Sherman chews excitedly on his latest cud. Marty stands waiting rather impatiently holding on to the propeller, nodding toward the rear cockpit. After I climb aboard, he swings the propeller twice to prime, then calls out, "Switch on!" which I repeat in our usual fashion.

On the first swing of the prop, the OX-5 starts, coughs twice and begins to idle. 'Glory be!' I think to myself, 'We are out of here! I'll be gladder to go than old man Sherman will be to see us go.'

In a few seconds Marty is standing by impatiently, gesturing with his thumb for me to get out and get into the front cockpit with the chocks and stuff we had out on the ground. Marty revs up the engine, swings the tail up and around and we go through the gap into the north field, taxiing slowly along. He warms the engine by taxiing with the tail skid not only down and dragging but held the stick back to make the skid dig into the ground, forcing the engine to run at a higher taxi r.p.m. than usual. Happily I know what that means. It means that when we reach yonder cornfield the engine will be hot enough so he can just swing her around and take off. It also means I would not have to get out and place the wheel chocks while he revved the engine up for a minute or two as we usually did beginning from a cold start. It's a great relief to me to now realize we will be ready to take off as soon as we reach the end of this second hayfield. Dragging along like this with bursts of engine power seems to take forever. Finally we reach the point at the end of the hayfield where the spinning propeller is only about 25 feet from the 10-foot high standing corn. Marty wastes no time, he guns the OX-5, pushes the stick forward, kicks the rudder pedals hard to the left. The tail end comes up to a horizontal position swinging around 180 degrees. Craning my head around the side of the cockpit I can see the rudder and elevators cutting a swift arc through the tall corn while the propeller blast had the stalks bent backward to the breaking point.

As Marty advances the throttle all the way to the limit we gather speed heading toward the gap. I can see Mr. Sherman well off to one side, nervously hopping about and undoubtedly highly concerned that Marty would lose control and unceremoniously send him to his Almighty without so much as a prayerful preamble. As we pass through the gap in the fence I wave to Mr. Sherman. Despite our speed of nearly 60 m.p.h., I can easily detect the rapid chewing motion applied to a larger than normal cud of tobacco. I can still feel the weight of the airplane on the wheels as we pass through the fence gap. We are now roaring along through the first hayfield, the one in which we had made our dead-stick landing. Up ahead I can see the slot we had made through the corn in our landing. The corn beyond that stood over 10 feet high. Gosh, it looks formidable! If we should hit that corn it could be almost like a wall. It would slow us down so much we'd never make it out.

We are still on the ground. The rumbling of the wheels on the ground and the vibration they transmit go up into the entire framework of the airplane. The forward controls are still in my cockpit and I am anxiously watching the stick for any slight rearward movement imparted by Marty to lift the airplane off the ground.

As we near the onrushing cornfield and its ominous swath, the stick moves back just a few degrees and I feel the ship lift off. We are now whizzing through the swath in the corn and climbing fast enough that it takes my breath away. Marty has certainly taken full advantage of the space available for our take-off. In a matter of seconds the cornfield is 100 feet below us and we are heading due west. At about 500 feet Marty starts a slow turn to the left until we are headed back east and over the Sherman farm. As we pass over I can see Mr. Sherman slowly plodding his way back to the barn. Then lo, and behold, I see portly Mrs. Sherman on the back porch staring skyward, shading her eyes with her dishtowel. Then good old Marty did just what I hoped he would do. He rocked the Waco's wings back and forth, blipping the throttle back and forth all in a salute to her wonderful breakfast and its seconds, thirds and fourth helpings.

Ahead I can see we are approaching what I will call the Southern Indiana Mountain Range, or my Dad refers to them as the Hoosier Smoky Mountains. It is a range of beautifully forested hills, not really high mountains. They are, or will be, a national forest for they are still one of the most beautiful scenes in America, still much like they were in the days of Daniel Boone when he explored the great expanse beyond the Appalachians in pre-Revolutionary days.

These forested hills extend from Fayetteville at the north end for 75 miles to the Ohio River at Cloversport near Cannelton at the south end. They average a width of about 25 miles. I figure we did our forced landing only about 5 miles east of the Jasper/Huntingburg highway where we took off. I get out the old road map I carry with my pocket Ben watch. Marty had said we are headed for a farmer's field just west of Paoli, which means we will be flying northeast from the Sherman's farm. According to my old road map, it will be about 30 miles over some of the prettiest part of the Hoosier Smokies. There is still a stretch of flatter farmland, but up ahead I can see those Hoosier Smokies. I'm excited to note we will pass directly over French Lick and West Baden Springs, those posh resort hotels in the Hoosier Smokies where the rich revel in the comforts and pleasures afforded them, while the ordinary folks like my Mother, Dad, Uncle John and Aunt Helen and I could also go and marvel at these great hotels. We could watch in awe and wonder, but never in jealousy, for we were allowed to habit the lobbies and beautiful grounds and to lunch in the coffee/dining rooms when dressed in our Sunday best—even during weekdays. The rich arrived mostly by rail, or by Pierce-

Arrow or Packard automobile limousines. Dad and Uncle John parked our ultra-modest Ford and Maxwell far away in the parking lot **so** that the mismatch with our dress would not be noticed by the upper crust.

We are now over the beautiful forested hill country of southern Indiana that my Dad always referred to as the Hoosier Smokies. After our last incident of the brushless distributor and its sudden forced landing, I am constantly scanning the terrain below, fantasizing where we will land if the OX-5 should conk out again. Even though it's all wooded hills below, there are a few small farms in the narrow valleys, just small pockets between the hills. These little farms do have small pastures or crop fields. We could land in those small spots but probably could not take off from any of them. I judge it is only about 30 miles from where we took off at Sherman's farm to Paoli. I look at my old pocket Ben watch, also I listen to the OX-5. By now I can tell pretty close what Marty's tachometer is reading in the rear cockpit, and from what he has told me of r.p.m.'s versus flying speed of the Waco, I can estimate our speed now at about 65 m.p.h. or 28 minutes from take-off to arrival over Paoli. We have been in the air now about 8 minutes, so we should be there in about 20 minutes.

Off to the south I can see all along the 75-mile length of the Hoosier wooded hill country. At this altitude I cannot see the Ohio River, but I can see the southern end of these Hoosier Smokies which means the Ohio River is there even if I cannot make it out. I spend the next 15 minutes savoring the scenery and languishing in the supreme feeling of being alive under these euphoric circumstances. Cruising along, enraptured with the vast beauty of only a small part of God's creation of this thing called Earth. Time does go quickly, all too quickly because down and off to the left there is French Lick and West Baden! I have been there before, but only by automobile. The beautifully manicured gardens and statuary of the richly designed French Lick Hotel is even more striking in its architectural richness from the air. The same opulence is reflected in nearby West Baden Springs.

During the past two weeks I have learned a lot about Marty. One of the many things is his cross-country navigation, which I found is made up of rather simple reliable methods. I wondered from the start how he knew where to land at his destination. There are no airports on most of his agenda. I found that he and other barnstormers exchanged information by mail prior to a barnstorming tour. Or they sometimes did so by Western Union telegram if time was short. The other thing they did was make fast friends if they could with the landowners that let them use their fields. During the winter months they corresponded with these folks. When the next summer season approached they essentially obtained permission or at least forewarned these friends of their intentions to land there again. Marty mentioned he had such a place selected for Paoli.

I had only been to Paoli once before on one of our auto trips to West Baden and French Lick. We had decided to check out the smaller mineral springs in Paoli. It is only a one-day trip, the distance being only ten miles from West Baden. But now I can see the town up ahead. The OX-5 is slowing down as we begin to slowly lose altitude. I had researched populations of these towns on our earlier auto trip. The Boonville Library's Indiana atlas of 1930 showed Paoli with 3050 residents. Marty had never been here before but obtained the Paoli field owner's name from another barnstormer. Then he contacted the field owner himself by mail. The other barnstormer had told him Paoli was a good place to rest from the so-called ardors of gypsy flying. A good place to join the town square loafers on a bench in the sun, to whittle on a stick of wood, philosophizing on the mysteries of life and other contemplative subjects.

We are passing over Paoli at about 300 feet altitude. I can see the courthouse square is the center of an intersection of two narrow highways, one from Bedford up north and the other from West Baden, 10 miles to the west. French Lick Creek stands out as it meanders through the town from West Baden and French Lick. The courthouse square is only a block north of a wide bend in the creek.

Marty makes a slow one-eighty turn to the south, heading back west. After a minute he does another one-eighty, heading back to approach Paoli again from the west, except this time he has throttled back, losing altitude. He seems to be lined up with the main east/west street going through Paoli. From that one trip two years ago I know it is Main Street, a street you drive in on from West Baden. Ahead I can see a stretch of level ground along the highway and the creek that is either mowed grass or hay. There are a few houses or barns back from the road to the north.

While I am mulling this over, Marty begins fishtailing the Waco and slipping it down into a landing mode. Before I know it he has flared into a nice three-point landing. We make one light bump on the springs of the landing gear, rolling to a stop at the far end of the field. He revs up the engine and taxis north about 100 yards and switches off the engine. As we slowly crawl out I notice a man making his way at a normal gait, coming down from one of the outbuildings. Marty starts off at a fast walk to meet the man. Being my naturally curious self, I tag along in a slow trot. The fellow is a clean man of about fifty, dressed in typical farm clothes, blue denim overalls and ankle-top, laced leather barnyard shoes.

Marty thrusts out a hand, quickly introducing us and gesturing to me to also shake the man's hand, who tells us his name is Galen Starr. This small acreage where we have landed is managed by him. It extends beyond the house and barns farther to the north. He and Marty exchange commentaries on their correspondence and also their mutual friend, the other barnstormer, who right now is somewhere over in Illinois. He tells us our plane will be safe where it is but suggest we taxi it up close to the barn in a fenced off space where the livestock will not bump into it or chew the fabric. He also tells us if we walk five short blocks east along the highway we will be in the center of town at the courthouse square.

The field where we have landed actually abuts the west end of Main Street. Main Street is actually the highway from West Baden as it enters Paoli. There are houses all along the street for three or four of those five blocks. Starr tells us there is a hotel and a couple of rooming houses near the center of Paoli. Also an auto service garage that sells gasoline and does repairs. He believes the owner would rent us an auto if we wished to drive back to West Baden for sightseeing.

With the Waco staked down, we pick up our light duffel bags, walking down to the road and its beginning of Main Street. Marty is stepping right along. I can hardly keep up with him. He says our trip thus far has been made up of riding in the plane or being driven in motor cars over short distances. So, now it feels good to take a good hike in this nice little town. Says he has been thinking a lot about what his barnstormer friend said about sitting on a bench and whiling away the time whittling on a piece of wood with his pocket knife. With that he drew out his pocketknife and gave me a wide grin. I then pull out my old Barlow pocket knife, a Christmas gift from my Grandma Baker when I was six or seven years old. Marty examines it carefully, but first handing me his two-blader by Case. We return each other's knives after a bit and Marty then begins to remark about some of the houses along Main Street and how they remind him of the nearest small town in Kansas when he was a lad. He also observed Lick Creek which lay immediately to our right and especially some well-worn places along the creek bank which were obviously used by the locals to do a little fishing. I remember a few of the cross streets running off to the left which either crossed Main Street or stopped short on Main because of the creek. This I remembered from the trips I took with my parents and uncle and aunt, when we had driven up to French Lick and West Baden. We came over to Paoli for a whole day, cruising around.

After a few blocks, the creek meanders off to the south about a block before it turns even further south, after passing the court square which we now approach.

At the court square, we sit down on a bench in the park surrounding the old courthouse. I discover that Marty has done his homework, as he always does. He doesn't carry any books or notepads or anything recording the research he has made before he began on the trip. His research always delves into the country where he will be flying his Waco for these two months. He especially concentrates on the history of the small towns. Where he digs all this up I don't know. Perhaps a lot of it, according to him, comes from the other barnstormers who have flown through this rural countryside.

I have done much the same thing myself because I've gone to our library in Boonville, which is less than a hundred miles away. So having information on these towns along our barnstorming route would not be too unusual for me to do since I am a Hoosier. But Marty had dug out details on all of these places, like Paoli, French Lick and West Baden, and he had done more of a thorough job than me. Between the two of us we talked over the history of Paoli. We both know that the old historic district here dates back to the founding of Orange County.

In 1816 Orange County was created by the Indiana legislature which subsequently appointed five commissioners whose responsibility was to fix a seat of justice for the county. A location along the north bank of Lick Creek in the approximate center of the county was chosen. The early residents were mostly Quakers from North Carolina seeking refuge from the slave-owning society of the South. They named the new county seat Paoli for the governor of North Carolina's twelve-year-old son who had died shortly before they moved to Indiana. The origin of the unusual name came from a famous Corsican patriot, Pasqually d'Paoli whose life extended from his birth in 1725 until his death in 1807. Paoli led the Corsicans as they fought a French takeover of their Mediterranean island in 1755 to 1756. The Corsicans were unsuccessful and Paoli was forced to flee to England where he was widely admired. One of his admirers was Samuel Ashe, later governor of North Carolina. Governor Ashe so admired Paoli that he named his son after him. As he became a popular governor and when his son Paoli died, the Quaker settlers of Orange County, North Carolina preserved his memory by naming the new county seat of their new home in Indiana, Paoli.

The Paoli historic district is significant as a town platted as a center of government. Within its boundaries the historic district contains many historic buildings of the late 19th and early 20th century as well as representative structures from the 1850's. The dominating feature of the historic district is the public square, which was platted and occupied by the impressive courthouse. The courthouse was built in the Greek Revival style.

We are now sitting in that court square which was platted back in the early 1800's. The Quakers are thought to have begun settling in Orange County as early as 1800, but the man generally given credit as the most important early colonizer was Zachariah Lindley who came to the head of Lick Creek in 1808 and soon erected a grist mill. The land on which the original town was laid out was purchased by Thomas Lindley and Thomas Hawker from the Federal Government on May 27, 1815. The land was then purchased from Lindley and Hawker. The county board appointed Jonathan Lindley a county agent. He laid out Paoli with 223 lots in April of 1816. The very early growth of the town was slow due to the large amounts of land purchased purely for speculation. By the 1830's, however, Paoli had easily distanced the other towns in the county in size and importance. Paoli had become the center of manufacturing and business for the county. Because Paoli was situated in an agricultural district, most of the early industries were connected to farm products. In 1828, David Adams began a business venture with ties to the Louisville, Kentucky area. It proved successful and consequently much of Paoli's business even today is connected to this area.

Paoli's early industrial development is directly related to the abundant water supply furnished by Lick Creek. There is little question that the commissioners had this in mind when choosing a site for the town. The first industrial site was located between Water Street and Lick Creek. Completion of the New Albany/Paoli Turnpike in 1838 quickened the growth of Paoli by providing better communication with the New Albany/Louisville area where Paolians did most of their business. By 1840 Paoli was large enough that the citizens sought incorporation with the county. Municipal powers were granted but were abandoned when Hiram Baxton, president of the town board was severely beaten. Paoli was finally incorporated in 1869. The need for a new courthouse and jail soon became apparent as the result of the dramatic growth of Paoli and Orange County and the county commissioners approved construction. The courthouse was completed in 1850 and the jail was completed in 1858.

Significant in the history of Paoli has been the large number of destructive fires.

Fires were the reason that most of the historic district's buildings are from the turn of the century. The first major fire was in 1879 when the beautiful four story Albert Hotel on the corner of South Gospel and Court Street burned. Six years later in 1885, the entire northwest side of the square was leveled in a disastrous fire. The sole surviving building was a corner structure on North Gospel Street. After the construction of this side of the square, another fire in 1891 burned the three buildings north of West Main Street. This fire started in a feather renovating plant on the southeast side of the square in 1894. The blaze demolished all buildings from South Gospel Street to the middle of the eastern side of the square. Shortly following this fire, concerned citizens started a water works to replace the bucket brigade, a system of passing buckets of water along a line of people.

An ordinance prohibiting flammable structures from being erected on the square was passed, nevertheless the fire demon struck again in 1917 when the old Arlington Hotel and adjacent buildings on the northeast corner of the square burned. The close proximity of the buildings made control of these fires virtually impossible with these primitive fire-fighting techniques.

Paoli grew steadily despite the frequent fires. An important contributor to this growth was the arrival of the Louisville, New Albany, and Cincinnati Railroad, commonly called the Monon in 1887. It was a spur from the main route to transport tourists to the resort towns of West Baden and French Lick, ten miles west of Paoli. As these towns flourished, elated Paoli businessmen devised a scheme to capture some of the tourist trade. A company of leading businessmen was formed: The Paoli Mineral Springs Company, and two mineral wells were drilled. The first, the Sulphur Springs, was drilled 250 feet to yield a strong sulphur water; the second, The Lithia Springs, was bored to a depth of 1055 feet. The Lithia water was touted as the world's finest, rivaling even the famous spas of Europe. The Lithia water was bottled at a bottling plant and shipped to Chicago. Gazebos were erected over the wells, and parks created around them. A lake was formed by damming Lick Creek below the Lithia Springs and named Lake Waterloo for the author Stanley Waterloo. He and his wife spent some time in Paoli making a study of birds and resting.

The disastrous fire of 1894 which leveled the southeast side of the square proved beneficial to the Mineral Springs company,, who quickly erected the impressive Mineral Springs Hotel. Water from the sulphur springs was piped into the hotel for bathing, and electric lighting was provided, a first for Paoli. The Mineral Springs Hotel quickly became not only a hostelry for guests, but also a gathering place for the wealthy and prominent citizens of the town. The Opera House was created to bring culture to Paoli. During the upswing in Paoli's economy, most of the commercial and residential buildings were built. Many large, fine Victorian style homes were constructed, notable among these are the Baxton, Patton, Reilly and Lindley houses.

Industries did far more than the unsuccessful bout with tourism to support the historic district. The resort idea waned as Paoli's neighbors, West Baden and French Lick became the playground for America's wealthy.

After our little discussion on the court square bench, we gather up our duffel bags, begin ambling around the square, sort of casing all four sides, looking over some of the stores and business houses, most of which had been there for many years. Of course as we had learned before, much of this square had been replaced over the years because of all the fires that had occurred over a period of seventy-five years. But even the buildings here in this year of 1933 look rather old to me.

Marty says, "Well, you had enough walking now? How about another couple blocks? Why don't we amble up a couple of blocks north of the square? According to Mr. Starr, one of the rooming houses will be a place for us. I think that would be a better idea than trying the hotel. What do you think?"

I said, "Okay with me, Marty. You're the boss and also the pilot of our Waco."

Marty quips, "I sort of like being boss." We walk up Gospel Street for two blocks, take off to the right, walk another block and then up a ways to the north.

We stop in front of a house which appears as though it had been built around 1895 or 1900 with a sign that is very prominently placed, a black background with gold letters: "ROOMS FOR RENT." We mount the front porch, ring the big doorknocker, and a lady of about sixty answers the door. We introduce ourselves, Marty explaining in great detail about how we had landed our plane over west of town and are looking for lodging for two or three nights. As he mentions Mr. Starr's name, her face brightens markedly. Before that I was beginning to wonder if she was going to turn us away, we being the gypsies we are.

The room she shows us is on the first floor with a bathroom connected to that room and one other. She explains, "Since that other room is not occupied" she will lock that one off so we have the facility for ourselves. She wants to know how long we will stay. Marty looks at me, back to her and saying, "Well, at least three days, and why don't we pay you accordingly."

"Sirs, with Mr. Starr's recommendation, I think it best that you just simply let us know when you're prepared to leave and we'll settle up then." Marty tells her that we expect to sightsee around the town and in so doing we would probably eat at the restaurants around or near the square. She introduces herself as Mrs. Kelley. She has lived in this house for 48 years. Her husband passed away ten years earlier. Renting of rooms in her house was her only livelihood, in addition to being a dressmaker.

Marty asks her where the Adams' garage is located. She explains it is two blocks to the west, on the other side of Gospel Street. She says, "It is a small place, a small building and has a gas pump. Most of the work Mr. Adams does is doing repair and servicing autos."

Marty turns to me, "Peyton, the day is wearing along, it's getting late in the afternoon, how about we walk down to that little restaurant we saw near the square and after we have a dinner, why don't we walk over to the Adams garage to see if it's possible we can lease from him an automobile."

The restaurant is excellent. We have a nice home-cooked pan-fried steak, mashed potatoes and gravy for $1.65. I thought that was a real bargain and so did Marty for he had the same thing, smiling from ear to ear with every bite. Then he grins, "Peyton, pull out your old pocket Ben. What time is it? We are just about through now, one more cup of coffee and we can hike over to Mr. Adams' garage and see if he has closed up."

I pulled out the pocket Ben, swiftly showing it to Marty as if I didn't expect him to take my word for reading the time on my own watch. The pocket Ben reads 5:45. Marty shook his head and said, "Well, Peyton, let's take another hike anyway. Perhaps he'll still be there."

The Adams' garage was aptly described as just that, simply a little two auto shed with a double door facing the street, on a lot all by itself. The doors were closed and locked. Marty strolls over to the house next door, raps on the front door asking the man who opened the door if he was Mr. Adams, who replies, "Oh no, he lives three blocks from here; he closes up at 5:30, but he'll be back at work as usual about 7:00 o'clock tomorrow."

With that we turned and headed back toward the court square, it still being daylight and too early to turn in. Marty pulls out his pocketknife, fondles it and I ask, "What did you have in mind down at the court square again? Most of those businesses are closing up, not too much open down there but a few people walking around is all I've seen."

Marty replies, his brow all furrowed, "Peyton, I had you figured for a more observant lad than that. You know when we sat down on the bench discussing the history of the town?"

I nodded. "Yes, I remember. I remember us discussing the history of the town on the bench."

"Well," Marty replies, "Did you look over on the other side of the square? A gentleman sitting over there on another bench?"

I said, "No, I didn't know there were any other benches."

"Well, as a matter of fact, there's a bench on each side, on the north and the south and on the east and on the west. We came in on the west side, we sat on a bench there. Well, the bench over on the north side there reposed an elderly gentleman who I waved at and you did not notice as we passed by going up Gospel Street."

"No," I said, "I didn't see him."

"Well, if you had seen him, what you would have seen was an old gentleman with a long stick of wood on which he was whittling away. In fact, he had a pile of sticks on the bench beside him and he had a small pile of shavings on the ground at his feet. We're going over and introduce ourselves to the old gentleman and I'll bet he's still there."

As we come down Gospel Street to Court Street, facing on the north side of the square, we see sitting over there on the bench an old gentleman with white hair almost to his shoulders. He wore an old black hat, even in this warm summer atmosphere, a long black coat, black trousers and ankle top laced shoes. He held a stick in his hands, which he had rounded out with his knife. He deftly used a beautiful, long bladed, folding knife and I wondered what it might be. I could see it glisten in the setting sun even as we approached.

Marty introduces himself unceremoniously, saying, "Sir, we are whittlers ourselves and I would like to introduce us. And you Sir, are ... ?"

The old gentleman looks up, chuckles, lays down his stick of wood and his beautiful, long, 4-inch blade Case knife. it looks as though it is a three blader and he is whittling with the longest blade. He introduces himself as Jasper Rusch. He explains, "Spelled R-u-s-c-h. I like to sit here and use a knife. A knife on wood is a peaceful thing to while away the time and one can be thinking too about what may be pleasant, what may be necessary to resolve a question in one's mind, or whatever things are important to the whittler or his friends. But there is a great deal of peace in whittling on a stick of wood with a nice knife that you're proud of. You fellows are the only ones I've talked to about whittling in many many years. I could tell you were whittlers when I saw you before over on the west bench. No one seems to care much about it any more. Always pick up my shavings and put them in this paper sack over here and carry them away.

"Gentlemen, care to sit down on the bench here with me and get out your knives? I have plenty of sticks."

We sit here for two hours until it begins to get dark and the old gentleman decides that he needs to make his way home, which was only two blocks away. He has a cane laying on the ground beside him, picks it up, shakes hands with us, his old eyes moist, he says, "Thank you so very much for whittling with me."

But during that two hours it was the most fun I've had in years, especially when spending it with this genuine old person and getting a chance to try out my own knife along with someone else who really knew how to use one. As we whittled, the three of us talked about all sorts of things. Oh sure, airplanes, gliders and Mr. Rusch's farm that he used to have but no longer does, and many many other things, much of it real homespun philosophy. It brought Marty and I down to earth in a way that I had never experienced before, except for the times I had done this same thing some years back in the fall sitting next to the woodshed at my grandfather's place. He too was a great whittler.

Arch and Peyton Autry before 1933 at 420 Oak Street, Boonville, Indiana.

Falls of the Ohio before 1933.

Lanier Mansion at Madison before 1933.

CHAPTER X

The next morning we shower, put on fresh clothes, head down to the little restaurant again where we'd had dinner the night before, and to our great pleasure learn they also serve breakfast. They have been open since 5:00 o'clock. After a leisurely breakfast, we walk up to Adams's garage. As we arrive both the doors are open and a man of about sixty stands surrounded by four autos parked inside. one in the rear has the hood off and its engine torn apart. The head is off and he is grinding the valves.

Marty introduces us. Mr. Adams' face brightens, his eyebrows lift as he says very warmly, "I'm pleased to meet you fellows."

The thing that really caught his attention, he tells us, was our flight over Paoli the day before. We discover that Mr. Adams, while not a pilot, is very air-minded. He talks at great length to Marty about planes of different types. He has flown many times as a passenger. He is acquainted with the variants of Wacos, Travelaires and various other privately owned types of planes such as our Waco. And the engines fascinate him very much, of course, his being an auto mechanic. He has many questions about the OX-5, he has never worked on one but is full of questions and exceedingly curious.

Finally Marty gets around to asking him if it is possible for us to rent a car from him for three or four days. He shows us a 1930 Ford open touring car. He wonders if five dollars a day would be okay but we must purchase the fuel. Marty readily agrees, saying we would start off by filling the tank from his gas pump out on the sidewalk.

After checking the Ford's gas gauge, adding five gallons and paying Mr. Adams, we drive over to Gospel Street and then down to the court square, turning west on Main Street, the road to French Lick. Just out of town Marty pulls off on a narrow lane leading up to Mr. Starr's barn and our adjacent Waco. Galen Starr is not around at the moment. Marty says, "Let's look the ship over and make sure everything is okay, then we will head over to West Baden and French Lick and see what the grandiloquent are doing at those ritzy hotels you've been telling me about."

Before we rented the Ford I asked Marty if he considered taking the Monon train over to these two famous spas at West Baden and French Lick. He replies, "Well, I thought of that. The summer tourist trade is at its peak so the train should be coming at least once a day through Paoli here." Then he launched into a history of the Monon Railway, telling me things I already knew! The Southern Railway runs across southern Indiana's Ohio River valley from Evansville up to New Albany and Louisville, Kentucky. The Monon Railway is really a northern spur loop of the Southern extending from New Albany to serve towns such as Pekin, Connor, Salem and Campbellsburg, then on up north to Bedford and down to Orleans, Paoli, West Baden and French Lick, then on south to rejoin the main line Southern again.

The Monon serves the lush, sedate spa hotels of West Baden and French Lick so the affluent rich from the urban east coast and even the nobility out of Europe could reach these famous resorts by rail through Cincinnati and Louisville. Likewise, the rich industrialists of the Midwest could arrive from Chicago by rail through Indianapolis and then from Bedford on the Monon. One wonders if the Monon's origin had much to do with providing access to French Lick and West Baden by these great folks of means and social station.

When Marty said he'd asked the restaurant owner about using the Monon instead of renting an automobile, the man said the train passed through once a day but due to the short ten-mile distance to West Baden the train made no stops anymore. In an earlier day when Paoli itself was a mineral spa, the train stopped regularly. In those days there were three spas and the Monon arrived from the north to Paoli, West Baden and French Lick in that order, but no stops nowadays in Paoli. Instead it just passes through town.

The highway to West Baden is a narrow, paved, two-lane road but we barely get beyond the western limit of Paoli when Marty suddenly turns off left at Willow Creek Road. He says he'd heard of the old Lindley home and wants we should see it.

The Lindley house is a two story Victorian frame house still in beautiful condition. It was the home of Thomas Lindley, one of the two founders of Paoli back in 1815. It was also the home of Thomas Lindley who platted the original 223 lots of the town in 1816. Marty gets out of the Ford, knocks on the door to find no one at home. He then walks all around the place, looking it over just as though he plans to buy the place. We then return to the West Baden highway to French Lick. We pass along some very beautiful, scenic rural farmland, all very picturesque.

The ten miles to West Baden pass by very quickly. Up ahead I see West Baden and remember coming through there with my parents on a drive three summers ago, or was it even longer? Yes, my first time up here I was only seven.

We enter West Baden along the Abbeydell Pike. The road into town is straight but as we approach Lost River it is just a small creek, a tributary of French Lick Creek which runs alongside the Monon tracks north of our drive into town on Abbeydell Pike. As we enter town, the road turns in a wide sweeping turn to the south, then becomes Broadway Street.

I tell Marty to turn left on First Street, go over one block so that he can turn left again so that we can drive on Main Street. West Baden is a small town. We drive around in the central district for a while, looking at the Monon Station in West Baden. Marty seems to not be impressed by it. Perhaps he feels slighted because the train passes through Paoli and instead we had to rent an automobile to be able to reach West Baden and French Lick. We also visit the Mineral Springs at West Baden. Marty only shook his head when I teased him about drinking the stuff, after I had described in great detail the diuretic effect it had on my family when we visited here several years back.

We then drive on down on the main highway to French Lick, which is only about two miles. When we arrive at the French Lick Springs Hotel, Marty really comes to attention. He does not say much and the reason he doesn't is that he is so engrossed.

As we drive into the huge grounds and elaborately manicured long entrance driveway, we are motioned in to a secluded parking space by a uniformed attendant. But Marty stops, asking the "general"—as he referred to him to me—that he wants to park near the entrance where he can see other autos parked. The uniformed one sniffily asks if we are guests, being snootily obvious that he is aware that we are not. Marty just laughs at the question, then he says, "Yes."

The snooty one then peers at our front bumper, saying our vehicle guest tag must be prominently displayed. Then Marty replies, "We left it in our room." Then snooty one asks our names and Marty shoots back, "I'm Frank Taggart and my young friend here is Tommy Taggart."

The snooty one comes sharply to attention. "Pass on, sir. I'm so sorry for the delay."

I start to say something and Marty shot back a silent look that plainly says, "Shut up, Peyton." As we drive on, I blurt, "Marty, that's not our names and Tom Taggart is the old Chicago billionaire who built this place years ago."

Marty grins, "Peyton, shame on you. Tom is your first name, Peyton your second name and your last name is Taggart, at least until we see the inside of this joint."

The adjacent autos in the lot make us both so excited they alone are worth the trip. Even Packard deluxe sedans were the lowest grade of the lot. There were huge Lincolns, Cadillacs, to be sure, but also foreign limousines, a Rolls Royce town car that seemed over 30 feet long, open front and closed in rear with telephone to the chauffeur.

Marty is really taken with the gardens, which I had seen twice before, the last time three years ago. One could spend all day in the gardens without retracing the same path.

Entering the hotel one has several entrances to choose from. The main entrance is staffed by two uniformed gents who literally stared us down, even though politely. But even Marty elected to take the side entrance. The main lobby is a high, vaulted, circular room, which on special occasions serves as a huge ballroom. A circular two-level mezzanine overlooks the main floor of marble. In fact, the entire building, as well as surrounding structures are the work of European artists in marble, Bedford stone and terra cotta. The banisters and colonnades of the mezzanine struck Marty as an awesome work of Grecian and Roman style art.

I felt out of place just like I did as a kid twice before. I could tell Marty felt the same, but his forthright nature subdued it much more than I. He circled the room to an entry into a wing of the main hotel. It was a huge dining room in which luncheon was being served. It was absolutely elegant. High-class silverware, silver wine buckets, white tablecloths, and elegant French Provincial furniture. Everyone in the entire hotel is smartly dressed in summer suits and dresses. The men all wear summer silk shirts, white Palm Beach suits, collars and ties. Here we are, baggy pants, scuffed, run-over shoes and rolled up shirt sleeves, no ties. I noted then that Marty carries a large old soiled envelope filled with our flyers, those in which no price for a ride is quoted. The maitre d' of the dining room measures us visually and disapprovingly, but he allows Marty to place a stack of flyers on the counter. At the front desk in the main hall he does the same thing. He also hands a wad to all of the bellhops, doormen, waiters and room maids that he could approach. They all seem to welcome our red flyers. He talks the maids into placing a flyer in each room. Rooms in the main building are off each of the two floors of the mezzanine. Marty then turns to me, saying, "Let's get out of here. I'll come back some day when I'm a rich airplane manufacturer. I'll bring my white tie, tails and frock coat. I'll show 'em."

I laugh, "Can I come along too when you are rich?"

We take a look outside at one of the Lithia Water fountains and have a good laugh. We get in the Ford heading over to see the wintering grounds and barns of one of the great circuses. Either Barnum & Bailey or Hagenback & Wallace, I didn't know which. The circus was out on its regular summer tour all over the U.S.A. There are no animals on the grounds, just empty sheds and barns and a few caretakers.

We head back to Paoli and our favorite restaurant for dinner. The next day Marty says, as he got out of bed, "Well, let's go have breakfast and go to work flying some passengers."

I reply, "Do you think anyone will come out to Mr. Starr's farm? We haven't advertised here."

Marty looks surprised. "Have not advertised? How about all those hand-bills at French Lick? I told all the employees that we would fly the guests over the hotel so they could see it from the air. It's only 10 miles up there but further than we usually do, so those rich folks will not bat an eye at paying $35.00 each." I laugh and shake my head. But Marty did not crack a smile. He was very serious.

After a bountiful breakfast, which would likely have to last us all day, we drive out to Galen Starr's farm, parking the Ford up near the barn. Marty goes up to the small house to tell Starr we would like to taxi the plane down next to the road as we were expecting to fly passengers, if that was okay with him? I tag along as usual, all ears, but in strict silence. I had wondered all along on this trip if Marty and his correspondence with farmers like Starr, had he not only asked permission to land but also to carry passengers for several days, making repeated take-offs and landings. After listening to them talk, I conclude it to be a typical situation. It is obvious that point had been discussed and agreed upon in their letters. So our visit is merely a friendly courtesy.

Starr is saying, "I wasn't sure if it would be today, so I left the cattle in the field, so I'll just move them into the field over the hill. I don't let them into the hayfield anyway except to graze along the fence down to the road."

We cranked up the Waco, taxi it out from its little fenced off area near the barn, parking it down near the French Lick road near a gate. Marty had hand painted up a large sign over in Adams's garage, reading: "AIRPLANE RIDES. SEE FRENCH LICK AND WEST BADEN RESORTS FROM THE AIR. ENTER FIELD THROUGH GATE."

No sooner had we parked the Waco when an auto drove up to the gate. But it had come from Paoli, not West Baden. it was none other than Mr. Adams, the auto mechanic and spare time airplane buff. He is all excited with looking over the Waco and especially the OX-5. Marty even removes the cowling to give him a closer look. He would let no one else even touch it. Then Adams let us know he'd like a ride if that was okay. Marty says, "That's what we're here for. Tell you what, you gave us a good deal on rental of the Ford so we would like to give you a free ride. We are aiming to fly French Lick guests on a special low flight over the resort. I'd like to fly up there now to sort of emphasize the handbills we left there yesterday. We will also take Mr. Starr along. The two of you in the forward cockpit." Then he turns to me, "Peyton, run up to the barn and tell Starr to come on down. We are flying him up to the resorts."

Ten minutes later I show the two men how to enter the cockpit and strap up without putting a foot through the lower wing. I run back to the rear cockpit to do my switching duties as Marty swung the propeller. They taxi down to the east end of the field, swing around, taking off to the west, headed for West Baden. I take up my usual lonely vigil when Marty is in the air with passengers. There are no waiting passengers to talk to like that weekend at

Huntingburg. I think to myself, Dubois County was certainly a place with a lot of air-minded people. Just people who simply wanted to ride in a plane.

I could still see the Waco receding in the distance, but flying low at only 400 feet. Then I noticed an automobile up ahead which seemed to have stopped. The occupants got out of the vehicle, stood staring up at the Waco. Marty had seen them too because he circled the automobile twice, then headed back west again. I can see the automobile up ahead is again coming this way. I stand there waiting for a long while because it is approaching very slowly. Even a quarter mile away I can tell it is very different. As it draws closer, my eyes almost fall out of my head because I had seen only one automobile, one car like this once before. It was owned by a banker in Boonville who had bought it new and drove it for only a year, selling it to some gentleman in Chicago for a handsome price. The reason he sold it was not because it was not a fine automobile, but all the townsfolk began to talk so much about how wealthy he was and he did not want to be known as a wealthy man. But it was an automobile that I would never forget, a Pierce-Arrow, and this one approaching was a Pierce-Arrow with its headlights molded into the forward fenders in a rather unusual fashion. Something that is very unusual even today in 1933. This long sedan is in two colors, a crimson red body and a blue hood and ornate silvered chrome radiator.

As the Pierce-Arrow passed by, it then slowed about a hundred feet down the road braking to a stop, slowly going into reverse and backing up. As it reached the gate, the driver, an elderly man with a neatly trimmed white mustache, wore a chauffeur's black cap with a leather visor. He wore a white shirt, necktie and, even in summer, wore a light weight black jacket and trousers. The rear windows were darkened and I cannot see the passengers, but the chauffeur calls out to me, "Young man, is this where the plane lands?"

"Yes, right here. At the moment he is flying passengers up to French Lick."

He nods, saying, "Yes, we saw him. He circled our automobile."

I have difficulty paying attention to his questions, I am so enraptured with the Pierce-Arrow. The distinguished older gentleman driving it as chauffeur is now quietly engaged in conversation with the person in the enclosed and darkened passenger compartment. Then he asks, "Are you associated in any way with the pilot? And do you know when he is expected to return?"

"Yes, I'm his assistant and I am a pilot too," I fibbed just a little. I looked at the Pocket Ben and added, "He should return in about 20 minutes or so."

The elderly chauffeur relayed my message, then shut off the Pierce-Arrow's purring motor. Then the rear window rolls down and a very sophisticated female voice calls out politely, "Young man, may I speak to you? Please come forward and do an old lady many years your senior a delightful favor."

As I approach looking into the tasteful interior, I see an elderly but attractive, very erect, primly poised lady of regal bearing. She wore a light summer suit and skirt of exquisite tailoring and texture the likes of which I had never seen before, even in cities like Evansville. Her graying hair was done up like a lady of fashion. She wore a style of Panama hat that would have fit either a distinguished lady like herself or a distinguished gentleman. She introduced herself as Margaret Stockton and her driver simply as Jason. She went on to say, she was from New York City and staying at French Lick. It was then I said I'd noticed her license plates were New York State, and it must have been a nice but long drive from there. She replied, "Oh my, no. Jason and I travel by train to French Lick, shipping the automobile ahead, care of the hotel."

Her attention persisted toward me. "You are so young to be flying about with a gypsy aviator, but I do admire it. If I were your age I would not be just an assistant, but an aviator myself. My husband loved to fly. He was killed as a student pilot in the U.S. Army in 1917."

But then I blurt out a desperate effort to correct her erroneous impression. I tell her I am an aviator. I tell her all about my glider flying and my enroute flying of the Waco.

That really got her attention. She called out to Jason, "I want to fly with his pilot. I shall be ready down in the field here when the plane arrives."

I start to open the door but Jason is there, gently pushes me aside. It is his job I can readily see, but I say, "But, Ma'am, there is no place out in the hayfield for you to sit. We can taxi the plane right up to the gate."

"Nonsense," she retorts, "Jason has my folding chair, besides, I'm not helpless, young man." When she gets out I can see how right she was. I have never seen such a regal, erect and physically distinguished person in all my life. She reminds me of some of the regal roles played by Ethel Barrymore in the movies. In fact, Mrs. Stockton looks much like Ethel Barrymore, and her diction and air are uncannily the same. She excitedly questions me about my glider flying, my parents, where our barnstorming tour had taken us, questions, questions, and more questions. This lady is really alive. She had done a lot of flying as a passenger; and the pilots and planes that she names leave me in a state of perpetual awe. Planes I have only read about, have never seen, big planes, planes with two engines, planes with three engines, planes with four engines. She went on to say that other guests at French Lick Hotel had questioned the security of her trip down here to fly with aerial "gypsies" as a result of Marty's handbills. It is readily apparent that she has been literally sent by others at French Lick to check us out, and it is apparent also that she will be sending them down here in droves after her flight, even though she has not even met Marty, but she has seen the Waco in the air. She knew instantly it was a Waco Model 10 powered with a Curtiss

OX-5 engine. She knew her airplanes and I feel highly complimented because she has judged its aviators solely by her judgment of me, without even saying so to me. What a great lady!

After twenty minutes, Marty landed and both Adams and Starr were excited about their flight, even though Marty said they made several real tight turns over French Lick Resort. Starr's description instead was, "We did a couple dozen loopity-loops all over them millionaires at the hotel. We really scared the liver out of the whole lot of 'em!"

I had run over to help Adams and Starr out of the plane. The main reason for my job in helping grown adults in and out of the front cockpit is to make sure they put their feet on the step next to the side of the fuselage. This area was a 12-inch space between the two innermost ribs of the lower wing on the left side. That area is planked over with plywood on top of the wing ribs and covered over by the doped fabric covering the wings. A small hinged door is cut into the left upper longeron of the fuselage to get one's legs inside to reach the seat. There is no door and no step on the right side. Access is only on the left side of the cockpit. If one steps on the lower wing outboard of the 12-inch step, your foot would go right through the fabric of the wing in the 12-inch space between the second and third wing ribs.

While Adams and Starr make their way home, Marty, I could tell, was impatiently waiting to ask me who the attractive lady was sitting in the chair over by the gate. Of course, he saw the parked Pierce-Arrow, which he had buzzed only 30 minutes earlier. I told him her name and how I thought she looked and acted like Ethel Barrymore, and that she was anxious to take a plane ride, and that she had flown all over the world in some famous big airplanes like Ford Trimotors, Fokker Transports, big Flying Boats in England and Germany and you name it, she'd flown in it.

As I spoke Jason stepped over briskly, doffing his little black cap, introducing himself, then asking Marty, "Sir, Madame wishes to speak to you, she also wishes to engage your piloting skills aloft to view the resorts of French Lick and West Baden."

Marty went over to her quickly and he was the epitome of grace, dignity and diplomacy. To say the two of them hit it off would be the understatement of the century. They regaled each other with all sorts of exchanged stories and escapades, then she said, "Well, shall you and I fly or shall we keep on discoursing with this old lady the things which she adores that you and young Peyton do?" Marty told her we usually fly two passengers at a time if we can, and would Mr. Jason be coming along also?

She retorted, "oh my gracious, no. Jason has been with me for many years. He is not afraid of anything but he will not fly. I'm only joking, of course, but his typical concern would be to worry if we two were to crash.

He would not be here to drive my sedan back to the hotel." we all had a laugh on that one. But Jason stood firm and smiling, not saying a word. To do so would be out of place in his view, I'm sure. She turned to Jason making a silent but knowing gesture.

She arose and he proudly returned the folding chair to the Pierce-Arrow, then returned, approaching Marty aside. He handed several large bills to Marty, saying, "Madame wishes Peyton to accompany her." Marty looked at the two $50 bills, saying, "Peyton is not a passenger, he's my helper, he rides for free, besides you gave me too much. This is $100 here. Even if she pays for Peyton it would be twice $35, or $70."

Jason looked troubled. "Please, sir, Mr. Marty, Madame still wishes it to be $100. And Madame wishes Peyton at her side when aloft, sir."

Marty just shook his head, quipping, "All aboard." Then I see her making her way back from the limousine, the Panama hat is missing. She is carrying a beautiful white gabardine cloth helmet and goggles, the best money could buy. She said she'd flown 150,000 miles in that helmet.

I load her into the Waco first, return to my switching duties in the rear while Marty swung the propeller, then I get up alongside Miss Margaret, as Jason referred to her. We take off west as Jason waves us off, standing by his precious Pierce-Arrow limousine.

Marty really gives our gracious lady her money's worth. We buzz the hotel at French Lick so low and in such steep rolling banks I am afraid we will take the dome off the fabulous joint, and bring out the sheriff in force. Miss Margaret lets forth with yells of elation as we dive in low over the resort with the OX-5 throttled down in those low approaches. I am sure the guests could hear her very clearly. Most of them were expecting her and were standing out on the grounds and the driveways surrounding the elegant place. After repeatedly buzzing both French Lick and West Baden, Marty takes her on a long scenic ride to the south, deep into the Hoosier Smokies. She waxes eloquently on how beautiful they are and how they remind her of the German Black Forest, and the forest along the Hudson River in her own New York State, and also the area around her other favorite spa at Saratoga Springs, New York.

We return to Paoli after an hour in the air. Jason's obviously worried countenance shows great relief as I help her out of the Waco, he standing by like a worried old guard dog. She fussed that she wanted to stay and talk with us a while, but then she saw Jason's worried look and promised to return tomorrow to watch us fly the other hotel guests which she assured us would be here in force tomorrow.

It is getting late so we empty one of the gas cans from the Ford into the Waco, taxiing the ship up to its place by the barn, then head into Paoli for dinner and bed.

The next day we are down at Starr's place early, taxiing the Waco down by the road. At 10 o'clock they started showing up; Cadillacs, Lincolns, long sedans of limousine quality, two of the Rolls-Royce town cars, a Stutz sport coupe, which as I recall was known as a Bearcat. And then there were three Cords made up in Auburn, Indiana, a very fine automobile, and one especially exquisite is a Hispano-Suiza limousine town car owned by some noble person from Europe whose name and place of origin I could not pronounce let alone remember. And last but not least was Margaret Stockton and Jason leading the group in her Pierce-Arrow. She insisted the lot of them must fly with Marty. While they waited their turns, the gent in the Hispano broke out a bottle of champagne from a cooler for a few toasts and sophisticated socializing. The toasting and drinking are properly discreet.

For my part I am busy as the proverbial bird dog in a gamebird aviary, loading passengers and taking their money. I have never handled so much money in all my life. No one seems to expect or wait for change. Marty is way off the mark with his $35 fee. He should have made it $50, then the question, or lack of question regarding change from a $50 bill, would not have even come up. They kept on coming all day long. The road on both sides is parked with all manner of expensive large automobiles. Even the townsfolk of Paoli stand in the road ogling the fine folks from the resorts, gaping at and admiring the collection of autos.

Marty and I are even busier than those two days at Huntingburg. He flies them over both resorts with three or four passes, then returns for another load. The hotel has sent along bountiful picnic lunches and drinks for their guests. Miss Margaret and Jason stay all day. She made sure Jason provided both Marty and I plenty of sandwiches, soft drinks and coffee.

The 0 X-5 is not shut down all day and Marty is never out of the cockpit. He eats his lunch and drinks his coffee while in the air. We both marveled at Miss Margaret's lunches. It is the first time either of us has ever eaten caviar and fancy French pate sandwiches. This all continues until almost dark when the high classed entourage make their way back to West Baden and French Lick.

This first day repeats itself on the second day and also on the third day. By mid afternoon on the third day the number of limousines parked on the road dwindled to only three until 4 o'clock when all had left. The last to go were Miss Margaret and Jason. She gives both Marty and I hugs we will never forget. She is a very strong of heart lady. Her only tears were nothing more than a dab or two to her eyes with a silk handkerchief. Her verbal good-bye lasted for 30 minutes. She told us how she wished she could fly with us on our tour, sleeping out on hay stubble under the Waco's wings. She hated to go, but go they did. We would really miss her and would for years to come and we told her so, both of us at the same time.

On the fourth day we are down to flying a few local passengers at $3 per ride and we do this for almost a week. We still have the Ford but neither of us wanted to drive back up to French Lick. Neither of us said why but we missed our fine lady too much. Going there would only remind us of the vast space between her life and ours.

Marty counted up our take back at Mrs. Kelley's one evening. We had taken in $6400. Marty and I drive out to Starr's place, Marty explaining to him the unusual situation of flying guests from the resorts. It is something that will never happen again. Normally our cash take is so small we can only buy gas and eat. Not enough to pay field rental fees to landowners or care-takers who are so good to allow us to use their fields free. But in this case it is different. Marty handed him what appeared to be several hundred dollars and telling him if he came back next year he would not be able to pay him at all. Starr seems to understand, looking on it as a one-time bit of fortune. He also remarked that the rich guests enjoyed their flights and the field party immensely and had gotten more than their money's worth.

We stay at Paoli almost another week. Marty, I thought, never tired of flying as long as we had gas. But now the Waco sat idle at Starr's farm for a week, its fuel tank full to the cap. We make one trip a day out there to do a ten-minute inspection, then return to Paoli. We never drive anywhere else in nearly a week. Marty and I spend most of our time loafing around the court square, and most of that on the benches whittling with our pocketknives. Marty has whittled a bushel basket of shavings it seems from the sticks he carries from Mrs. Kelley's and Adams's garage. I whittle also but I tire of it in two days, but I enjoy the discussions Marty has with the other locals. Sometimes I take an hour or two at the library which is very interesting.

I knew our next step would be flying to Salem, which lay only twenty miles due east. I was there last year with Marvin Northrop to pick up my Mead Glider and to deliver my Hocker monoplane. It would be interesting to see the fellows again who had built the old Mead Rhon Ranger.

Next morning we arise at the usual time and walking down to the nearby restaurant for breakfast. As Marty sips his coffee, he says, "Well, Peyton, you ready to go over to Salem?" After somewhere between one and two seconds, I said, "Yeah!" so loud it drew attention from the other customers. We walk back over to Mrs. Kelley's, packed our meager belongings, paid her our room rent and drove the Ford over to Adams' garage, paying him our auto rental. Adams insists he drive us out to the plane, but Marty is even more determined to walk the one-mile out there. It is a nice day and still a cool forenoon. We talk with Adams for nearly an hour, then bid him farewell until next summer, as Marty put it.

When we arrive at the plane it is still wet in the morning dew which glistens on the silver wings. We are disappointed to learn from Mrs. Starr that her husband had departed to Grangeville up northeast eight miles on farm business. We unstake the Waco, start it up and taxi down near the road at the east end of the field, swing around to the west and take a leisurely five or six minutes to warm up the OX-5. We take off to the west, climbing slowly to about 500 feet. I wonder if Marty is going to make a pass over French Lick. I decided no, he would not do that, but he kept on going.

As we pass over the hotel at 100 feet, he rocked the wings back and forth three times. I could see the limo parking lot below very clearly. There was no Pierce-Arrow, but back near the storage garage, far behind the hotel I could see a red Pierce-Arrow poised to be readied for shipment. I could also see the Monon train moving east through West Baden, headed for its junction at New Albany with the Southern Railway, which in turn joined other lines from Cincinnati and on to Philadelphia, Washington and New York.

As I mulled the idea of buzzing the train and how hard it would be to communicate the idea with Marty over slipstream, propeller and engine noise, he began nosing the ship down and speeding up the OX-5. Hooray! He's doing it! As the train turned east out of West Baden in a clear area, he pulls by the train a little more than the same speed as the train. So slow, I was afraid we'd stall. We are less than 50 feet over the fields almost at the eye level of the passengers at their windows. Then he climbs over the train on the other side, repeating the show for the passengers on that side. I could not see Miss Margaret but if she was on the train she would certainly see us.

We then climbed up to 500 feet again and in a couple of minutes we are over Paoli and headed east for Salem.

There are two things that stand out in my interest regarding Salem. As a teen age Civil War history buff, I am aware that Salem figured importantly as the site of an invasion by the Confederates in 1863. The second thing of interest was my truck trip from Boonville to Salem only last summer with famed World War I flyer and used plane dealer Marvin Northrop of Minneapolis.

The only two Civil War battles which were fought in the north both occurred in July 1863. The much more famous one was at Gettysburg, Pennsylvania, but the one remembered by Hoosiers was at Corydon, Indiana. Both were turning points in the war, although Gettysburg, of course, was much greater in size and casualties. For six days, Confederate raiders terrorized Southern Indiana, causing a half million dollars damage. The roads on which they galloped were unpaved then and for a long while thereafter. This raid into southern Indiana was led by Brigadier General John Hunt Morgan. Morgan lived in Lexington, Kentucky before the war. Most of Morgan's men were Kentuckians with a nucleus from the Lexington and Frankfort bluegrass area. They also included conscripts from counties farther south, whose return in force it was hoped would be welcomed by a state which had deeply divided loyalties, despite the refusal of the Kentucky legislature to secede from the union together with its formal declaration of neutrality.

Morgan commanded a considerable force, his battle-tested division consisted of two brigades of four regiments each. In all there were 2460 mounted men and four pieces of artillery, which started out enthusiastically from Alexandria, Tennessee on June 11, 1863. They had hoped for a friendly welcome as they entered their native Kentucky on June 29, but they were forced by loyalists into several bloody skirmishes. As they crossed the Green River on July 4, Lieutenant Thomas Morgan, a younger brother of the commander, was among those killed. About 9 a.m. on July 8, Morgan's advance units reached the bluffs above Brandenburg, Kentucky, 40 miles west of Louisville on the Ohio River and two miles upstream from Mauckport, Indiana. The Union gunboat "The Lady Pike" was driven off by Morgan's artillery. The captured steamers "Alice Beam" and "John T. McCoombs" were used as shuttle transports to the Indiana shore and then scuttled.

Morgan marched with his men directly north to Corydon.

On July 9, 1863, the battle of Corydon occurred. From there he marched on north to New Salisbury and from there to Palmyra, and then from Palmyra on northward to Salem.

After a long while at Salem, carrying out much destruction and looting, Morgan headed directly east for Vienna, then to Lexington, Indiana, then turned north to Paris and North Vernon, turning again to DuPont, Bryantsburg, then north to Versailles and Osgood, then turned east again to strike the Ohio border at Harrison. He burned the gateway bridge at Harrison on the Whitewater River, heading on through that old state line town, pressing his horsemen to ride hard all night down the improved Ohio road. Thereafter, it was strictly "hare and hounds," Morgan was at the Ohio-Pennsylvania border when he was finally captured by Hobson on July 19. Even then he himself escaped, although most of his worn-out men were transported to Union prisons. General John Hunt Morgan was killed in 1864 near Grainville, Tennessee by a Union soldier named Andrew G. Campbell who had infiltrated Confederate lines in the Knoxville region. His end came near the home of Andrew Johnson, the Tennessee loyalist U.S. Senator who was elected Vice President on the Union ticket with Abraham Lincoln in 1864.

For several generations wide-eyed Hoosier children recited verses about "Morgan, Morgan; Morgan the Raider." Early in the march Morgan had seized 500 fresh horses, seized at Corydon. Morgan's main column easily took New Salisbury. He met some resistance near Palmyra while foraging for food and more horses. His far ranging patrols looted Greenville to the east in Floyd County and Paoli to the west in Orange County. Nobody knew just which way the raiders would turn, but at 9 o'clock the morning of July 10, they reunited on the courthouse square at Salem, seat of Washington County. The few militia there surrendered without firing a shot. The plundering at Salem was the most wanton of the entire expedition. "There was a senseless and purposeless mania for pillage," wrote one of the raiders years after the war. When terrified citizens fled their homes, they were thoroughly looted. Those families, which dared to stay, were treated as sympathizers by the Confederates and received cavalier immunity. Morgan's telegraphers informed him that the Union regulars were coming up from Louisville and New Albany, so the railway tracks, now known as the Monon route, were torn up for a distance south of town and the Salem depot and nearby bridges were burned. Large ransoms were exacted from Salem's gristmills.

After revelling in Hoosier Civil War history, I now turn my attention back to last summer's trip to Salem with Marvin Northrop.

Marvin Northrop was an American volunteer pilot with the British Royal Flying Corps during the First World War. After the War, he returned to his native Minneapolis, starting the largest airplane jobbing supply house west of Ohio. When Peace had been declared in 1918 and Northrop left the R.F.C., he noted the great supply of surplus planes in Europe, planning on returning one day. It all gave birth to his idea of starting his airplane supply business immediately after the war. Beginning soon after the war, he still makes pilgrimages abroad to keep abreast of the latest foreign developments and to purchase surplus airplanes and parts for selling and trading on both a national and international scale.

The Versailles Treaty greatly restricted German aviation and aircraft construction. Gliding by German youths and recreationists was not restricted however. Consequently, the Rhone (or Rhon) Mountains became the region where gliders were designed, built and flown in great profusion in the 1920's. A common primary training glider was known as the Zoegling, or German for fledgling. On one of his trips to Germany, Northrop brought back detailed blueprints of the Zoegling, which he sold profusely in the U.S.A. until here in America the Zoegling became Northrop Primary. I purchased a set of Northrop's plans, built the glider and taught myself and friends to fly it. it and acquired my Mead Rhon Ranger Primary Glider the club in Salem, where we are now headed. The Mead is very similar to the Northrop and it, too, has its origin in the Rhon Mountains of Germany and the source of its name, the "Rhon Ranger" as dubbed by its maker, the Mead Cycle Company of Chicago.

Last year I purchased a single place monoplane built by Albert Hocker of Evansville in 1930. It is powered by a 4-cylinder, in-line, air-cooled Henderson 27-horsepower engine. I first saw it in 1931 when the plane was hangared in a small doorless hangar at the old Fairfield Airport in east Evansville. The hangar and entrance to the field is at the intersection of Vann Avenue and Pollock Avenue. The field is a huge grass field about the equivalent of four or five city blocks square. I first saw the Hocker in its hangar after it had been flown by Al Hocker for a year. He completed the airplane in 1930. I first saw it during a big fly-in at Fairfield. I saw many airplanes that day that I'd only seen pictures of in magazines like *Aero Digest, Aviation* and *Popular Aviation*. Two other locally owned planes was a De Haviland "Moth" owned by a dentist pilot of Evansville. Another owned by a young man whose wealthy grandmother lived on Lincoln Avenue. It was the very unusual new Buhl "Bullpup" one-place monoplane powered by a 3-cylinder, 45 horse-power Szekely radial air-cooled engine.

This young man later crashed the "Bullpup" in his grandmother's front yard but walked away unhurt. Another at that show was a neat bright red, sleek, strutless, full cantilever winged Cessna Model A. During that show I kept going back to look at the little Hocker in the hangar. Little did I know that 2 years later I would own it. It had been sold to Howard Webb of Boonville. I purchased it from him. One axle had been broken on the left wheel and repaired with a large, long King-bolt inserted into the axle's tubing stub. The new "axle" was rugged but a bit too loose. When I would reach 35 miles per hour the wheel would shimmy so badly I ground-looped the plane four or five times and finally gave up. The axle needed a rebuild by welding back to its original configuration. All of these flight attempts occurred on East Oak Street in Boonville where Oak intersects on a right angle turn to the Pelzer Road (present site of Oakdale School). I tried to take off from this east corner on a west by southwest heading, which would have brought my climb-out over Old Lake in Boonville (now City Lake).

After several months I wrote used airplane dealer Marvin Northrop in Minneapolis. He mailed me a check saying he'd pick up the plane that summer. Northrop had used airplanes on "hold" and storage all over the U.S.A., Canada and Central and South America.

That summer Marvin Northrop arrived in Boonville in a brand new flatbed Chevrolet truck to pick up the Hocker monoplane. It was the first time I had met him after all of this correspondence and glider plans purchasing. He was a distinguished, tall blond man, well dressed in a summer suit, tie and sailor straw hat and looked about 40 years of age. The thing that impressed me was that he did not seem a bit fazed that I was 15 years old, but tall for my age. Our discussion was air-mindedly enthusiastic, friendly and business-like. He hit it off with my parents in a grand fashion. He told us of his background in a very un-egotistical fashion. He told of the War; he told of all the airplanes he had bought and sold all over the world, some in South America, such as a Fokker Tri-motor which he purchased and sold without even seeing it. He told of barnstorming and mainly selling surplus Jennys and Standard J-1's to barnstormers. In fact, once at a big fly-in at St. Louis (where Lambert Field is now located) in 1923 he had several Jennys and Standards for sale. Many purchasers had never flown. Charles Lindbergh was at this same fly-in which lasted for such a long time that the place became a permanent airfield and later an airport. (Now in 1999, an international airport, Lambert Field.) Northrop hired Lindbergh to train Northrop's novice plane buyers to the extent they could depart with their new purchase. (Incidentally, Lindbergh himself describes this Northrop episode in some detail in his book *The Spirit of St. Louis*, which was published in about 1953 and later, made into a motion picture of the same name. James Stewart had the part of Lindbergh. It made me feel good in 1953 when the book was first published that I had this story told to me first hand by the subject of the story twenty years earlier.)

Northrop told me he believed he had sold the Hocker to a fellow in Salem, Indiana by the name of Ralph Denien who was president of the glider club there. He would have to bring Denien down to look at the Hocker in Boonville. Would I like to come along? I said Yes in one blink of the eye. He said he had also taken in a Mead primary glider on the Hocker; would I be interested in it? I said I'd love to see it and meet the Salem group. Salem is 80 miles from Boonville on the two lane county and state roads of this year of 1933; it took us all day to reach Salem. We stayed the night in a small Salem hotel. Next morning we drove southeast a few miles to near Pekin where a man by the name of Lowell Boss had an airstrip on a farm. There we met a small wiry fellow by the name of Ralph Denien and his friend Ralph Kendall. I looked over the Mead and admired it very much but could not make up my mind. Northrop, of course, wanted me to take it since the truck was going back to Boonville empty otherwise. But Marv Northrop was not the pushy sort, simply ready and not one to belabor the obvious. In any case, the four of us jammed into the truck and headed back to Boonville, arriving there long after dark. Next day Denien checked out the disassembled Hocker, ran the engine and decided to take it. He then loaded it up and returned to Salem. Of course I did not really need to go unless I decided to take the Mead after all. So I went back and two days later Northrop and I returned to Boonville with the Mead loaded on the truck. So that is part of the story of Marvin Northrop, the old Hocker (Air Commerce registration 441-Y) and the Mead Rhon Ranger (Air Commerce Registration 12864).

Now here I am a year later and Marty and I are in the air in his Waco heading back again to Salem and Pekin and hopefully to see Denien and his friends. We are in the air only twenty minutes from our take-off in Paoli when Salem is dead ahead. As we pass over Salem I see the old stone courthouse with its bell tower. I've sketched out to Marty the road leading southeast to Pekin and the Boss airfield where we should see the Hocker, probably in plain view. Marty swings the Waco in that direction and in a few minutes I see the airstrip, but not the Hocker. Marty makes a nice approach and touches down, taxis up near a small hangar housing a small enclosed monoplane, but not my old Hocker. Marty switches off the OX-5 as an auto drives up to the hangar. I immediately recognize the short stature and bald head of Ralph Denien. And also with him is his soft-spoken and quiet friend Ralph Kendall. Denien tells me that the first few months after he had the Hocker he had nosed it over upside down demolishing the wing. It is now in storage in Salem. He, Kendall and two others are preparing to restore it, possibly with an entirely new wing. I am saddened to hear his tale of woe. I had hoped that he would not do as I had done, but instead restore the left wheel axle by welding it up to its original design. He did fly it three times, each take-off a hairy one because of the wheel shimmy, and its tendency to ground loop. On the fourth take-off he was not so lucky.

Denien took us into Salem for the night in a rooming house he had used the year before. Next day he drove us about town, feeding Marty all the history and local library treasures, which Marty literally devoured while Ralph and I discussed our experiences with the Hocker and the Mead. Next morning Denien took us down to Pekin to see us off, because Marty seemed anxious to get back down to the river towns along the Ohio to the southeast.

As we take off from the Pekin grass airstrip with our friends waving their good-byes, I get to thinking how Marty and I had discussed many times before this up-coming particular part of our tour of the Ohio River country. I had told him how twice before my parents had taken me upriver into this beautiful country above the historic "Falls of the Ohio." On an early trip we drove the 125 miles by automobile, we in Dad's new Essex and Uncle John, Aunt Helen and daughter Edith in their Willys-Knight. That was in 1926 and a year later we made the trip via a stern-wheeler steamboat, the "Tom Greene" from Evansville to Madison with various stops between, the main one being Louisville, Kentucky. On both trips we had stayed in summer cabins in a large flat area on the river but well above, on a bluff, about 75 feet above the river. This large field lay below the Hanover Heights on which reposed the picturesque and historic small town and college of Hanover. Hanover and Hanover College are west of Madison, founded in 1827. It is the oldest private, four-year, liberal arts college in Indiana. It is on a breathtaking, 500-acre hilltop campus overlooking the Ohio River.

Always the air-minded one at all times, I had fantasized on both trips about the place where we stayed below the Heights of Hanover. There were about six of these cabins in a row, rented to summer vacationers like us. They all faced the river, of course, with an unpaved lane behind the cabins for auto access. The field in back of the cabins was nearly a mile long and a half-mile wide. Beyond that the land was wooded and rose to the north and west to form the large knoll that was Hanover Heights. The road down the hill to the cabins was narrow and paved to just the bottom of the hill and from there auto access to the cabins was out on the open field of grass.

Back to my air-minded fantasizing about this place. On both trips to this place I dreamed of how the large field behind the cabins would be an ideal base for a barnstormer or a flying vacationer. Our cabin's landlord also owned this huge field and he patiently and amusingly had tolerated my questions if planes ever landed there and if not would he let them? His answer had been an emphatic "Yes," if especially they rented his cabins or paid a usage fee to fly paid passengers. Now here I was, six years later, about to find out.

Marty's plan was to fly directly to the area north of the river at New Albany, which is across the river from Louisville, Kentucky. He did not want to fly over any widespread city. We would then head upriver to Charlestown, Hanover and Madison, but he wanted to see the historic "Falls of the Ohio" from the air. He did not seem to realize that the river is navigable in that stretch. The river runs northeast from New Albany to Madison but in a zigzag fashion, therefore Hanover is five miles north of our old cabin site. We have now passed over the little village of Providence and can see New Albany, Jeffersonville and Louisville dead ahead in the distance.

CHAPTER XI

As we pass over New Providence flying southeast, we see up ahead the sprawl of New Albany, Jeffersonville and Louisville with the meandering Ohio River dividing them. I knew, and I knew that Marty knew, that the "Falls of the Ohio" is right in the center of it all, but in spite of the falls, flatboats and steamboats have navigated the falls since the early days when men had used the river as the main avenue to the fabled land stretching far west of the eastern mountains. I knew that Marty yearns to see the historic "Falls of the Ohio" but I also knew he avoided flying over broad expanses of settled terra firma made up of streets, houses, business districts, telephone poles and their electric wires, and big trees along residential streets.

If our old Curtiss OX-5 conked out over such cities or large towns we would find ourselves landing in streets, playgrounds or athletic fields. The likelihood of our clipping our wings on trees or telephone poles would be very high. Worse yet, we could injure or kill someone on the ground. Even at best we would probably have to dismantle the Waco's wings and have it towed to an airport or field well outside the city. It would likely be the end of our Hoosier Barnstorming tour. I could not help but think of what had just recently happened over the Sherman farm east of Huntingburg, or the carburetor trouble Marty experienced over Hawesville and Cannelton. Then I got to thinking of our motor trip to Hanover a few years ago when Dad and Uncle John had to drive through New Albany and Jeffersonville with the Essex and Willys-Knight in 1928. It took us two hours to make our way through the streets trying to follow Indiana Highway 62 through the adjacent towns of New Albany and Jeffersonville.

Oh Boy, just the thought of being forced to do a power-off landing in that area here five years later is scary as the dickens. In those five years it has grown even more and hence, even more scary to do a dead-stick landing without hitting a tree, a house or telephone pole, to say nothing of going through a maze of phone wires and electrical wires. As I get more and more apprehensive, all of a sudden I am brought to the realization that Marty and I are of amazingly like minds. He is turning to the left and after about a forty-five degree turn, he is heading straight east and away from the approaching New Albany. I dig out of my hip pocket a much folded and soiled roadmap segment. Judging about where we started our turn just south of

New Providence, I deduce that we are now headed straight to Charlestown on the Ohio River, upstream from Jeffersonville and Louisville about fifteen miles. I calculate we are about 25 miles from Charlestown and will arrive there in a little over twenty minutes.

Charlestown is about two miles back from the river as I recall it, when we drove through there five years ago on our automobile junket to Hanover. I remember thinking at the time that the flat area between the town and the river would be an ideal place for gypsy barnstormers like us to land and entice the locals with plane rides for whatever the traffic would bear.

I have looked up history on Charlestown in the Boonville library along with other Hoosier places along the Ohio River, which I shared with Marty before we took off. Charlestown was platted in 1808 when it was Indiana Territory. It was surveyed by John Hayes and Charles Beggs. The town was names for Beggs. Situated in Grant 117 which had been granted to General John Girault of Louisiana, one of the men in General George Rogers Clark's army. Clark's men received the land grants for their service. Barzillah Baker and James McCampbell purchased the grant from Girault. The 149 lots were 80 x 200 feet. Lots were also given for public use and the town square. The Clark County Courthouse was situated here. Charlestown served as county seat from 1812 until 1868 and all roads in the area led here. Houses and buildings were mostly of brick. Charlestown's proximity to the Ohio River and its higher elevation contributed to its importance in the early westward movement of pioneers. Many important and influential people lived here, the most illustrious being Jonathan Jennings, the first governor of Indiana. Jennings was a young lawyer from the east, arriving here in 1809. He was instrumental in leading the fight to prevent Indiana from entering the union as a slave state. He defeated the territorial governor, William Henry Harrison, a slave owner, and became governor when Indiana attained statehood in 1816. He married Ann Gilmore Hays, whose family had settled here after moving from Kentucky. During his life he served as a Congressman from the Indiana Territory, Indian Commissioner, and again as a Congressman from Indiana. He died in 1834 at his farm near Charlestown. Jennings died of alcoholism at a time when the illness was not understood resulting in the unceremonious burial of a great man who had served his state and country well. Later his remains were located and moved to a more suitable and honorably marked burial site. In the late 1800's and early 1900's Charlestown became a tourist center because of Rose Island Resort and Amusement Center.

As we cruise along at 65 miles per hour, we can see the river and the sprawl of Louisville, Kentucky on the other side. I look below and all around us there are plenty of beautiful fields within easy gliding range and I feel a lot more secure now, and the old Curtiss OX-5 up front is clacking right along with not the least sign of weariness. I am glad we put in the new distributor back on the Sherman farm and the venerable engine seems to be even happier with its new lease on life.

A mental and optical wandering had caused me to lose track of time. Just over the nose cowl I can see Charlestown and the adjacent river and the flat stretch in between. At the same time Marty has throttled back the OX-5 and we are coming in over Charlestown at about 500 feet, then settle even further down to about 200 feet, turning about thirty degrees to the left so that we are cruising over the long flat field paralleling the river. I get to wondering if Marty is going to land along here somewhere. There are plenty of good hayfields as well as large cornfields. Of course we will not land in the corn, but there are lots of hay fields that have been freshly cut. We pass over a large cornfield but up ahead is a large field of freshly cut alfalfa. There are no farmers or farm machinery in sight. Then I feel the OX-5 throttle back and we are down to 50 feet over the corn, then down to 20 feet as we enter the alfalfa field still coming down, then throttle back some more into a three point attitude and the gear is rolling along the field, then the skid is down and we are slowing down to a smooth taxi. Then we come to a full stop, with the OX-5 on slow idle. I turn and yell to Marty, "We are out in the middle of nowhere. Are you going to shut down?"

He shouts back, "No, stay in the ship. I just want to say I landed at Charlestown. This is a perfect field but no roads and no passengers. Nearest passengers are up there in Charlestown. We'll taxi back, turn and take off again, after we sit here and keep cooled off behind our idling propeller," he quipped. After ten minutes of lollygaging, we take off and climb back low over Charlestown, make a U-turn and head back upriver toward Hanover.

As we swing down to the river, following it upstream, I dig out my battered little fragment of old road map and estimate we will be heading northeast for fifteen miles until we reach the little river town of Bethlehem, Indiana. Then the river turns directly north for fifteen miles after which we will reach our destination near Hanover. At Hanover the river turns sharply eastward for five miles to Madison, Indiana. Flying up the river with the Waco throttled back to a slow cruising speed of 65 M.p.h., the ethereal view is nothing short of magic to my young mind even though I do not think of myself as young. More like I am on the fence between young and old and not able to decide. But I am more concerned with the thrilling sight I am seeing. All of it is country I had seen twice before as new and exciting when we traveled along this river by automobile and on another vacation occasion by stern wheeler steamboat, the old "Tom Greene." Now I can't believe the sheer reality of seeing it all now, almost all at once by air. The convergence of all my dreams, the airplane, not just any airplane but my favorite old Waco biplane with open, breeze blown cockpits. Oh great and good God of all wonders, how wonderful it is to be alive. If heaven is better than this I can hardly wait to get my call, but, hold it, Bud! not right now, I'd have to leave this. Aha, fifteen minutes have passed and we are approaching Bethlehem down and ahead on our left on the Indiana side of the river.

Marty noses down, throttles back even a bit more. We pass over the tiny village waterfront, rock our wings back and forth in salute and continue on up river, climbing back up to about five hundred feet. Now I am really getting anxious about what it really looks like up ahead, all the time remembering the Hanover Hill and the wonderful old tourist camp and the flats below along the river. How much has it changed in the past five years?

The day before Marty and I took off from Boonville for Richland, I had enticed my mother into writing the manager of the Hanover tourist camp and reminding him of her son's pestering inquisition about future barnstormers using his field and that we were on our way and, hopefully, could land there and stay in one of the cabins. But, of course, I could not predict when or whether we would reach Hanover. But at least it would give him warning and by the time he had answered her letter we would have been long gone and out of reach by mail, phone or telegram. Or at least that is what I thought. I had explained to Marty about our trips five years before. It really appealed to him and who wouldn't? Our own long field plus a nice cabin by the river!?

Up ahead I can see the hills stretching back into Indiana from the river and the flatter terrain south of the hills. Then I started worrying. Suppose the tourist camp had been torn down and abandoned? After all it was nothing but farmland along the river, the tourist camp was only a summer camp with summer cabins. If the owner of the property below the camp thought the land was more productive in crops, he'd tear down the cabins. Then my heart pounded suddenly and I could see the hilltop far ahead was in fact Hanover. The flats below the near side of the hill would be our field. But all I could see was a row of trees along the river. The same trees that grew in a row in front of our cabins on the 75-foot bluff above the river. But I could see no cabins; then we were over the river and nearer to the Kentucky side than the Indiana side. I turned in the cockpit and waved Marty to swing to the north so I could see what was on the landward side behind the trees. He replied with an abrupt 90-degree turn to the left and held it there until we were over the Indiana shore, then he did a 90-degree to the right. Dead ahead and below I could see the cabins. God bless! Thank the Lord for saving them for us all these years. Not only had he held all six of them, he had added two; I now counted eight. Another thing I noticed, and I'm sure Marty noticed, the field immediately behind the cabins had been freshly mowed a full mile length of the field in a swath that looked to be about five hundred feet wide. The eight cabins were at the far end of the field, each separated by about 100 feet. I remember it so well and there they are, just like I remembered them.

Marty glides down to an altitude of 100 feet, flying over the grassy auto-mobile lane behind the cabins. At the far end of the field, the big knob of hill known as Hanover Heights looms ahead. As we pass the cabins, Marty banks gently to the right and over the river. Five minutes later we are abreast of the Madison river front. What a beautiful town it is and from the air it is really something to behold. We are flying at only two hundred feet and it's like we are seeing Madison from a two hundred-foot tower in the middle of the river. I can see the road from Versailles coming down into Madison through the valley between the Hanover hill on the west and another large hill to the east, which I recall, is known locally as Telegraph Hill.

Marty does a couple of circles out over the river until he has climbed up to about 1500 feet, then he heads back over Madison, then gradually back over the little town of Hanover and below I also can see the high campus and buildings of beautiful Hanover College, which I remembered visiting so well in both 1926 and 1928, now five years ago. Ahead and below I can see our field and the tourist camp cabins, and Marty is cutting back on the OX-5's r.p.m. and we are slowly losing altitude. At about 500 feet we pass over the hill and on to the south or far end of the field to swing north and get lined up for an approach and landing. We set down gently in the hay stubble and begin the long taxi up to the first or southernmost of the cabins. We taxi nearly a quarter of a mile before we reach the southernmost cabin. There are no autos parked at the southernmost cabins so I gesture to Marty to keep on taxiing to the northernmost cabins. My experience from past trips with par-ents I remembered that tourist renters parked their autos behind the cabins. Now there were only two autos, one at each of the first and second cabins at the northern end. When we taxi abreast of the first two cabins a man ap-proaches us from the first cabin, waving vigorously and smiling broadly. I recognize him as the same manager who dealt with my parents five years ago, and the same man I pestered so much with questions about future use of his field by barnstormers. I gestured back to Marty and he cut the OX-5 to idle and we come to a standstill. As the man hurriedly approached, Marty cut the switch.

The man called out, "I'm Henry Johnson," and pointing to me he said, "You must be Peyton. I received a letter from your mother. I remember you from five years ago. You've grown a lot," he added as I climbed out.

Just like I remembered from five years ago, Henry Johnson was a very congenial and helpful man. He and Marty hit it off immediately. Johnson is exceedingly curious about our aeronautical exploits, and particularly the places we had landed on this trip. Marty was just as curious about Johnson and the Hanover-Madison area. When Marty gazed at the row of cabins, Henry Johnson caught on quickly. "You can have any you wish except the first two. This first one I use in the summer for a bed and my office. Also on one side I built an extension for a small camp store. I carry staples such as canned goods, and also fresh bread each day and a small refrigerator with some meats, milk and soft drinks. The second cabin is occupied by an elderly couple who stay here all summer each summer. All of the other cabins are available right now. It's nearing the end of summer and all of the occupants have gone home to put their children back in school for the fall term."

Marty looked at me for approval, which I gave instantly with a nod when he told Johnson, "I think we'll take the last one down at the south end and tie down the plane in the field just behind it. Also, can we rent an auto, motorcycle or bicycles so that we could tour the area and conduct our small amount of chores and alleged business such as we have without having to hike the few miles up and over Hanover Heights to get to Hanover and Madison?"

Henry Johnson grinned broadly. "You can use the old Dodge here, the only vehicle we have. You can ride up there with me the few times I need to go, or you are perfectly welcome to use it any time. I might even let you do my shopping for me so that while you are out I won't need to bother," he laughed.

Marty replied, "That's wonderful. We will see the Dodge's gas tank is kept full. Another question: how do you feel about us flying passengers from here? and if you agree I would like to find a printer who will do some handbills for us to direct the populace on top of the hill, and those over the hill in Madison, to come down and fly with us."

Henry Johnson's face lit up. "I'd be greatly disappointed if you didn't fly passengers from here. As to the handbills, there is a small shop in Hanover who could almost do those while you wait. And I think you have already announced to the folks here that you are flying passengers when you circled all around the area just this afternoon. Also your young friend primed me on barnstorming from here when he was here five years ago. Since then he has been flying a gliding machine he built himself. What a small world. His mother wrote at length on his glider flying!" he laughed.

Marty said, "I expect to pay you for use of the field for plane rides."

Johnson grinned broadly again. "After all you are renting a cabin. The passenger activity brings attention and business to my camp here. I won't charge you a flat fee for the field because I don't want it to turn out that such a fee costs more than you take in for passengers. How long you think you might stay with us?"

Instantly Marty replied, "At least a week," which quickly and happily lifted my eyebrows in pure delight. We shook hands, then started up the Waco and taxied back to the last cabin, staking down the ship in the field about 100 feet behind.

The so-called cabins are a one-room affair, built off the ground on five foot stilts with the front facing the river with wide front steps to an open narrow front porch. The flat wood walls extend only four feet up from the floor on all four sides of the room. Wire insect screens extend from the top of the low walls to the high ceiling on all four sides. Sheets of corrugated galvanized tin are hinged above the screens on the outside. These can be kept raised horizontally by draw ropes extending inside. They can be lowered and battened down during windy, rainy thunderstorms that pass up the river about once every other week during summers. The interior can be divided off by simple draw curtains to separate the kitchen, sleeping and sitting areas. All of these cabins appear to be identical with a simple square floor plan, measuring about 18 by 18 feet. Electrical lighting consists of two hanging 20-watt bulbs. Cook stoves consist of one single hotplate and a gasoline pressure stove.

After staking down the Waco and moving into the cabin with our meager personal gear, we take a stroll along the trees bordering the high bluff in front of the cabins. The view is fantastic, up and down and across the river. Not infrequently a paddle-wheel steamer makes its way past the place. Near our cabin a long flight of narrow, rickety wooden stairs make their way from the bluff down to the river's edge where a very old small houseboat lays anchored. Marty insists we go down and look it over, which of course we did. The vertical descent of the steep stairs must be at least fifty feet. As we near the old houseboat, we hear someone moving about inside. Out the door and onto the tiny dock stepped an old gent with a very rough beard and tousled gray thick hair. He wore old tattered jeans, seemingly patched for at least three or four decades. One remaining suspender cast over one shoulder, its mate obviously gone the way of long and arduous use. "Howdy, fellers," he said. "Lookin' ta git ye some nice channel cats? I got some good 'uns right here in them floatin', slatted fishboxes," he said matter-of-factly. He bent over and lifted one box half out of the water to reveal several catfish in 12- to 15-inch lengths. He then raised a second box to show some very much larger ones, which he said ran from 10 to 15 pounds each. "You fellers stayin' up yonder? You'ns must be the plane pilots just landed, I betcha." Marty nodded, saying nothing, his attention on the fish boxes.

"Ever eat these little fiddler cats? They is the best eatin' fish in the world. So's these big channel cats. I git 'em on my trout line out there, and my channel nets down river a piece."

Marty introduced us to the old gent, which surprised me as I thought it was unnecessary but I could tell Marty liked and was fascinated by the old man. The old fellow said his name was Sam Jones, said he was born in a log cabin on the other side of the river 86 years ago. Never left this stretch of river, fishin' his life.

Marty said, "I like catfish. Only ate good river catfish once in St. Louis. Peyton here grew up on them a long ways down river at a place called Yankeetown. Ever hear of it?"

"Naw," he replied. "Never keered fer Yankees." At that Marty said, "Later we'll come down for some catfish; not this evening though."

This evening we heat up pork and beans, plus bread and milk from Henry Johnson's store, then sat out on the front steps and watched for paddle-wheel steamers plying the waters of the Ohio. We each have cots with good mattresses and sheets and sleep like logs. Except for just two or three nights this past month, we have not slept in a bed, so this is absolute bliss. I know Marty must have snored but I was too soundly snoring to hear him. Needless to say we slept in next day long after daybreak.

Marty remarks, "Peyton, let's drive Johnson's Dodge up to Hanover and live it up by ordering breakfast at that little cafe you and Johnson said was near the college. Also, we'll look up one of those print shops to print some handbills. Then we'll look around at things and later spread the handbills if they are ready."

The drive up the hill to Hanover impressed Marty very much, also he was visibly impressed with the river view which is some four hundred feet above the river. Then we seek out the little cafe, which is just like I remembered it five years ago. At breakfast I tell Marty of the many interesting things to see in the Madison-Hanover area. All it did was make him anxious and fidgety. A lot of what I told him I, of course, remembered from previous trips. But on the last I was only eleven years old but it had made a lasting impression. But on the evening before Marty and I left Boonville, I reviewed our early trips to Madison with my parents and memorized the places I should show Marty.

After breakfast, we go over to the college and admire the campus and buildings. Marty bullies his way right into the Registrar's building asking questions. They are very helpful and invite him to use their library, giving him pamphlets on the history and curriculum. Next we find a small newspaper and print shop and Marty writes his handbill for them. What surprised me was they would be ready later in the afternoon. The shop also gives us an illustrated brochure and map of all the things to do and see. Marty immediately begins reading it and firing questions at both me and the printer. He began to frown and shake his head, saying, "Peyton, it would take us a week to really see all of this without even flying a single passenger all during the week. So let's see all that we can today."

The printer urges us to see the scenic grounds at Madison State Hospital, just north of Madison. It is known as Cragmont. Marty showed an unusual interest, much to my consternation, for I knew it was a hospital for the insane. It would remind me of Woodmere at Evansville, also a beautiful, large, landscaped grounds and impressive large buildings. I always dreaded even driving by Woodmere. Here five years ago I felt the same way about Cragmont. It was built in 1906. It overlooks Madison, sitting on a high plateau 400 feet above the Ohio River, it commands a sweeping view of the river with the curving Indiana and Kentucky shores. The hospital group consists primarily of 27 buildings on a farm of 1265 acres. Beautiful, large Clifty Falls State Park joins the farm on the east. Cragmont is the most beautiful institution site in the state, the brochure says. It says each year thousands drive through the grounds to enjoy the fine view, so Marty had to do it, and so we did. Marty, the perceptive one, perceived my disappointment and could not help teasing me. "What's the matter, Peyton, are you afraid they will declare you insane and not let you out?" I knew him well enough to tease back and I replied, "You are the one they won't let out; anyone crazy enough to inspect this loony bin." All we did was drive through the place and wonder at the scenic beauty of its well-kept landscape and idyllic farmland. I had to admit I liked it and even more that we did not go in to see the patients. It did not take all day, but over half of it.

We drive back to the print shop to find the flyers all printed and ready to go. We leave a stack in the cafe as well as on the literature table at the college and all of the stores and offices and restaurants we could find. Back in the Dodge we head down to Madison and repeat the performance by leaving handbills wherever we can. I urge Marty to take in the old Lanier Mansion on First Street facing the riverfront. It is truly a beautiful old southern mansion built in 1840. Madison was the seat of early Hoosier culture and wealth. James. F.D. Lanier gained enduring fame by financing his government in the Civil War with an unsecured loan of one million dollars. It is truly the home of a southern gentleman retained in its original elegance and exhibiting heirlooms of the Lanier family handed down through the generations. The grounds from the mansion down to the river are elegantly landscaped with varieties of antique flowers, dwarf fruit trees, exquisite gardens of Lanier's day. Francis Costigan was the architect who designed the Lanier mansion. He built his own home in 1851 just up the hill from the Lanier place on Third Street.

Old Marty literally wallows in the enthusiasm and curiosity of his visit to Lanier. When the tenant politely tells us it was 5 p.m., closing time, Marty turns to me, saying, "Peyton, since we still have plenty of money left from Huntingburg, wouldn't you say it would be really stupid to go back to the cabin and heat up another can of pork and beans?" I grin. "Yeah, what you got in mind?" He answers by going out to the Dodge and we drive to a nice checkered tablecloth restaurant on Main Street. Boy, this was really living compared to what we have been doing for the past month. We both order the same thing: Steak, fried potatoes, coffee and homemade blackberry pie. That morning Marty had urged me to dress my best. We both had pressed our trousers under the mattress during the night; Marty had a good shave and trimmed his little mustache, and I touched up what little there was in my coming undeveloped beard. So, Marty the crafty one, has planned this dinner early this morning. He is a crafty one.

We drive back to Henry Johnson's river camp in the dark. When we arrive he greets us laughing, not the least bit worried. Marty grins like he always does when he is about to spring a surprise and says, "Well, Mr. Johnson, you've been extra nice to us. Tomorrow we are going to fly over the area to lend some attention and emphasis to our handbills, which we have spread all over Hanover and Madison. We would like to take you along."

"Great," he replied, "and here are some fresh eggs and bacon for your breakfast." Then he added, "Sam Jones was up here today, says he's hoping you will want some catfish and he'll show you the best way to fry them."

Our little cabin is a welcome and comfortable friend. It's been a long day. First we do a walk-around inspection of the old Waco out there alone in the dark, poor thing, but it was okay. I'm sure Henry Johnson made sure of that in our long day's absence. Boy, does my little cot feel good tonight! Sleeping on hay stubble night after night is all very adventurous, but this bed is just like home back on 420 Oak Street in Boonville. As I lay here I start a relaxing discourse on the day's happenings, only rewarded with a loud snort initiating what is to be his nocturnal symphony for the evening. I promptly slip off in a dream world of Wacos, fluffy white cumulous clouds, and a little blond angel by the name of Katherine.

Next morning I awake slowly and become quickly aware that I was not awakened by any noise but by the smell of bacon and eggs. Marty stands back in the corner grinning as he turns the morning repast in a skillet on the gasoline stove. "Rise and shine, Champ! and sink your chops in these breakfast morsels," as he hands me a plate and a cup of coffee.

I sit on the edge of the cot, devour the breakfast, gulp the coffee, then get up and dress, then wash the plates in the little sink. Suddenly a rap on the screen door and in walks Henry Johnson, grinning from ear to ear. "Just thought I'd shoot the breeze with my intrepid guest pilots," he quipped. Marty quipped back, "My, you are eager. The dew isn't even dry on the plane yet. Since you are so eager you must be yearning to join us in some loops, inverted cruise, sudden stalls, long spins and the works."

Johnson holds up both hands in defense. "No, I've never flown before. Just straight and level, please, and I don't want no parachute."

I answer for Marty out of turn. "We don't have 'chutes and don't do loops, but if we are going to advertise we have to do more than straight and level. We have to wag our wings, blip our engine and fly low and do tight turns and stuff."

Marty casts me a critical eye. "No, Peyton gets carried away. We just have to attract their attention without folks thinking we are reckless daredevils. You'll enjoy seeing your hometown from up there." With that he leads us out to the Waco, waving me into the back cockpit and swinging the prop a few times with the switch off in the usual start procedure. I notice Johnson looking real worried, approaching Marty who waves him back away from the propeller. Then I realize that Johnson thinks since I was in the pilot's cockpit I was going to fly the Waco with he and Marty as passengers. At first I laugh, then the pangs of hurt feelings. Marty swings the prop on "Switch on" and the OX-5 begins to idle. Then Johnson gets to Marty's ear, talking earnestly. Good old Marty, at first he grinned over at me and nodded his head, then shook his head and in a few words tells Johnson I'd been flying for two years, age or no age, and that no, I wasn't going to fly this trip, he was.

I help Johnson climb in the front with me alongside. We taxi to near Johnson's cabin at the north end, then swing around and with a short warm-up, take off to the south, climbing to five hundred and turning back upriver toward Madison, climbing all the way until we reach about 2000 feet to give our camp manager a good look for miles around, slowly circling so he can see it all. Then Marty does something he'd not done before on this trip. He dove the Waco steeply, with the OX-5 throttled back and began a steep spiraling descent, not a tailspin but what Marty later laughingly called "a poor man's tailspin." Mr. Johnson later said if that wasn't a real tailspin, he'd hate to be in a real one. He held on to my arm like a vise.

Ahead over the engine cowl was a slowly rotating, nose down view of Madison. When we reached about 300 feet, Marty leveled off flying up river about a mile, then turned back steeply, coming down to 100 feet buzzing the Madison riverfront. We did this four different times, then climbing back up to 1000 feet, heading back upriver. Up ahead we could see Cincinnati in the distance about 50 miles and I pointed it out to Mr. Johnson. Marty then turned back downriver in a slow descent, swinging in over Madison, then Hanover Heights and down to a neat landing in the mile-long hayfield of Johnson's camp. As our passenger climbs out of the Waco he is beside himself with enthusiastic excitement. He never ran down on the subject all during our stay. As we approached over his cabin at the north end, I note there are six autos parked near his cabin. We doubt potential passengers or curiosity seekers. They turn out to be both.

Before Marty shuts down the OX-5, the newcomers inquire about rides. About fifteen people, mostly students and faculty from the college up the hill. I immediately take over, telling them it is $5 each, then run over to Marty and the Waco for his okay. He looks at the gas gauge, saying we could take them all but would have to get more fuel for the next day.

I load in the first two, then Marty takes off for the usual fifteen-minute spin until he had flown them all two hours later. After the last trip, Marty shuts down the OX-5, climbing out, saying, "Let's take the Dodge up to that little gas station we saw on the way to the Versailles Road. I saw he had several 5 and 10-gallon cans. We can fill those 10's and one 5 will do us for a couple days at this rate. By late afternoon we return with 35 gallons of gas and use of the cans as loaners. The 10-gallon cans weigh over 60 pounds and are much too heavy to carry up on the wing step and be raised high enough to pour into the funnel inserted into the filler neck. So, instead, we have to transfer it into the smaller 5-gallon can, 5 gallons at a time, straining it through the filters before lifting it to the funnel. Johnson says there are no tank trucks in the area, the nearest are up in Versailles or North Vernon who service the two gas stations in Hanover and Madison. Too far to deliver 35 gallons to us down here.

After we finish gassing up the Waco, Marty says, "Tonight we are having catfish. Peyton, run down to Sam's houseboat and bring back a dozen of those little fiddler cats and have Sam dress them out. I'll go up to Henry's and get a can of cooking oil and we'll deep-fry them on our stove."

Old Sam is really happy I show up wanting fish. He cleans all of the dozen in about 5 minutes. He says, "You'ns come down here and I'll fire up my fire pit out here on the shore and I'll fry up two of them big 15 pounders and we'll have ourselves a real feast."

I love catfish and Marty gobbles up seven of the dozen and I gobble the rest. Boy, are we gonna sleep tonight! Whew! and our cabin sure smells like fried catfish! Even on a full belly it still smells good. Marty is now real hooked on catfish. We sit out on the steps till dark, then back to our soft cots, bone tired and sleepy.

I wake slowly next morning to birds hopping and pecking on the tin shutters raised outside. Another gorgeous day. I raise up and see the old Waco, its silver wings, red fuselage gleaming in the low sun. Even though the opened-screened windows run the length of all four walls, the place still smells like fried catfish. All three local cats are out on the porch meowing at the screen door. They are nuts about all fish, especially Ohio River catfish. Today will be a busy day, especially for Marty when passengers start driving down the hill from Hanover and Madison. He yawns and gets up. By that time I dress and fry us up some eggs and bacon and burn a little toast and heat a pot of coffee.

All during our trip I have written letters or cards to my folks and mailed them where I can, so I got out a hasty note and take it up to Henry's store to be picked up by the rural carrier. By the time I do that and visit with Henry and have coffee with him, three autos pull up and want to know where the airplane is. Henry tells them it's down at the other end but don't go there. Later, he says, the pilot will bring it up here to do plane rides.

He tells them where to park their autos in rows to have some order when the others show up. I hurry on down to give Marty the news. We crank up the

Waco and taxi up to Henry's place leaving the engine running. I collect $5.00 each from the first two to pull out their money, then put them in the front cockpit. Marty takes off to the south, then turns, coming back over us. So starts another day of flying passengers. Three more autos arrive, carrying from two to four in each vehicle.

Marty told me last night he'd told Henry he'd give him $2.00 per passenger for use of his field, which he found more than satisfactory. We keep up a steady pace of flying passengers all day much like we did at Huntingburg. Our tank of gas for the Waco, 35 gallons, will go just a little under four hours. We brought down 35 gallons last night but it did not all go in the plane because it already contained several gallons. Allowing for the time to load passengers when the engine was only idling, plus the residual in the tank, I figure it will take almost six hours before we use up all of the fuel in the plane now, including additional fuel we have in the cans. At the beginning of each day, of course, we will have to refill the gas cans at the Hanover-Madison gas station. This, of course, is all based on having a steady flow of passengers. It turns out today we have plenty of passengers, it being after 5 o'clock before we shut down, parking the Waco in the field near our southern cabin. Marty takes the cowl off the OX-5 and checks it over for nearly a half hour, then closed it up saying, "Peyton, we haven't eaten since your breakfast eggs. Let's go down to Sam's and try out his riverbank catfish picnic."

"I said, "Okay with me, but I thought you had all the catfish you wanted last night."

"Let's go," he says.

Sam is delighted. He hoists a big 15 pound channel cat out of the box, lays him out on the dock, bashing his head with the same big club he used for this purpose for 75 years, dressing it out on a table out on the sandy beach, lit the fire in a pit, pouring oil in the kettle and after several minutes throws him in. He has some benches around a table and a big coffee pot over the fire next to the kettle. We spend the evening eating chunks of catfish, swilling coffee that did not keep us awake and enjoyed long-told river tales from Old Sam as an occasional stern-wheeler went steaming by. Marty really marvels and revels in the old man and his unwritten history. He would listen intently, saying nothing and gazing wistfully off into the great distance of the river like he could see it all before his very eyes. All hundreds of years of it. He would never admit it, but I have come to believe that my good pilot harbors the soul of a poet. Poems he composes and recites to himself.

After dark, as we make our way back up the stairs to our cabin, Marty begins talking rather wistfully. "You know, Peyton, you've been on this trip nearly five weeks now. In just a few days your school starts again. I can get you home quickly. Boonville is 110 miles on a west by southwest shortest route from here. We could be there in less than two hours. Now your Dad said if you reported to school a week late you would have a good educational excuse with your BHS principal who was a pilot in France during the First War. If you shoot home on a straight line, the river on our route would be several miles to your left and we will be north of the route we took up here. If you stay another week, we could either loaf along the river, stopping to fly passengers at many of the places we landed coming here. The other alternative is to fly straight west into new country, taking longer legs and not stopping so frequently. We would head west first to Bedford, then Vincennes, then down through Petersburg, Princeton, Oakland City, and Boonville."

It didn't take long for my reply, "Let's stay another week after here and go the Vincennes route. I know about other pilots in that country north of Boonville all the way up to Terre Haute."

The next four days were made up of me doing the early eggs and bacon, then our morning trip up the hill to fill the gas cans, flying passengers all day, then snoring on the cots. Two dinners were at the two cafes in Hanover and Madison, the other dinners were down on the river beach with Old Sam, devouring his catfish steaks or the handier twelve inch fiddlers, while Sam regaled us with his river stories as gas-lit steamboats churned by in the dark.

One day we quit flying early due to a scarcity of passengers and old Sam took us out on the river in his long skiff to run his nets. He said the biggest cat he ever caught weighed 150 pounds. Finally the passengers quit showing up so we parked the Waco just south of our cabin, out of sight from Hanover Road and Johnson's cabin. We set about telling Henry good-bye and making a few last trips to Hanover and Madison. We tell Henry we will be leaving for Bedford the next morning.

We both sleep in till 8:30 when the birds hopping on the tin shutters woke me up. I did the breakfast again, washing the dishes and putting the cabin and beds the way we found them. All the while, Marty is shaved and ready. We had gassed up last night and returned the cans to the station. We throw our gear in the plane, get the OX-5 going, swing around back into the field and taxi up to Henry's cabin and swing around south. He comes up to the plane, shook our hands almost tearfully with a loud, "Come back, please." Marty gave him a polite salute, opened the throttle, raised the tail, and we go roaring down the field, up and away for Bedford.

As we climb up over the river, I remember that Marty had pointed out that Bedford lay about 60 miles due west. He had also said we would be there in less than an hour, but he had also said that we had no reason to take that straight line route. We could take a more circuitous route and still go to Bedford. All the time I could tell he hated to leave the river valley country. He also had made references to the fact that our only excursion across the river into Kentucky was at those few times when we had flown a few miles beyond Hawesville, Kentucky when we were based at the farm in Cannelton, Indiana. My, that now seemed so long ago.

As we level off at about 1500 feet, we are headed south since our field had run along the river, which in this stretch ran north and south, so I expected Marty to make a ninety degree turn to the right, which would have put us flying directly west toward Bedford. But instead he just keeps on going. But heck, he is the pilot, I should worry, I'm just going along for the ride. But, I also have a curious mind. I like to know where we are and where we are going. I knew that the river goes directly south to the little town of Bethlehem where we buzzed the place on the way to Hanover. At Bethlehem the river changes course from due south to southwest. We will reach there in a few minutes. At Bethlehem the river flows southwest all the way to beyond New Albany and Louisville. If Marty continues to follow the river, he will have to make a forty-five degree turn to the right to stay over the river. If he, at last, decided to take the direct route to Bedford, he will have to make a full ninety-degree turn to the right. Up ahead I see little Bethlehem. Soon we are over the river just abreast of Bethlehem. Marty should now be making a forty-five degree right turn to follow the river. I wait and wait but he just keeps on going south. In a few minutes the bend of the river at Bethlehem causes it to be off to our right at a forty-five angle and it gradually is farther and farther away from us.

I raise up and look back at the goggled Marty. He simply grins back at me in a very mischievous way. I get out my little scraps of road map, which has bits of Kentucky. If we keep up this southern course we will soon be 40 miles south of Bethlehem into Kentucky and about 40 miles east of Louisville. Before long I conclude that was a good estimation because I can see the city haze of Louisville on the horizon directly off our right wingtip. And Marty just keeps on going south. At this rate in an hour or so we will be in Tennessee!

I now begin to really scrutinize the tattered Kentucky portion of my old road map. There are a number of little villages and small farms but the countryside is hillier than north of here in Indiana. If the OX-5 should quit, we might have to land on sloping fields. I can only guess at the small towns, but one seems for sure to be Shelbyville just off our left wingtip. I note on the map that if we continue on south we will come very close to flying over Bardstown where my parents and I drove down to during our stay at Hanover. Bardstown is famous for the southern mansion in which composer Stephen Foster is said to have written the words and music for *My Old Kentucky Home,* published in 1853. The mansion was the plantation house of the Rowan family and known as Federal Hill. The two-story brick mansion was begun in 1795 and completed in 1818. Even as early as the Civil War, Federal Hill was widely accepted as the composer's inspiration. On our trip back in 1928, my mother photographed the Federal Hill plantation known as My Old Kentucky Home with her little old box camera. I cannot make out Federal Hill for certain as we pass over Bardstown. Clumps of trees I notice may be shrouding the garden of the mansion and the old home itself.

Marty still holds a steady southern course and I again consult my battered old map. Then all of a sudden, Marty makes a slow turn of forty-five degrees to the right, now heading on a due southwest course. I note on the map that this means we are headed directly toward Hodgenville, Kentucky. It is the birthplace of Abraham Lincoln. We drove there five years ago in 1928, from My Old Kentucky Home at Bardstown. The Lincoln's old birthplace one room log cabin is enshrined there in a temple-like structure of marble and granite, with many steps of granite leading up to the temple on a rise of ground. I will never forget it. Abe Lincoln's history was taught in my Boonville school with an air of devout reverence, shared by both teachers, students and town folks. Lincoln was a local son, too. In his youth he had self-studied law in the Boonville Courthouse, and lived in nearby Gentryville in his formative years.

As we fly along the beautiful Kentucky countryside to Hodgenville, I pay close attention because I know we should be able to see the large Lincoln shrine from the air. It is so white and expansive the way I recalled it five years ago. According to the scale on my map it is, I guess, about 30 miles from Bardstown and we should be there in about 25 to 30 minutes. I set about remembering all I had learned in school and our 1928 visit of the Lincoln National Historic Site at Hodgenville.

Thomas and Nancy Lincoln bought a 300-acre farmstead at what is now Hodgenville in 1808. It was named Sinking Spring Farm for the fine spring that flowed on the property, which also included one building, a simple one-room log cabin. On February 12, 1809, a son Abraham was born to Nancy. Two and a half years later the Lincolns left the area. Many years later in 1860, when Abraham became well known near the outbreak of the Civil War, the remains of the cabin was moved to a nearby farm. Presumed to be the original, this modest structure was returned to Sinking Spring Farm in 1894. In 1911, on the very hill where the cabin originally stood, a grand and imposing marble and granite shrine was erected which contains the humble restored birthplace of the Great Emancipator. As visitors approach the temple-like memorial, they must climb 56 granite steps, one for each year of Abraham Lincoln's life. Inside, the visitors find a 12 by 17-foot log cabin with a single window, its oak and chestnut walls chinked with clay.

As we approach Hodgenville, I can easily make out the shrine from the air. In my exuberance I rise up and turn to Marty, gesturing down, and find myself exasperated in not being able to tell him what it is over the sound of the Waco's engine and propeller. Marty's nod assures me that he not only sees it but knows what it is. Then it dawns on me in even greater exasperation this is why he flew directly south from Hanover. He never once mentioned his intention. He cuts the OX-5's power and we circle over the memorial at about 300 feet. Each time we pass the stepped white granite threshold he rocks our wings in salute and blips the engine by advancing and retarding the throttle. I am surprised that he does not seem to have any intention of landing and inspecting the memorial. But all I can guess is that he keeps thinking of how little time is left for our Hoosier tour and how much more we still have to do. I feel a little sad only because of that and I feel that he's sitting back there at the controls feeling the same way. We both peer back at the Lincoln Memorial as we turn on a northwest heading toward Elizabethtown, Kentucky. Judging from the turn angle and my tattered road map, I estimate we will pass directly over Elizabethtown and if Marty stays this same course we will cross the Ohio River at Brandenburg, Kentucky and the small town of Mauckport across the river on the Indiana side from Brandenburg. Then I recall that Mauckport was where General John Hunt Morgan landed his Confederate Army in his invasion of Indiana and Ohio during the Civil War. Up ahead and already I can see what must be Elizabethtown. It must be since it is the largest town on our course and the largest I can see to either side of our course. So I feel like a real excellent dead-reckoning navigator, depending only on memorizing the angles of our turns ever since we left Hanover, and mentally judging those on my old beat up map.

My front cockpit in the Waco has no compass. Only Marty's instrument panel has a compass. Now we are passing over Elizabethtown, and the next larger town up ahead will be Radcliffe on our right and smaller Vine Grove on our left. Even in the distance I can make them out. Doggoned it, I am really good at predicting Marty's navigation. We are headed directly between what appears to be Radcliffe and Vine Grove.

On the map I notice something else I had not noticed before. Just beyond Radcliffe is Fort Knox where America's gold is Allegedly all stored in vaults below ground. But the old map confirms what I had always taken as a rumor about all that gold being stored. The old map says simply: "Fort Knox, U.S. Bullion Depository." Then I start laughing out loud to myself alone in this front cockpit when I start thinking: Boy! I'm amazed that old Marty back there has not landed at Fort Knox and wanted a tour of the place so he could see all that gold.

As we approach Radcliffe, I look off to the left at about a sixty-five degree horizontal angle and note a very dark cloud in the low horizon. I look on the map to estimate its location and quickly conclude that it is over the Ohio River Valley at about the Tell City and Cannelton area, and undoubtedly is moving upriver as storms always do. At that distance I guess it must be nearly 50 miles wide and straddling the river. Then I note with a start lightning strikes coming down from the cloud and the height of the dark mass rose steadily higher with each passing minute. But Marty keeps on going on the same course. I loosen my safety belt, raising up, turning to him, pointing at the approaching storm. He nods that he sees it and probably saw it before I did. Then he advances the OX-5's throttle and we pick up a bit more speed, probably going from 65 up to 70 or 75 m.p.h. Before I sit back down, Marty points with one hand straight ahead indicating he wants to get as far north from the river into Indiana as he can to try to bypass the storm. By the time we reach the, river at Brandenburg, the top of the huge black cloud is at an elevation of about 40 degrees above us, and is moving fast upriver. The storm appears to stretch about 25 miles to the south of the river and another 25 miles to the north of the river. As we reach the river at Brandenburg, Marty turns right thirty degrees which puts us on a course that will skirt the eastern edge of the Hoosier "Smoky" Mountains, so that if we have to land we can go down in the flat farm land instead of the forested hills which stretch for over 60 miles and are 30 miles wide.

On my map we are now on a straight course to Bedford. At first I wonder why Marty doesn't turn 90 degrees right heading straight east flying directly away from the storm. Then I recall he once said the Waco was not fast enough to outrun one of these Ohio River storms. It would only gobble us up. The best tack is to get out of its way. By now I can see what I believe to be Corydon up ahead and to the right of our course. And now the immense coal black cloud top is almost directly overhead, and there are bolts and flashes of lightning stabbing the ground below from its upper reaches. Soon now, winds as great as our own speed will hit us broadside, coupled with torrential wind-blown rain. Marty has descended now to an altitude of about 500 feet to assure that he can see the ground when the dark cloud envelops us.

No sooner than I make these observations, the Waco suddenly begins to buck up and down and roll wildly from side to side and the nose pitching up and down. Then as suddenly, we are drenched in a driving downpour as if we were flying through a huge waterfall. In seconds, head and shoulders are soaked in a chilling cold torrent. I can't believe the OX-5 is still running in this torrent. The windshield seems about to be torn loose from the screws that hold it to the forward cowling. I crouch down as low as I can get to the cockpit floor amid our stashed duffel bags and tie-down ropes. I dare not loose the safety belt because the airplane is tossed about so much I'm getting my first taste of air-sickness. I peek out to the left and see only wooded high hills, and to the right a town in the storm-swept vista. The land from here to there is flat farmland. We are flying only at 300 feet and ground visibility is still very poor. Just up ahead a lightning bolt in a size beyond my wildest imagination hits the ground in a flash that even illuminates the darkest corners of the floor boards in my cockpit. The crash of thunder followed it by only 4 or 5 seconds and was so loud it drowned out the noise of the storm sweeping through our little plane, and even the now feeble noise of the struggling OX-5. I look out again to the right and see a fence pass by at an altitude of less than 100 feet, and I realize Marty is attempting to make a full-power landing. The broadside force of the storm keeps lifting up the left wing and yawing the tail with such force he can not hold the wing down. And if we do land it is going to be on the right wing and wheel and we will crack up in a terrible ground-loop. The ship, and us, will be tossed all over the fields below even after we have made the so-called landing.

Marty corrects the situation by turning the tail 90 degrees to head directly into the storm. The OX-5 is running at full power. Our ground speed relative to the fences and fields that I see passing by 50 feet below is less than 10 miles per hour. We are flying at a virtual standstill in the teeth of the storm. Then our altitude drops to only 20 feet and I realize we are landing. I come immediately to the realization that once we are on the ground and right side up, I am going to have to get out fast with my tie-down ropes and Marty will have to stay in the ship to fight the wind with the power of the OX-5 and the control surface. Visibility is only a few yards in this cloudy driving rain.

Suddenly we are only half airborne, the wheels hit the ground in some unknown field with a bone-jarring jolt, then in the air again and another hard jolt. This phenomenon repeats itself three times until we are down and "taxiing" at full power but at a standstill, the wings rocking violently from side to side and the tail pitches up and down as Marty struggles to keep it from nosing over, or worse, being flipped over backwards on its back.

Stern wheeler Tom Greene as seen from Hanover Camp before 1933.

Hanover Camp beach/bluff as seen from atop Hanover Hill campus before 1933.

Cabins at Hanover Camp prior to 1933. Shown are (from left) Norma Fluhrer, Helen Fluhrer, John Fluhrer, Peyton Autry and Arch Autry (Peyton's father).

CHAPTER XII

I look back to see Marty's rain-drenched head as he shouts, "Stay aboard until I tell you to get out and tie down." Turning to look forward I see he is laboriously edging the ship into a fence corner. I get the message and I know what to do as we slowly inch our way up as near as we can without the spinning propeller getting nicked on the fence. I bail out on the ground with my armload of ropes, stakes and mallet. I tie a rope to each left and right forward wing strut with the ends of each firmly tied to a fence post. Then I tie a rope on the tail skid, tying it down to a deeply mallet driven stake. Then I go back to each wing strut, lashing ropes, staking each one of those down into the ground. Marty stays at the controls keeping the engine running to counter the force of the storm's headwind. He motions me back into the front cockpit. We hunker down in our respective cockpits to ride out the storm. we are huddled up in our cockpits for nearly an hour while the gale rages on. Finally the wind drops down to a gentle 35 m.p.h. Marty switches off the OX-5. But the torrential rain and wind persists.

We dig out the cockpit cover tarps using them as covers for our rain-soaked bodies. I am cold and shaking. Marty calls out that he is colder than I am because he is older. Always humor in the teeth of adversity!

Visibility is so poor we cannot see where we are and no one seems to know we are here. In staking down the ship, I note the field is soft and muddy even though grassy, like a livestock meadow. The underside of the Waco is muddy. The wire spoke wheels are completely encrusted in mud. Would we ever get out of here?

After two hours huddled up in our cockpits, the wind finally subsides to a mild 10 m.p.h. but the rain now becomes just a good steady rain but no longer the torrential downpour. We dig our slickers out of our duffel bags. At least they keep us from getting any wetter than we already are and do ward off the cold. I hear Marty stirring in the rear cockpit as he stands up to don his slicker. He says, "Well, we just as well get out and see what's around us and if there is anything we can do about it."

The grass is long and the field has scattered clumps and mounds, typical of a cow pasture. The soil is soft and the tracks left by our wheels in landing are deep and muddy. It all looks very distressing to me. Paradoxically, the 65 m.p.h. wind in which we had landed had actually saved us. If we had landed at our usual ground speed of 45 to 50 m.p.h. in this field, we would have nosed over and cracked up for sure. I made this observation to myself but Marty put the same thought to words. He makes his way over to the fence. The field on the other side is newly mowed hay. We walk around finding the surface relatively hard in spite of the rain. Also, typically for a hayfield, it is smooth and flat, but how to get the Waco over here even if we uproot the fence posts and roll up the wire? The Waco's wheels are so deeply mired that the propeller tips whipped the grass with less than 2 inches of clearance with the ground. If the wheels had gone in any deeper in landing, we would have bent the propeller that would have ended our tour right then and there.

It is still dark, cloudy and raining even though the day is far from over. About a quarter mile to the east we can see a house and barn, a light shown in the rear of the house, probably the kitchen. As Marty stands surveying the fence, I become interested in the house, wondering if I should walk down there for help. Then I notice a farm implement road runs along the fence to the house; then I notice a vehicle's single headlight appear out of the barn, turning into the road and apparently headed toward us. I tap Marty's shoulder, pointing to the oncoming vehicle. No doubt a tractor with a single headlight.

The storm has made things so dark I guessed the driver turned on his headlights so we'd know he'd seen us and was coming to either help us or accuse us of trespassing. He was approaching as fast as the tractor would travel in high gear. Even at that distance its whining drive-train could be heard far away. Two things are certain: either he sensed our distress and is responding to it as any good farmer would do in an emergency, or he is eager to express his anger at our trespassing and just wants us to leave as quickly as we had arrived.

As the tractor roars up the driver dismounts quickly, leaving the tractor running. He is a young man, not as young as me, but about Marty's age, dressed in well-worn denim overalls and rubber boots, a battered straw hat on his head. He is excitedly relating in detail how he had observed our landing and Marty's struggle to keep the Waco from being blown away. I'm relieved that our trespassing seems to be the farthest thing from his mind. The Waco fascinated him and his questions come in rapid fire order, seeming not to care whether we answer them or not.

Presently Marty gets in a word edgewise. "Sir, I believe if we could get the ship into the hayfield over here the ground is hard enough despite the downpour that we could take off. I believe the storm will pass well before dark, then we will be able to bother you no more with our unceremonious emergency intrusion."

The young guy eyed Marty quizzically as though he did not fully fathom Marty's eloquent excuse. He shakes his head saying, "No, you could'a got yerselves killed right here in my cow pasture. Now we can pull up the fence stakes which are easier to get out than buried wood posts. These are the new angle iron stakes. We just wiggle 'em back and forth and they just jerk right out. This is all woven wire; we can lay it and the stakes down flat and the wheels of the plane will roll right over it without puncturing the tires, 'cause there is no barbed wire." With that he ran over and started wiggling a fence post and Marty and I ran over to the others mimicking his maneuver. After pulling the stakes on both sides of the fence corner, we laid the wire down flat. The young guy grabbed a coil of rope from the tractor, tying a length to each of the Waco's two wheel axles, gathering them together on the tractor, saying, "You fellers hold the plane's tail down when I pull the wheels out of the mud," he instructed. He puts the tractor in low gear and within five minutes we have the Waco over in the hay field. Marty shook the young fellow's hand and passed him a twenty dollar bill for damages and inconvenience. But he would have none of it. His face became somber and his cheeks blushed. Marty quickly caught on, "Sir, we are very appreciative and indebted to you nonetheless," as he returned the money to his pants pocket. The young fellow just nodded, saying, "It was an emergency, just good to help."

Marty and I did a careful walkaround inspection. We could find no damage and the controls operated normally. But the underside of the lower wings, behind the wheels and the lower side of the fuselage were splattered with mud. It was still raining but no wind at all now. Off to the north, our route to Bedford, we could see sun in the distant horizon which extended up to the edge of the clouds at an angle of 15°. That angle was slowly getting larger as the storm moved on up the Ohio River valley.

The young guy helps us pick up the Waco's tail swinging the ship around for a takeoff to the north. The hayfield is nearly a half mile in length. After we start up the OX-5 and tell our good friend good-bye, Marty slowly taxis down the field for about half its length, testing it for hardness and any standing water, then returns to the starting point. Without further ado he blasts the tail up, swings around at full throttle without lowering the tail and we head out for Bedford.

We climb to 1000 feet. It is still raining but five minutes later the rain stops. The helpful fellow had told us his farm is only two miles from French Town. As we cruise along I dig out my battered road map which has gotten pretty wet, so it was a good idea anyway to unfold it and let it dry out. I find that French Town is just southeast of Marengo. I thought back years earlier when my parents had taken me on a Southern Railway excursion train from Boonville to see the famous (famous to Hoosiers anyway) Marengo Cave. We had spent the day touring the dark caverns with a tour guide and his lantern to learn all about those scientific word definitions of icicle-like formations all ending with 'cites.'

By now the edge of the black storm cloud is over us and to the east about 45 degrees and our old Waco is bathed in the afternoon sun. I can see on my map that we will soon be passing our old familiar town of Paoli only about five miles to the west of our course. I could not help but think of that fine lady who had thrilled us with her charm and the patronage of she and her rich friends from French Lick Hotel. What an experience that was! My parents won't believe a word of it when I tell them.

Instead of passing east of Paoli, Marty flys directly over the town for it is obvious he had a soft spot in his heart for the place the same as I did. He drops to 300 feet, rocking our wings back and forth several times as we pass over Paoli. It is only about another twenty minutes to Bedford as Paoli recedes behind us. I note we are approaching the little town of Orleans. I remember it well because my father and I had driven there to a trap shoot at the Jenkins Brothers Gun Club only two years ago. The Jenkins Brothers are well known champion trap shooters having broken hundreds of clay targets, one after the other, without a miss. Dad and I do that as a recreation at the old Boonville Gun Club, so a sojourn to the famous Jenkins Club was a trip neither of us will ever forget.

Next we pass over Mitchell and Spring Mill State Park where we once visited in our old Essex and mother took pictures of the old Spring Mill and its waterwheel.

Marty has told me several times of his friend John Ragsdale's farm located southeast of Bedford and just three miles north of the little village of Buddha. He established a friendship with Ragsdale last summer on a barnstorming tour of central and northern Indiana and he had landed there only a week before he arrived in Boonville on this summer's tour. So he knows this place very well.

I have been to Bedford twice before, the last a few years ago, each time on our drive to Indianapolis to see Uncle Harmon. I was struck by the numerous limestone quarries surrounding the town and even in the town itself as well as the stone mills which fashioned the heavy products of the quarries.

As Marty now circles the town to look it over again from the air, I am even more impressed with the number of quarries than ever before. They are great sheer rock cleavages, cliffs if you will, in the surface of the earth, sometimes bounded by smooth vertical walls of stone, nearly a hundred feet in depth. I've read that by 1875 there were five limestone companies employing over 600 men in Bedford and the immediate vicinity, overtaking agriculture and other businesses in bringing income to the town. The stone industry continued to be the city's largest employer of men and by 1900 25 cut-stone mill companies operated. Mill blocks were obtained from 32 quarries within a radius of 5 miles of the city. By the beginning of the World War in 1914, there were 39 cut-stone mills employing 4,000 men. Bedford became Stone City and is now in 1933 almost a one industry town.

After circling Bedford twice, Marty heads to the southeast, beginning to lose altitude. Up ahead, I can see what might be the little settlement of Buddha, but then Marty suddenly makes a sharp turn banking to the left with the nose down sharply. I can see a long hayfield with a house and barn at the far end. Then Marty noses down even more, throttling back, fishtailing and side-slipping so I knew that must be the Ragsdale farm. We pass over a fence at about 50 feet, sitting down in a pretty three-point landing with not even a bump.

John Ragsdale is a tousled, auburn haired fellow about Marty's age, his prominent teeth bared in almost a perpetual grin. Quickly I learn he is a really jovial fellow. He and Marty had seen each other briefly only two months earlier, greeting each other with informal light hearted repartee. My introduction to Ragsdale was just as carefree, both he and Marty laughing at my blushing reluctant acknowledgement at being introduced as the only southern Hoosier glider pilot. The first thing we did was taxi the Waco up near the barn. He has a gas engine pump hooked up to his water supply. I am then given a hose, rag and a brush to begin washing all the mud off the Waco's underside as well as the wire spoke wheels and landing gear struts. It's quite a job, taking me until almost dark. But I knew that next morning the old ship will glisten anew in the morning sunshine.

Ragsdale lives on the family farm with his mother, a vigorous lady of sixty-five. Her husband had died ten years ago. Her three other children are married and live on Lawrence County farms of their own. Her dinner is one to behold. Marty and I enjoy every bite and tell her so at least a dozen times. She only shakes her head, saying, "Oh pshaw, it's not much to brag on." John asks Marty what our plans are. Marty without hesitation, replies, "Leaving in the morning for Vincennes. Few more stops to make. Got to get Peyton back to school." It depresses me to think of it. I'd like nothing better right now than living this life of being an aeronautical gypsy forever. John looks at me and laughs loudly, while Marty smiles sympathetically and knowingly. Both Marty and I know it's best without saying so.

The Ragsdales put us to bed in the bunkhouse which is as clean and neat as my bedroom in Boonville. Next day we are up to a crowing rooster that even Marty's snores cannot defy. The first thing I do is inspect the Waco. It gleams in its bright cleanliness in the morning sun, just as I thought it would. I just had to go out and admire it. Then we partake of Margaret Ragsdale's bountiful breakfast! We take plenty of time saying our good-byes and go out together to turn the Waco around to face the other end of the hayfield, prepare to take off westward for Vincennes. Marty and I do a walkaround inspection, then shake hands with the Ragsdales again. I climb into the rear cockpit while Marty stands at the propeller. Then I am out and Marty is in while I retrieve the chocks and haul them into the front cockpit. We make our take-off, climbing to about 200 feet. Marty takes a last turn over the Ragsdale farm, then up to about 500 feet and swings over Bedford for a last look. I am impressed even more with all the stone quarries but as we head toward Vincennes, there are still more quarries in the western outreaches of Lawrence County as we pass over the communities of Fayetteville and Silverville. I pull out the crumpled old road map from my hip pocket and note that a direct heading for Vincennes would be about 15 degrees south of due west, which seems to be what Marty is doing for I can see what must be Silverville and it is off on our right lower wingtip. I have my usual fun of estimating and conclude that at our present speed of 70 m.p.h. we should be over Vincennes in a little over 45 minutes. I take a look at my old pocket Ben and estimate our start time over Bedford as five minutes earlier for we have been in the air five minutes already.

I am shaken out of my navigational doldrums when the stick begins quickly slanting against the inside of one knee and then as quickly against the other. Marty wants me to take over, which I eagerly do, but after several weeks of this I now can do it and relax enough to enjoy the scenery and look for the small towns along our route from my wrinkled old map, even though I am flying the airplane. I have long since learned to stay on course because whenever I have strayed from his compass heading, Marty has let me know in no uncertain terms by shaking the stick, throttling back almost to idle so that I cannot ignore his shouts and open palms banging on the cowling behind my head. I am still holding Marty's course and it now appears he has set it more southwesterly than a straight line directly to Vincennes. Judging from the small towns off to our right which I guess to be Raglesville, Epsom and Cornettsville, that we are heading directly to Washington, Indiana which is 20 miles directly east of Vincennes. Washington is the home of my Uncle Harmon Autry's wife Fae. Uncle Harmon, my dad's brother, has worked for many years for the Indianapolis Water Works as a stationary engineer at the spotlessly clean Rock Creek Pumping Station with its huge Peerless, triple expansion steam engine, its huge, low r.p.m. flywheel rim requiring two full floors of the station. Uncle Harmon is as spotlessly clean as the Rock Creek station. He always wore a white shirt and necktie to work. He would sit and watch the huge steam engine with limitless pride. Uncle Harmon always loved to come down to Boonville to quail hunt with dad and I with our pointer dogs. But his hunting clothes and Stevens pump shotgun, 12 gauge, were spotless too. His Chevy coupe reflected his and Aunt Fae's bent toward cleanliness and neatness of attire. So anyway, I will be happy to tell them on their annual fall hunting trip to Boonville only a month away that I flew over Washington, Aunt Fae's home. Sure enough, what surely is Washington appears over the nose of the Waco up ahead. On two occasions before my folks and I had visited Washington so I had some recollection of the town.

My Washington ruminations are rudely interrupted by shaking of the stick, a retarded blip of the throttle to which I quickly respond by holding both arms vertically and removal of my feet from the rudder. Marty throttles back, dropping our altitude to 200 feet. We are directly over the east-west Vincennes/Washington/Loogootee Highway. Then Marty drifts over to the north a bit from the highway so I can see he was going to fly right down Main Street. He drops the Waco to 150 feet giving us only a clearance of 50 to 75 feet with the tops of most of the buildings. On several occasions I had mentioned to Marty that Aunt Fae's parents and siblings lived in Washington as well as liberal descriptions of her and Uncle Harmon's fastidiousness so I guessed he knew I'd tell them all about the trip and how we had flown over Washington. So good old Marty, he wants to make sure Aunt Fae's family are fully aware of it. As we roar down Washington's Main Street, I can see the White River up ahead as it meanders its way south along the west edge of town. Up ahead I can make out a dim visage of Vincennes on the horizon as Marty climbs up to a more leisurely altitude of 1000 feet, one that would avail a better choice of emergency fields if the OX-5 decided to take a pit-stop without warning. I'd made only two previous trips by auto with my parents to Vincennes but had made only a brief visit to the O'Neal Airport founded by Frank O'Neal in 1926.

O'Neal is a true pioneer aviator and widely known throughout the Midwest. He has trained a large number of the early Hoosier pilots. Most of what I knew of O'Neal until now was what I had eagerly read and retained from the Evansville Courier and Evansville Press. Marty, on the other hand, has known O'Neal for a long time, in fact, he has visited O'Neal Airport on two previous barnstorming tours of the Hoosier state. Vincennes and O'Neal's Airport has been the starting point for Marty's previous tours of Indiana, beginning in early summer and ending there on the way back to Kansas in the early fall. But to me now the impending meeting of Frank O'Neal has set my heart a-beating so fast I am afraid I would not be able to speak when introduced by my intrepid pilot friend. Marty had explained and I had also previously read that O'Neal's first airport was only one mile southwest of Vincennes on the south 6th Street Road in 1923. But poor water drainage from seepage from the Wabash River forced him in December 1926 to move the airport just across the river to its present location on the Vincennes/ Lawrenceville, Illinois highway. This pioneer Hoosier aviator did a lot of barnstorming around the Midwest and in Indiana and Illinois in particular. I believe he made stops more than once at our old field west of Boonville long before I had my primary glider. His first airplane was a Standard J-1 which he used to barnstorm southern Indiana, in fact at least six or seven years ago,

1926 or 1927, I had a ride in a Standard J-1 piloted by a Hoosier pilot whose name was lost to posterity before I knew or had heard of Frank O'Neal. Later, as I read of O'Neal, I believe he was my pilot when I was 10 years old. Now when I meet him soon I will ask if he ever barnstormed at Boonville. From all I've read and from what Marty has told me, O'Neal's flying career is worth putting down in this book.

Frank J. O'Neal is not only a pioneer aviator but an astute businessman. He was born in 1900 in the small southern Indiana settlement of Oatsville, which is a short distance east of Princeton, Indiana. After high school he became an elementary school teacher in the public schools of Francisco, Indiana, at the age of 18. Francisco is seven miles east of Princeton. In 1918, he entered the service in a special training unit which was terminated when the war ended. Like many other young men fascinated with the impact the airplane had made in the war, he gave up teaching in the public schools for an aviation career. He began this career in 1920 by taking up a partnership with a wartime pilot by the name of Joe Walker. They purchased a surplus Standard J-1 training plane located in Wisconsin. Surplus Standards and Curtiss JN-4 Jennies were all that were available. This was before the production of airplanes for new commercial use, which did not even begin until five years later. Joe Walker with O'Neal as passenger flew the Standard from Wisconsin back to Wheatland. Wheatland is just east of Vincennes on old Highway 50. This was in May 1920. A hangar for the Standard consisted only of roping it to a tree on a piece of land owned by a friend. Walker gave O'Neal one hour of instruction, then for some unknown reason, left for California. It wasn't until years later that he returned for a short visit with Frank O'Neal.

With an airplane on his hands and no one to teach him to fly it, O'Neal began a series of self-instruction lessons which he accomplished alone through careful patience and plenty of slow experience. He taxied the airplane many times up and down the field, lifting off only a few feet at a time, then setting it down until he eventually soloed. As a man of intellect with an astute business acumen, his business grew from there to the same O'Neal owned and operated airport in this year of 1933 that offers all aviation service, including flight instruction.

Initially, after barnstorming locally for three years, he tried to locate his first airport at Princeton in the period between May 1920 and 1923, proposing it be done at an estimated cost of $12,000 to the city fathers of Princeton, but the deal was never completed. His next move was acquisition of the land on the South 6th Street road at Vincennes, which was the real beginning of his career as a commercial aviation operator. In December 1926, he re-established O'Neal Airport just across the Wabash River from Vincennes at its present location. His first field on the South 6th Street road became untenable because for many weeks during the year, due to seepage of water from flooding in the Wabash River, the field often was wet, saturated to the point where it sometimes took many weeks for the field to dry out well enough for take-offs and landings.

As we fly in over Vincennes on a direct west compass course, I notice something about Vincennes I had not noticed before when I had driven up there with my parents. Its streets are not laid out with north/south streets crossing streets going east and west. Instead they are at 45 degrees to the compass, evidently to get a normal relationship to the frontage on the Wabash River. Those streets running northeast to southwest cross those running northwest to southeast. Up ahead I can see the Wabash River facing the western edge of Vincennes. Beyond the river I can easily make out O'Neal Airport, a metal hangar plus some smaller buildings and a few airplanes parked outside the hangar.

Marty makes a wide turn circling the airport, approaching from the west. We are now about three miles into Illinois. He then swings around lining up with the field. We begin a slow descent touching down mid-field, taxiing up near the hangar and switching off. A fellow in slightly soiled white coveralls approaches in a friendly greeting. It is obvious he recognizes both our Waco and Marty. They shake hands, Marty asking, "Is Frank around today?" The young guy replies. "Yep. In the hangar, just outside the office, bent over those boxes."

My heart is all a-flutter; I am about to meet my hero at last. All of a sudden he stands up when he hears us approach. His face is not a surprise to me because I realize the pictures I'd seen of him in the *Evansville Courier* were good likenesses, except now he is not wearing the cloth helmet and goggles of the newspaper photos. He is not tall but not short either. He is noticeably taller than Marty and I know they are both 33 years old because I knew from the *Courier* that O'Neal was born in 1900 and Marty had told me he was born in Kansas in 1900. I conclude the *Courier* stories were accurate in describing him as an astute businessman because he wears a good looking tweed coat over a matching vest, white shirt and tie and dark serge trousers, not pressed, even slightly rumpled, showing him to be a businessman who isn't afraid to mess his attire to get his job done. I'd even heard that he often tore down an engine without soiling nothing more than a little grease on his hands. He steps forward to greet Marty, asking, "Well, Marty, so it's back from this year's Hoosier tour. How was it?"

Marty, in his eloquent but brief way, filled him in on the highlights of our trip. Carb trouble on the OX-5; the forced landing east of Jasper; the disconnected contact on the distributor, stormy landing south of Paoli, and so on. I could not believe how Marty could tell it all so completely and yet so briefly. It brought forth a string of chuckles and outright laughter from Frank

O'Neal, then Marty said, "Excuse me, Frank, this is my assistant, Peyton. He did the entire trip; has built and flown a primary glider down at Boonville just west of town, a field you may recall. He tells me he thinks he may have had a ride with you in your old Standard when he was a lot younger."

When we shook hands I asked him if he ever flew passengers in his Standard at the field at the foot of Orphan's Home Hill. He nodded emphatically. "Sure, several times. I never knew it was Orphan's Home Field but it was in the west edge of Boonville on the north side of Highway 62. The field's owner's name was a man by the name of Hart."

My eyes must have bugged out because I blurted out, "Yeah, that's it. I flew with you in your Standard J-1 at Roy Hart's field. That's where I fly my glider now. We use a car tow to take off and climb." He smiles broadly and gives me a pat on the shoulder. I feel like I will never wash this shirt again, at least not the shoulder.

But then suddenly the businessman in Frank O'Neal comes out.

"Marty, what can I do for you?"

Marty winked at me thoughtfully replying, "Well, it wouldn't hurt to top off my gas tank, then we head south to take Peyton back to school, and a stop or two down around Princeton, Oakland City and Petersburg, then on down to Boonville. Then I will make a non-stop trip back up here and have you overhaul or put in a new carburetor and distributor. Then I head back to Kansas and ride a few passengers in Illinois and Missouri on the way."

O'Neal calls his mechanic over to gas up the Waco while we look around the place. Frank, or F.J. as they call him, tells us he has two other planes in the air now flown by students practicing cross-country flying. A parked airplane, apparently owned locally or by a visitor, an O'Neal patron, is a Stinson JR 4-place, powered by a Wright J-6 engine of 150 horsepower, a high-wing, strut braced cabin monoplane. Another is a Curtiss Robin powered by an OX-5 engine with its variable airflow shuttered radiator, a 3-place, high wing cabin monoplane. I believe I saw the same Curtiss Robin last year set up on display with a "For Sale" sign on its propeller hub at the Warrick County Fair in Boonville. The Robins are built at the Curtiss-Robertson plant in St. Louis and several were produced with the OX-5. With the OX-5 they were the most inexpensive priced cabin plane, because of the cheaper OX-5 engines. Two of O'Neal's early planes are put in a rear part of the hangar and one outdoors, temporarily or otherwise. One is the venerable old Standard J-1. The engine on the Standard is covered in canvas but it looks as though the old Hall-Scott engine had been replaced by an OX-5, also the one I flew in several years ago before, presumably with O'Neal, was powered by the Hall-Scott, but also had the triangular cabane struts on the top side of the upper wing to carry brace wires to the outer section of the upper wing. But this one has the cabanes replaced like the Lincoln Standard with struts extending from the lower ends of the outer bay struts to the under side of the outer section of the upper wing. The other airplane is an OX-5 powered Waco Model "9," the predecessor of our Waco "10." Both Wacos are very similar. The "10" has the so-called split-axle spring shock absorber landing gear where the "9" has a shock-cord axle landing gear similar to the Jenny and Standards. The tail surfaces of the two are of a different shape. The 10 has a streamlined head rest for the pilot, the 9 does not. Otherwise the airplanes are nearly identical except the 10 has ailerons on both upper and lower wings, but the 9 only has ailerons only on the upper wing.

Presently our ship is gassed up and we bid O'Neal good-bye.

With Marty it's only temporary. With me I have a gnawing feeling I will never see my hero Frank O'Neal ever again. Before we climb in our old Waco 10, I ask Marty why he does not want to stay in Vincennes and check out the really special history of the place, the George Rogers Clark Memorial and the story of Clark is really special. He replies that he has already done that before on his previous trips here, but I press him on the subject anyway, cross-examining him on the subject to make sure he understands its true impact. Also I have hinted about both Vincennes and Terre Haute all during this trip. He has nodded and talked about it at night and over meals all the way from Richland to French Lick, Paoli, Salem, Madison, and up to Bedford, but he has also pointed out that there isn't time to do everything. After all, we've been on this trip nearly two months and as it is I'll be late to school. Still we talked of the pioneer exploits of George Rogers Clark and the early plane designs of 25 years ago in Terre Haute, by the Johnson Brothers. Years apart, but history.

The Piankashaw and the Shawnee Indians called the Terre Haute area home. They hunted buffalo, raised corn and tobacco, reared their families, fought the French, British and the Americans; lost their homes and were eventually moved to Oklahoma. Their arrowheads and stone tools are all that remains. The French trappers came early and stayed long. They built their cabins, cleared some land, married Indian girls, reared their families and many stayed. The missionaries came; they witnessed, taught and established congregations, names like Gibault, Rivet, Brute, and others are familiar in local history as are names which have a romantic sound. Such as Busseron, Vigo, Dubois, Richardville, Godare and of course Francois-Marie Bissot Sieur de Vincennes.

Vincennes was commissioned to construct a fort on the Wabash River to counteract the expansion of the British. He completed the fort here in 1732. Four years later, while on a campaign against the Chickasaw Indians in Mississippi, he was captured and burned at the stake. The fort was named Poste de Vincennes in honor of Sieur de Vincennes for his bravery. After the 1763 British victory in the French and Indian War, the flag of France was to fly no more on the banks of the Wabash. In its place the British flag floated in the breeze over the fort at Vincennes. During the American Revolution, British Lieutenant Governor Henry Hamilton arrived in Vincennes in December 1778 and immediately began to repair and improve the fort, which was renamed Fort Sackville. The fort stood in defiance of a small band of volunteers under the Virginia Colonel George Rogers Clark. Clark had captured Kaskaskia and Cahokia in the Illinois country during the summer of 1778. Then he prepared to do what was considered impossible. The Illinois country was flooded and the British were approximately 180 miles to the east, safely quartered for the winter in a well-constructed fort with cannons at Vincennes. Governor Patrick Henry of Virginia received a short statement from Clark. Quote: "Great things have been effected by a few men well conducted. Our cause is just. Our country will be grateful." With that report to his Commander in Chief, Colonel Clark and 175 men began a trip which would change world history and would echo for more than two hundred years. He marched on Vincennes and captured Fort Sackville. The British flag was hauled down and Hamilton was taken to prison in Virginia. The Redcoats were gone from the banks of the Wabash. Coming through the breech opened by Clark and his little band of volunteers, there emerged a new nation that began to stretch westward. Its feet were implanted in rich prairie land that destined to become the heart of America, and the breadbasket of the world. A new flag flew over Vincennes. Ohio became a state; the Indiana Territory was born, encompassing the present states of Indiana, Illinois, Michigan, Wisconsin and a part of Minnesota. A new capitol for a new land was established at Vincennes.

On the banks of the Wabash, William Henry Harrison, Governor of the Indiana Territory, and later the 9th President of the United States, built a mansion of such beauty and durability that it still stands as a monument to the man and to a people. Tecumseh, Chief of the Shawnee and his medicine man and brother, the Prophet, came to parley with Governor Harrison. They could not agree and the battle of Tippecanoe and the ensuing War of 1812 ended the Indian control of the upper Wabash. Known to any normal youngster, America began to grow and develop its muscles. A University, Vincennes University, was begun by Governor Harrison in 1801. A newspaper, the Indiana *Gazette* began operation; several churches were founded; the first Masonic Lodge in Indiana was started. The first courthouse, the first nursing school, the first hospital and many other firsts concerning Vincennes are recorded in the annals of Indiana history. The buffalo no longer crossed the Wabash but many wagons loaded with settlers moving to the new country were using the ford at Vincennes. In one wagon came Abraham Lincoln, destined for fame as the 16th President of the United States. Many other now well known men and women lived and visited here throughout the years and each left his or her footprints in the historical sands. There are monuments to some who have been recognized for their achievements. Others are remembered by a headstone in a cemetery.

Marty is also fascinated with my research on the history of the Johnson monoplane, which I had gathered from newspapers and library with connections with those in Terre Haute and Vincennes area. All of that had happened 25 years ago in the Terre Haute area. But I still thought it would be a great idea to fly to Terre Haute and look into their news morgue, the library there and talk to those who remembered the Johnson Brothers and their historic flights. And here again he simply nodded wishfully, "Maybe next year. But we only have so much time to do our barnstorming tour. You young bucks want to do everything now. So do I. But you also have to get back to school—and not too late." So during these past weeks we would talk on about the Johnson Brothers as we munched our lunch or slept under the stars and under the lower wing of the Waco.

The Johnson Brothers of Terre Haute, Indiana fared well because of their experience in building small marine engines for powering fishing boats on the Wabash River. The Johnson's technical success in designing and building both a flying machine and a special aero engine was nothing short of phenomenal in 1907 to 1915. Had they continued in aviation their names would have been emblazoned with pioneers like the Wrights and Curtiss. Their first attempt in 1907, a wood structure, was abandoned, but in 1909 they began an all-metal steel and aluminum, fabric covered monoplane in which Lou Johnson taught himself to fly in 1911. He carried on these flights frequently for a period of five years. The brothers, Harry, Lou and Julius Johnson designed, built and flew their creation as a team, just as they had carried on their marine engine business. The engine for their monoplane, built from scratch, was a 4-cylinder V-type, water cooled, 2-cycle design of 60 horsepower, weighing 160 lbs. The complete machine weighed 700 lbs. Wingspan was 36 feet, wing chord 8 feet, length 34 feet, propeller of laminated wood, diameter 8 feet, pitch 4-1/2 feet. All metal aluminum and steel fuselage wing and empennage. Wing and tail surfaces were fabric covered. The tricycle landing gear was equipped with wheel brakes, a feature that did not come into wide aircraft use until many years later. The method of lifting off by lowering the tail in the tricycle configuration was apparently eminently successful in making their machine comparatively easy to fly, in a day when dual instruction was essentially unheard of. The machine was balanced and trimmed such that the tail produced no lifting load and only a minimal amount of download for trim stability and control. Even the scant literature indicates the Johnsons paid close attention to these kinds of details, much to their credit.

An outstanding innovation of the Johnson design was the cooling system. At a time when Curtiss and others were using honeycomb radiators of 100 percent frontal area for cooling, the Johnson cooling system presented essentially no frontal area drag since it had no conventional radiator. The fuselage structure consisted only of a large metal tube on which the pilot's seat and controls were mounted. The radiator was an integral part of the fuselage and engine mounts, aside from a small reservoir ahead of the pilot.

The Johnson shop on the Wabash River was hit by flood and tornado in 1915, destroying everything. That natural disaster of fate no doubt cost aviation a famous name that would have otherwise prevailed. Discouraged, they later moved to northern Illinois to continue their marine engines. But even though their name did not become a historic watchword of aviation, it did become very famous. Ever hear of the Johnson Outboard Motor? They are one and the same!

After this unique all metal monoplane and engine combination was flown extensively for five years, the engine in 1915 successfully outperformed competing engines in a grueling 10-hour government test at Mineola, Long Island. The Aero Club of America at that time was trying to interest Secretary of the Navy Daniels in developing engines that would be superior to those used in foreign aircraft during the European War. The summer of 1913, their airplane was flown by Ross L. Smith, also of Terre Haute, Indiana, who took it on an extended tour of the Middle West. This was undoubtedly part of a serious promotional program to sell and produce their creation. A Johnson Brothers brochure from about that year displays a photo of a plane flying over Terre Haute housetops, and it reads in part: "Johnson Brothers' 60 horsepower steel monoplanes, Ross L. Smith, aviator. Johnson Brothers Motor Company, Terre Haute, Indiana." Smith also made a number of spectacular take-offs from Meron Bluffs, using the available run of only 200 feet. This stunt was a feature of the historical Meron Chautauqua on which occasion William Jennings Bryan was a platform speaker. The Johnson monoplane was not without some national recognition in spite of its secluded origin in the southern Hoosier hinterlands. A September 30, 1911 issue of Aero Magazine carried a 500-word article and photo which went on to describe the machine, its builders and the flight test exploits of Lou Johnson. A large, tapered steel tube formed the fuselage proper, atop which the pilot's seat was mounted, tapering down in diameter from the front wing spar to the elevator hinge. The engine mount consisted of three longitudinal steel tubes extending from front of the engine to aft of the wing trailing edge. These three tubes straddled the main fuselage tube in a triangular disposition, two at top and one at bottom and were structurally attached to it. In addition to forming the engine mount, these tubes were finned throughout their length, serving as a complete radiator for the engine, with essentially zero frontal area cooling drag. This basic fuselage engine mount was probably very efficient from a frontal area, weight, strength and space standpoint but it did have the pilot's body partially exposed to the slipstream which would have been superimposed within the fuselage frontal area of the conventional machine. The coil spring oleo strut was something of an innovation in a day when looped elastic shock cord was normally used. Landing gear geometry became a skid if the spoke wheels failed. Wheel brakes consisted of a pilot operated skid pivoted on the main axle. Wing warping for lateral control was accomplished with an ingenious evener system that applied uniform tension wireload, down or up, at three spanwise stations on each wing.

As we take off from O'Neal Airport, I look back wistfully at Vincennes and O'Neal Airport. I know we still have three more days before I have to show up at high school, nearly a week late. But Marty said we would take the long way home from Vincennes and spend at least one more night sleeping out under the Waco's wing, and reminiscing about our aerial odyssey. We have stocked up on sandwiches and soft drinks at O'Neal's airport so eating would be no problem. A good way to end our last nights together. At least that's how I feel about it, and Marty seemed all during the tour to sense my feelings about what we were doing. These past two months we have talked a lot when not in the air about things we knew the most about or cared the most about. At this late date I had one pang of regret, I had talked too much about my own life and its environment and he had encouraged it and persisted with questions about it. He seemed to have a thirst for knowledge about me and my environment. It had become a bond of friendship. He had a keen, amused curiosity about me and of course I had reveled in telling him about myself, my family and the southern Hoosier area in which I had grown up. But now, belatedly, I realized that it had robbed me of knowing much about Marty's far more interesting background. Sure, he had told me a few fascinating things of his life but they always seemed to have had a conclusion and ended then and there. I felt I had deluded myself, even cheated myself; I did not blame Marty, it wasn't his fault. I felt I had over-shared my experiences and dreams without getting his in return.

The route he was now taking back to Boonville was a good example. Just before we had taken off from Vincennes, he said he would cruise down the Wabash to Mt. Carmel, then out over the Illinois prairies west of Mt. Carmel where I could hopefully imagine and even see my grand uncle Albert Baker's farm where our family visited in the summers of my earlier youth just like I had told Marty several times. He was all ears. Then we would head back to Mt. Carmel, then on east to Princeton, then up to Petersburg, then back down to Oakland City, Lynnville, Folsomville and Boonville. At Oakland he wanted to land at a field that he knew about and greet a friend there that he had met once at O'Neal's Airport. We'd lay over there for the night, then go on to Boonville. The last letter to my parents was mailed nearly two weeks ago and in barnstorming one has learned not to set exact arrival times. One gets there when one gets there and the expectors are simply saddled with the indefinite of it all. My poor parents, I did feel for them, despite our basic agreement that this tour was a good thing for me and for them.

As we cruise down the Wabash, I get to thinking of Marty's fascination with the Wabash Valley from Terre Haute to Evansville as the origin of two famous brothers. One was Paul Dresser, the famed song writer who wrote the world famed song, *"On the Banks of the Wabash."* His brother, Theodore Dreiser, is one of the 20th century's most acclaimed novelists. Both lived in Evansville and Terre Haute and points between at various times in their early lives. Marty seemed especially intrigued with the troubled life of Theodore Dreiser and the reasons for the difference in spelling of their last names.

As we now approach Mt. Carmel, Illinois, I began to think of our very early motor trips to my mother's uncle, Albert Baker who had a small farm on the prairies some twenty miles west of Mt. Carmel. Our family, Mother, Dad, myself and Uncle John, Aunt Helen and their daughter Edith took from 3 a.m. to 9 p.m. one summer to drive to Uncle Albert's farm in our open touring cars; Dad's Maxwell and Uncle John's Model T. There was no auto bridge or regular auto ferry over the Wabash at Mt. Carmel, only a railroad bridge. We crossed on a makeshift, but regularly scheduled ferry comprised of an old barge, restrained by a cable to keep it from being drawn downstream. It was driven by an old skiff, powered by a one-cylinder inboard engine lashed to the side of the barge-like ferry. I will never forget Uncle Albert and Aunt Mary Baker's young grandson my own age; his name was Brown Alka. His mother was Albert and Mary's daughter. Brown's father had been killed in France in 1918. He was a motorcycle dispatch rider. I remember going to the old one-room Baker chapel crossroads church just a few miles from the Baker farm. Brown's father is buried in the churchyard cemetery. My mother once took Brown's picture standing by his father's gravestone. A fine proud young lad he was, deeply interested in farming and showing Edith and I all of the beauties and pleasures of rural life.

As Marty now turned 90 degrees to the west, we cruise all around the area, but from the air I could not locate the old church or the Baker farm. It has been ten years and the old church may have been rebuilt or moved and the little farmhouse of Albert and Mary may have been improved or rebuilt beyond recognition from the air, even though we sometimes flew as low as 200 feet. After a while Marty turned and headed back to Mt. Carmel on an easterly course to cross the Wabash again and head for Princeton, Indiana. Mt. Carmel to Princeton is only 20 miles so it only takes us 15 minutes. We cross the main north-south highway, U.S. 41, which runs from Evansville all the way to Chicago. I always remembered Princeton not by the one trip my parents had taken me there, but my cousin Floyd Taylor's aunt lived there and would come for Floyd in Boonville and bring him back to live with them in summer school vacation in Princeton. Floyd's father Jesse died in a mine accident, leaving poor Floyd fatherless as a young lad. His mother Artie was my father's sister. Floyd's aunt's husband's name was Jesse Bolin, a big friendly man who drove from Princeton to Boonville in his 1925 Essex (new at the time) to pick up a highly enthusiastic Floyd.

We fly straight east down Broadway, the main east-west street of Princeton. Princeton is the county seat of Gibson County. We pass over the beautiful old courthouse in the center of Princeton at Broadway and Main. It was built in 1884, the third courthouse since the first one in 1814. It is only 15 miles now to Oakland City and on the road between the two towns is the little hamlet of Francisco. It is Francisco where Frank O'Neal at age 18 became an elementary school teacher. As I look down on Francisco, I get to thinking again about Frank O'Neal and how I had just met him for the first time, and how he had been my aviator hero for many years.

Yes, many years to me at age 16 are like all of 5 years. Yes, Frank O'Neal had been my hero all of those years, but it now dawned on me like a bolt out of the blue, something I'd known now for weeks, that another hero now sat behind me flying this old Waco biplane. Yes, buried in my conscience, knowing it all along these past two months without consciously thinking about the fact that I did know that he would always be my hero. And also the fact that the end of our Hoosier sojourn was only a few hours away has now brought it all home to me. I now knew that our paths might never cross again. I don't like to think about that right now. But what I do know is that I will always remember and treasure this aerial odyssey through the southern Hoosier hinterland. And I will always remember Marty and that we were friends for two months on a first name basis and, in his case the first name basis was obviously only a nickname. As we fly over Oakland City, I remember that my cousin Floyd had come up here also on summer vacations with his uncle Jesse Bolin as well as at Princeton because Bolin had lived in both towns over the years.

Then Marty throttles back, beginning a slow turning descent to the north, then turning back to the south, lining up on a field on the north side of the highway east of Oakland City. I thought of the man who had flown the three place open cockpit OX-5 powered biplane in 1929 to the Poor Farm Field in Boonville with the thirty plane statewide air tour. He had told me he was a teacher in Oakland City. I will never forget he was well dressed, wearing a new white cloth helmet and goggles, but also in a full length rubber fireman's raincoat. He had said that during a rainstorm one could get very wet in an open cockpit, but what amazed me was the fact that it was a hot, sunny August afternoon! But after the drenching we received recently on the Ohio

River, I did not see him now as looking so foolish after all. I could have used that raincoat of his just two weeks ago.

Marty lands gently in the smooth hayfield, taxis up near the road and switches off. We get out and stretch for an hour or so hoping Marty's friend, the field's owner, would show up. There is little traffic out on the road. Those that drive by only gawk at the plane. It is getting late and a bit cool because it is now well into September. The trip down from Vincennes only took two hours. We had spent another two hours at O'Neal's looking around and talking to F.J. and his mechanics.

Finally Marty says, "Okay, let's taxi back to the north end of this field, eat our dinner, get our bedrolls out, plan for a good night's sleep in this nice green hay stubble." I climb up in the rear cockpit to man the switch while Marty swings the prop over for a quick start. He comes around, waves me to remain in the rear cockpit while he climbs in front. Using the front controls he taxies the ship a half mile to the north where we switch off and unload our gear.

After a hearty dinner of cold O'Neal Airport hamburgers and still cool Orange Crush, we unroll our bedrolls under the Waco's right lower wing. Dusk of the late afternoon has become twilight. Dress all during this trip has been trousers and shirt sleeves, no sweaters or coats. The evening now is strictly the brisk onslaught of autumn. We lay in our bedrolls, talking for a while until our weary bodies become bored with our conversation. All I can recall after that was on three occasions being awakened by Marty's raucous snoring. My hero!

The next morning I am awakened by Marty who lets forth with a loud yelp and muffled muttering that sounds a lot like some kind of curse. He had sat up suddenly from his sleep with a start, ramming his head into the lower wing. I laugh loud and long. It is really funny. He retorts, "Okay, you young laughing hyena, get up and get the breakfast out of the ship. It's cold and the coffee is cold. Then we'll take off for Boonville, and get you back in school and put an end to your lollygaging all over Indiana with an aeronautical tramp, the likes of me." Then he grins impishly. His retort not only woke me up but sobered me up. He could read my face too well. How I hated all of this to end. Last evening he had said he too was real sorry it had to end. But he also said he was anxious to get back up to Vincennes and get the OX-5 into preventive maintenance so he could get started back to Kansas before any early snow.

The suddenly cool turn of weather, even in just the evenings, seems to arouse his anxiety. Soon it will be October. Weather in the western Midwest has often proven it can produce early snowstorms to aggravate the unwary, and Marty is a careful pilot, definitely not unwary. Marty's friend, the field's owner, has still not shown up and Marty seems not at all anxious to hang around any longer. We pick up our gear and crank up the OX-5 in the usual procedure. The field is very long and the air cold, clear and still. Instead of taxiing the three quarter mile down to the road at the south end, Marty takes off directly to the south. We clear the road and its phone wires by nearly 100 feet. With all of his seeming hurry, I see he is not reneging on his flight plan of showing me my old favorite towns on the way to Boonville. He does a turning climb back to the north. I know he is going up to Petersburg where our family had friends and also this year where I had gone with Dad to hunt up a fellow on a farm near the White River who had built a two-place Pietenpol Air Camper powered with a Model A Ford engine. I hoped we could land on his wheat stubble strip along the river and visit with him for a few minutes. It is less than twenty miles north.

Off to our right I can see the town of Winslow where my Dad said some of his friends worked in an underground, deep-shaft coal mine. I think I can see the mine. We have good friends who live in Petersburg, Paul and Donna Ruff and their young grandson Donny. As we approach Petersburg I can see the old courthouse and then I am oriented to the neighborhood where the Ruffs live in the south part of town, near the intersection of 6th and Maple Streets. Maple is four blocks south of Main, so I wave to Marty to come in from the south over what I know to be 6th Street. He is at about 150 feet. At the north end of town we do a one-eighty, repeating the process going south just over the treetops, and high enough to clear any steeples or the court-house if we were to stray off course. We then turn again northwest along the White River. I recall my Pietenpol builder's place as along the river north-west of Petersburg. We hunt all up and down the zigzag river's course and I cannot spot his farm or the little T-shaped wooden hangar across the road. Finding something by auto as Dad and I had done was a lot different than finding it by air, as I was certainly discovering.

White River forms the entire north border of Pike County along its full width of 21 miles, so after about ten minutes of following the crooked stream in the northwest stretch more than once, I finally signaled Marty to give up and turn back south to our inevitable course to Boonville. It is only seven-teen miles due south to Lynnville where Dad and I quail hunted and also participated in the bird dog trials of the Southwestern Indiana Field Trial Club. I can well recall one trial held on the Wilson farm where my saddle horse was fidgety about wading a creek and tried to jump it. Instead he fell headlong, throwing me with my new riding boots, new white Stetson hat and all into the muddy creek.

Lynnville also is the family roots of some of my Mother's side of our family. It is a tiny place. Most of the familiar places are farm houses and barns within a mile or two of the town. At Lynnville we turn southwest to Folsomville which figures strongly on my Dad's side of our family. It also has another name dating well beyond my own memory into the past. Its nickname is Lickskillet. My great, great grandmother Narcissus is buried here in Folsomville. She, her husband Samuel, her sons and other siblings, among them my grandfather William, were caught up in the battle of Shiloh on their farm in Tennessee. Samuel, a Confederate recruit, was never heard from after Shiloh. My grandfather worked as a steam traction engine operator for a sawmill in Folsomville. Folsomville is another region of "persimmon hills" where Dad and I quail hunted with our pointer dogs and ran dogs in the Warrick County Field Trial Club trials.

Heart and mind go back to times-of-yore stories I've been told by the family even long years before I was born. It is a simple backwoods place but a special tiny non-town well hid in the spirit of my soul, purely unsophisticated in its starkly beautiful lack of sophistry.

We circle the old cemetery as I gaze down wistfully at the familiar bare handful of old frame buildings as we continue in our southeast course to another tiny hamlet, Tennyson. Tennyson is roots to, and home of others of Grandma Autry's family. Also Grandpa Autry in other years operated a steam powered sawmill here like that in Folsomville. In Tennyson, some of grandma's family, the Mundys resided. A sister, as I recall, and cousins my age or a bit older on Sunday visits in our Maxwell with grandma in tow to see her sister. They visited while the cousins and I played out back throwing wet corncobs at the back wall of the barn, and at each other. Tennyson is very small, less than a half dozen houses, so our Waco does one 360 circle around the place while I gawk down in my reminiscing.

Then, alas, we turn west for Boonville. It is only twelve miles as the so-called crow flies—or a Waco. In less than a minute I can see the old Warrick County Courthouse on the low horizon. A due west course from Tennyson will take us two or three miles north of Boonville allowing us to come in from the north to my old glider field at the foot of Orphan's Home Hill, our take-off point in this Waco nearly two months ago. All too soon we are north of Boonville and turning south toward our field. Marty is throttling back for a slow descent. I had not asked or even hinted before that he fly low over Oak Street to announce our arrival. My parents only knew we should arrive in September, but no idea at all which day, or much less the time of day. I knew that Marty knew if I wanted him to buzz Oak Street I'd have asked him. I knew also that if we did announce our arrival my parents would have insisted he remain at least until tomorrow, only adding to his frustration. He genuinely enjoyed our town and its people—especially us. But I am sure he also sensed Dad would be very persuasive, which Marty would find frustrating in the face of his anxiety to get back to Kansas, now that the barnstorming season was over. Beating the weather to get home was the mark of a good aviator—a fact he and I understand better than my parents.

We land down at the north end of the field, taxiing up to within 300 feet of Highway 62, the main road from Evansville into Boonville. We swing the Waco around to the north, drop the tail and switch off the OX-5. No one seems to notice because we landed from the north. A few autos are going back and forth on the highway. We climb out and Marty helps me retrieve my meager gear. He looks up at the empty cockpit, quipping, "That was your home for the past two months." We both say, "It's been great," almost in unison, which drew a simultaneous laugh from both of us. He shook hands with his other hand on my shoulder seeming to say, "No risky hugs for a 16-year-old who suddenly had to quit a two month barnstorming trip." Then with the old grin he says, "No sense, lad, to tarry. Man the switch once more while I twirl the prop." I climb down from the idling Waco as he climbs in, reaching out a final handshake, opens the throttle, raises the tail and gathers speed to the north. Once in the air he does a turn over the center of the field, rocks the wings, heads north in a climb. I watch till he is out of sight, pick up my bag, walk up to the road and up Orphan's Home Hill. At the St. Charles Hotel I make a phone call to home.

A month later I receive a winter scene picture postcard postmarked from Wichita reading, "Hi, Peyton, thanks for your good help and partnership. I ran into snow traversing Missouri. I'm off now for the south—by train. Marty." No return address.

Just after Thanksgiving I receive a second picture postcard from Arizona reading, "Hi, Peyton; Aviation is here to stay. Stick with it. But barnstorming is not. The barnstormer's day will soon end. My regards to you and your fine parents. Marty." Still no return address. I guess it must be the stamp of a true aerial gypsy.

ABOUT THE AUTHOR

Peyton Autry has been a published author for over 65 years. Over a hundred features published in nationally circulated magazines. One other book of non-fiction was published in 1986, titled *Warrick County*. A novel set in the Great Air War of 1914-1918, titled *The Eagles of Warrick*, was published in 1990. Two additional novels by Peyton Autry await publication, one with a setting in the Pacific Northwest, the second in a fictional small southern Hoosier town during the Great Depression. Peyton Autry has had a keen lifetime interest in aeronautics since 1923. He joined the airplane preliminary design section of the engineering department of the world's largest producer of jet airliners (Boeing/Seattle), retiring after 41 years.

Peyton Autry was born January 29, 1917, in Boonville, Warrick County, Indiana. His lifelong fascination with aeronautics began at the age of six. In his early teen years, he built and flew the early primary gliders. This was followed by an early career of designing and engineering light airplanes, which occurred prior, during, and well after a six-year curriculum with Columbia Technical Institute, D.C. (Airplane Design) and Westwood Aeronautical Institute, L.A. (Advanced Aircraft Stress Analysis). He joined the Boeing Engineering Department in 1940, retiring in 1981. He married Leta Ellsworth of Portland, Oregon, on March 2, 1945. They reside in Seattle. Motivation for writing this book began years ago, but was put off by other tasks in a busy life until now.

9 781681 623320